W9-AFM-090

FOOD AND SOCIETY IN CLASSICAL ANTIQUITY

This is the first study of food in classical antiquity that treats food as both a biological and a cultural phenomenon. The variables of food quantity, quality and availability, and the impact of disease, are evaluated and a judgement reached on the health of the population which inclines to pessimism. Food is also a symbol, evoking other basic human needs and desires, especially sex, and performing social and cultural roles which can be either integrative or divisive. The book explores food taboos in Greek, Roman and Jewish society, and food-allocation within the family, as well as more familiar cultural and economic polarities which are highlighted by food and eating. The author draws on a wide range of evidence new and old, from written sources to human skeletal remains, and uses both comparative historical evidence from early modern and contemporary developing societies and the anthropological literature, to create a case-study of food in antiquity.

PETER GARNSEY is Professor of the History of Classical Antiquity in the University of Cambridge, and Fellow of Jesus College. He is the author of, amongst other titles, *Famine and Food Supply in the Graeco-Roman World: Responses to Risk and Crisis* (1988), *Ideas of Slavery from Aristotle to Augustine* (1996) and *Cities, Peasants and Food in Classical Antiquity: Essays in Social and Economic History* (1998). He is also a co-editor of *The Cambridge Ancient History* Volumes XI, XII and XIII.

KEY THEMES IN ANCIENT HISTORY

Editors

P. A. Cartledge
Clare College, Cambridge

P. D. A. Garnsey
Jesus College, Cambridge

Key Themes in Ancient History aims to provide readable, informed and original studies of various basic topics, designed in the first instance for students and teachers of Classics and Ancient History, but also for those engaged in related disciplines. Each volume is devoted to a general theme in Greek, Roman or, where appropriate, Graeco-Roman history, or to some salient aspect or aspects of it. Besides indicating the state of current research in the relevant area, authors seek to show how the theme is significant for our own as well as ancient culture and society. By providing books for courses that are oriented around themes it is hoped to encourage and stimulate promising new developments in teaching and research in ancient history.

Other books in the series

Death-ritual and social structure in classical antiquity, by Ian Morris
0 521 37465 0 (hardback), 0 521 37611 4 (paperback)

Literacy and orality in ancient Greece, by Rosalind Thomas
0 521 37346 8 (hardback), 0 521 37742 0 (paperback)

Slavery and society at Rome, by Keith Bradley
0 521 37287 9 (hardback), 0 521 37887 7 (paperback)

Law, violence, and community in classical Athens, by David Cohen
0 521 38167 3 (hardback), 0 521 38837 6 (paperback)

Public order in ancient Rome, by Wilfried Nippel
0 521 38327 7 (hardback), 0 521 38749 3 (paperback)

Friendship in the classical world, by David Konstan
0 521 45402 6 (hardback), 0 521 45998 2 (paperback)

Sport and society in ancient Greece, by Mark Golden
0 521 49698 5 (hardback), 0 521 49790 6 (paperback)

Religions of the ancient Greeks, by Simon Price
0 521 38201 7 (hardback), 0 521 38867 8 (paperback)

FOOD AND SOCIETY IN CLASSICAL ANTIQUITY

PETER GARNSEY

CAMBRIDGE
UNIVERSITY PRESS

PUBLISHED BY THE PRESS SYNDICATE OF THE UNIVERSITY OF CAMBRIDGE
The Pitt Building, Trumpington Street, Cambridge CB2 1RP, United Kingdom

CAMBRIDGE UNIVERSITY PRESS
The Edinburgh Building, Cambridge CB2 2RU, United Kingdom   http://www.cup.cam.ac.uk
40 West 20th Street, New York, NY 10011–4211, USA   http://www.cup.org
10 Stamford Road, Oakleigh, Melbourne 3166, Australia

© Cambridge University Press 1999

This book is in copyright. Subject to statutory exception and to the provisions
of relevant collective licensing agreements, no reproduction of any part may
take place without the written permission of Cambridge University Press.

First published 1999

Printed in the United Kingdom at the University Press, Cambridge

Typeset in Baskerville MT 11/12½ in QuarkXPress™   [SE]

A catalogue record for this book is available from the British Library

Library of Congress Cataloguing in Publication data

Garnsey, Peter
Food and society in Classical Antiquity / Peter Garnsey.
p.   cm. – (Key themes in ancient history)
Includes bibliographical references (p.   ) and index.
ISBN 0 521 64182 9 (hardback) – ISBN 0 521 64588 3 (paperback)
1. Food habits – Greece – History. 2. Food habits – Rome – History.
3. Food supply – Greece – History. 4. Food supply – Rome – History.
5. Civilization, Classical. I. Title II. Series.
GT2853.G8G37   1999
394.1'2'0937 – dc21   98-38424   CIP

ISBN 0 521 64182 9 hardback
ISBN 0 521 64588 3 paperback

836819

In memory of Conant Brodribb
archaeologist, educationalist, raconteur

839813

Contents

Illustrations

Acknowledgements

I wish to thank the following for permission to reproduce illustrations: the Soprintendenza Archeologica di Salerno, Avellino e Benevento (nos. 1, 7, and 9), the Cambridgeshire Archaeological Field Unit (nos. 5 and 6), Dr Jane Renfrew (no. 2), and the Museo Nazionale Preistorico Etnografico 'L. Pigorini', Sezione di Antropologia, Rome (no. 3).

Abbreviations

AHR	American Historical Review
AJAH	American Journal of Ancient History
Annales ESC	Annales: Economies, sociétés, civilisations
AJPh	American Journal of Philology
ASNP	Annali della Scuola Nazionale di Pisa
BAR BS	British Archaeological Reports: British Series
BAR IS	British Archaeological Reports: International Series
BCH	Bulletin de Correspondance Hellénique
CAH	Cambridge Ancient History
CPh	Classical Philology
CQ	Classical Quarterly
DArch	Dialoghi di Archeologia
DHA	Dialogues de l'histoire ancienne
G&R	Greece and Rome
GRBS	Greek, Roman and Byzantine Studies
JHS	Journal of Hellenic Studies
JRA	Journal of Roman Archaeology
JRS	Journal of Roman Studies
JSOT	Journal for the Study of the Old Testament
JSQ	Jewish Studies Quarterly
MEFR	Mélanges d'archéologie et d'histoire de l'Ecole française de Rome
PG	Patrologia Graeca, Migne
PL	Patrologia Latina, Migne
RE	Real-encyclopädie der klassischen Altertumswissenschaft, Pauly-Wissowa (-Kroll)
REL	Revue des études latines
RHDFE	Revue historique de droit français et étranger
SC	Sources Chrétiennes
TAPA	Transactions of the American Philological Association
THES	The Times Higher Educational Supplement
TLS	The Times Literary Supplement

Preface

Greeks and Romans, rich or poor, were obsessed with food. For most people, life was a perpetual struggle for survival. Among the well-off minority, there developed an elaborate *haute cuisine*, and, in reaction, a rhetoric (and in certain contexts, a practice) of rejection or continence, in the service of politics, morality, philosophy, religion or health.

This book presents food as a biocultural phenomenon. Food is at once nutrition, needed by the body for its survival, and cultural object, with various non-food uses and associations. Food functions as a sign or means of communication. It governs human relationships at all levels. Food serves to bind together people linked by blood, religion or citizenship; conversely, it is divisive, being distributed and consumed in accordance with existing hierarchies.

Historians and archaeologists have long been interested in the material aspects of food in classical antiquity. They have traced the origins, diffusion and evolution of particular foodstuffs and catalogued and discussed what was eaten, from where it came, how it was produced and distributed, how it was processed and cooked. Their findings form part of the background of my research, and to some extent I have followed in their footsteps. Some of the early chapters of this book reflect my previous work on systems of production and distribution, and patterns of consumption during times of both relative normality and stress. But I go on here to pose the question of food-availability. Did ancient populations get enough of their staple foods to provide the food-energy and protein requirements for good health, and were the deficiencies of their staples in certain vital proteins and vitamins made up by complementary foods? I develop a thesis which is likely to be controversial on the nutritional status of the population, with the aid of evidence not normally adduced.

A less traditional interest, which marks some recent work by a new generation of historians, lies in the social, religious and cultural functions of food and its metaphorical uses. Their explorations have influenced the composition of the later chapters, but again, within the confines of this book and my own preoccupations and limitations, I have not followed up all their lines of inquiry. In general, I have found those studies most useful for my purposes which are informative about the nature of Greek and Roman society. Thus, for example, I particularly welcome the attention given to communal drinking (the symposium) and banquets. In any society, group eating and drinking highlight social attitudes, relationships and hierarchies, and these matters form a central part of my subject. My aim is to use the universal activities of food and eating as a way of clarifying the distinctive nature of Graeco-Roman society and culture. Food and eating (in the parlance, 'food and food-ways') are a good entrée into a society, an introduction to its cultural traits, social institutions, individual and collective attitudes. Studies of food, however informative and entertaining, do not escape the charge of antiquarianism unless they fully contextualise their subject.

This point has been better understood by social scientists than historians, on the whole. The most interesting historical writing on food has been aware of and in dialogue with anthropological studies. In the English-speaking world, I have in mind a work such as Stephen Mennell's *All Manners of Food*, a historical sociologist's investigation of tastes and manners in France and Britain from the Middle Ages to the contemporary world. A historian of food who neglects Claude Lévi-Strauss, Jack Goody, Mary Douglas and Marvin Harris, to select a few of the more prominent names, will have difficulty asking intelligent questions of the evidence for food from antiquity or from any society whatever. The potential contribution of *physical* as opposed to social and cultural anthropology to the historical study of food and nutrition is of a quite different nature, and has been exploited as yet hardly at all, as regards ancient Mediterranean societies. One of my aims is to begin to rectify this omission.

Between ancient history and modern social science (not to mention biological science) there is a large but not unbridgeable gap. Opportunities have been lost on both sides. Little use has been made of classical antiquity, even as a source of *exempla*, by social scientists working on the subject of food. This is not surprising. Anthropologists have other societies, often experienced at first hand, to serve as reference-points. One would not expect Lévi-Strauss to refer to ancient sources on the roasting of meat, and it is something of a surprise to find that he cites Aristotle twice on this subject, even if via a secondary source, in his classic paper 'Le triangle culinaire'. At the other extreme,

Mœurs des sauvages amériquains (1724), by the ethnographer Fr Joseph François Lafitau, is built around an extensive comparison of the customs of Native Americans with those of the classical Greeks and Romans. That work is a 'period piece', its approach and methodology dated. Among contemporary anthropologists, Jack Goody stands out as one who has made fruitful use of the comparison with Graeco-Roman antiquity (in investigating the family and literacy as well as food and cuisine). Goody's examples of peoples who developed a *haute cuisine* include, naturally, the Chinese and the French, but also, unexpectedly, the Greeks of the fourth century BC. This is a quite legitimate deduction from an eccentric work called *The Deipnosophists*, or *Professors of the Dinner-Table*, composed by Athenaeus, a minor writer in Greek, born in an obscure Greek town in Egypt and surviving in what may be a cadette, but is still a lengthy, version. Athenaeus himself flourished about the turn of the second century AD, but drew heavily on classical and Hellenistic Greek sources. Again, there would have been no debate on the dietary laws of the ancient Israelites without the intervention of anthropologists and other social scientists such as Douglas, Harris and Simoons.

On the other side, if we except the work of French historians of ancient Greece, especially Vernant, Vidal-Naquet and Detienne, in their structuralist explorations of the role of food in Greek society, anthropology has been slow to make an impact on ancient historical scholarship in the area of food studies. Few ancient historians appear to have asked why the ancient Israelites imposed food prohibitions on themselves whereas the classical Greeks and Romans on the whole did not. Even synthetic studies such as *Consuming Passions: The Anthropology of Eating* by Farb and Armelagos, despite its lack of reference to antiquity, have much to teach students of the ancient world, in setting an agenda for historians to follow. I for one am impressed by their demonstration that material and symbolic aspects of food can be combined profitably in a single study.

This book on food was fed by research begun around two decades ago, and was already in rough draft in 1992, when it was first delivered as lectures to senior undergraduates at Cambridge. My thanks go in the first place to the participants in this course, and to my former graduate students who were already, or became, experts in various aspects of the subject, in particular, Sue Alcock, Sarah Currie, Justin Goddard, Neville Morley, Jonathan Thompson, Jeremy Toner, Onno van Nijf and Greg Woolf. I owe a heavy debt to Paul Cartledge, Robin Donkin, Richard

Gordon, Richard Hunter, Tim Jenkins, Vivian Nutton, Walter Scheidel, Malcolm Schofield, Dorothy Thompson and Frank Walbank, who have read and improved part or the whole of this book in earlier drafts. Other friends who have helped me over the years and/or have given me sundry, vital assistance in preparing this book include Filippo Cavassini, Giovanna Ceserani, Gillian Clark, Lin Foxhall, Paul Halstead, David Hanke, Chris Hayden, Caroline Humfress, Ted Kenney and Richard Smith. I am grateful to a number of experts: in third world studies, to Barbara Harriss-White, in the field of nutrition, to Roger Whitehead and his team at the Dunn Nutrition Unit, and, in physical anthropology, to Sara Bisel, Paola Catalano, Corinne Duhig, Gino Fornaciari, Valerie Higgins, Estelle Lazer, Patricia Macadam-Stuart, Roberto Macchiarelli and Theya Molleson, among others. I owe particular thanks to Paola Catalano and Roberto Macchiarelli, who invited me to collaborate in their projects at Vallerano near Rome and Isola Sacra near Ostia, respectively. Finally I acknowledge the assistance of the Wellcome Trust, which awarded me a Research Leave Fellowship in 1987–88.

Food, substance and symbol

There is no god like one's stomach: we must sacrifice to it every day.
(From 'Hunger', a Yoruba song)[1]

I hate the belly: it dogs you shamelessly,
making you remember it willy nilly
in the midst of stress, in the midst of sorrow of heart.
(Homer, *Od.* 7.216–18; transl. A. J. Bowen)

Food comes first. No food, no life. In myth, the satisfying of this primary
need was a struggle and a burden. The sin of Adam (issuing from the
gut rather than the loins) condemned humanity, the flower of creation,
to getting its food the hard way, through tilling the soil. Prometheus,
Adam's counterpart in Greek myth, through his act of stealing fire from
heaven, brought upon the human race the harsh necessity of agricultural labour, without which the seed, sunk in the earth by a vengeful
Zeus, could not be converted into an edible plant. Agriculture was a punishment imposed upon mankind, and a diet of cereals a drastic come-
down from the divine menu of nectar and ambrosia, or from the free
produce of the Garden of Eden.

In antiquity, as in all pre-industrial societies, most people were of
necessity engaged in food-production. In the Mediterranean environment this was often a hazardous enterprise carried on in hostile sur-
roundings. The grimness of the terrain worked by the people of
Palestine is reflected in the prominence of miracles of feeding in the
New Testament, and in the Old Testament prophets' dreams of a
Promised Land of abundant food and drink (Is. 35:1; Ezek. 47:7–12).

It used to be orthodoxy among anthropologists that the transition
from hunter/gatherer to agricultural economies in prehistoric times

---

[1] In Chinweiza, ed., *Voices from Twentieth-Century Africa* (London, 1988), 423–4.

enhanced the quality and stability of food supplies and improved the health of the community, while reducing the burden of labour on producers. More recently, under the impact of the models of the economist Boserup and newer anthropological literature on hunter/gatherer societies, the view has gained ground that the adoption of sedentary farming, while bringing 'progress' in its train in the form of demographic growth, cultural development and, in time, sophisticated civilisations, also had undesirable consequences, namely, poorer diets, lower nutritional status and greater vulnerability to famine and malnutrition among ordinary members of the expanded communities.[2] A modified version of this theory denies population growth the status of an independent variable, and argues for the adaptability and equilibrium-seeking tendency of human communities in the face of social and economic change. I aligned myself in earlier work with this last position. I stressed that Mediterranean peasants and urban communities employed a variety of strategies in response to the risk, and reality, of harvest shortfall and food crisis, and I concluded that they were largely successful in heading off real catastrophes, that is, famines. I did find, however, that food shortages which were less than famines, and the human suffering that attended them, were a common occurrence in Graeco-Roman society.[3] In this present work, I shall take the further step of arguing that endemic undernourishment or chronic malnutrition underlay those periodic shortages, just as it underlies the famines that afflict developing nations today.

It is not difficult on the basis of the sources from antiquity to establish the regularity and inevitability of crises of food shortage and hunger. The literary texts are haunted by the spectre of famine, food crisis, and the resulting *episodic* malnutrition and hunger – as distinct from the *endemic*, long-term, malnutrition and hunger to which I have just referred. The upper classes, from whose ranks the authors of those writings were inevitably drawn, may not themselves have been commonly exposed to food-shortage and temporary hunger-stress. But the communities they presided over *were* thus vulnerable, and this made their position as political, social and economic leaders insecure. Food crisis threatened the dominance of the elite and the stability of the society over which they presided.

Anxiety over food is manifested, for example, in the establishment, survival and centrality of the cycle of religious rituals and celebrations

---

[2] Boserup (1965); (1983); Cohen (1977); (1989).   [3] Garnsey (1988).

in honour of food-associated deities such as Demeter in Greece and Ceres in Italy. It is also shown, more practically in our view (not necessarily in theirs), by the laws issued and institutional arrangements made to safeguard the supply and distribution of food. An additional, general, indication of the fragility of the food supply, and the vulnerability of the mass of ordinary people to dearth and hunger, is to be found in the very obsession of the sources with food and its lavish consumption by the rich. The conspicuous consumption of food was an important index of wealth, status and power. This was appropriate in a social context where food was a relatively scarce, highly valued and unequally distributed commodity.

Directly and indirectly, the ancient sources testify to the reality and fear of food crisis. On the other hand, one would have one's work cut out if one wanted to demonstrate that *malnutrition* was the normal condition of large numbers of people in antiquity. The literary sources identify no such phenomenon. It is easy therefore to argue against its existence, and that has occasionally been done, largely by a priori reasoning. How, it has been asked, could the dazzling civilisations of Greece and Rome have been built on the backs of malnourished people? Students and observers of antiquity more often do not even consider the possibility of widespread malnutrition, while those who give attention to food commonly write as if most inhabitants of the ancient Mediterranean world enjoyed an adequate diet and a satisfactory health status during their lifetimes. The probability that those lifetimes were severely abbreviated has not been allowed to cast doubt on this assumption.

The problem of the absence of malnutrition from the texts can be resolved by a two-stage strategy. One must first escape the perspective of the upper classes, as reflected in the literary sources, by drawing on quite different kinds of evidence, both ancient (human skeletal remains, an important and hitherto under-utilised source of information on nutrition and health status) and comparative (from other historical societies, including the contemporary developing world, in which malnutrition is a familiar and much-studied phenomenon). That done, one can then turn back to the ancient literature with new questions and hypotheses.

Food, then, was a vital concern in the advanced societies of antiquity, much more so than is now the case in the developed West, which has long since slipped the net of famine, food shortage, malnutrition and hunger. For most of us in our affluent society food is part of the routine of life. It comes to us almost automatically; we have to do little to secure it. We are aware of hunger, but as something that exists somewhere else. Unlike the Old Testament prophets, we do not need to dream of paradise, because we have no personal experience of the meaning of hunger. Hunger in our society has to be artificially induced by war (the siege of Leningrad of 1941–42, the blockade of Holland in 1944, more recently, the siege of Sarajevo), or it is the result of a tragic accident. An air-crash in the remote Andes in 1972 made cannibals of The Old Christians rugby team from Uruguay. For the two who survived, the return to civilisation was the Garden of Eden rediscovered.[4]

In so far as there is concern over malnutrition in our own society, it is principally over the malnutrition that is associated with overnutrition or unhealthy diets. Ancient medical writers, too, sometimes asserted that excessive eating could endanger health. (However, when Anthimus, a Greek doctor of the early sixth century, addressed the King of the Franks in these terms, his main target appears to have been overindulgence in raw meat and other uncooked foods![5]) Today, the fascination of food is reflected in publishers' lists, but most of the books that load the booksellers' tables are written for gourmets, dieticians or food-faddists. Among scholars, food is studied chiefly by anthropologists, and for its non-food uses and symbolic significance. Only in the contemporary developing world does food stand centre-stage as indisputably a biocultural phenomenon, a subject fit for biological scientists and social scientists alike. So it could be for students of antiquity.

THE FOOD AND NON-FOOD USES OF FOOD[6]

Food is food, in the first instance. It is substance taken into the body which can satisfy hunger and give nourishment. Other items consumed, as is written in al-Biruni's *Book on Pharmacy and Materia Medica*, are poisons, or drugs which may be taken against poisons but none the less weaken the body.[7] A primary question therefore is, what was the quality of the diet or diets potentially available to residents of the ancient Mediterranean? The quantities of foods actually consumed are beyond our grasp, just as they are for other pre-modern societies. But the consequences of diets of such-and-such quality and quantity for the nutritional status of consumers can be pondered. For certain select populations the direction of the inquiry can be reversed, where skeletal

---

[4] P. P. Read, *Alive: The Story of the Andes Survivors* (London, 1974), 227–42.

[5] Anthimus, *De Observatione Ciborum*, pref., with Grant (1996).

[6] Fieldhouse (1986), pref., lists 19 non-food uses of food.   [7] Hamarneh (1973).

data (relating to stature, or the presence of deficiency disease) point to the adequacy or inadequacy of diets. Also, the likely incidence of hunger and malnutrition can be investigated with the aid of comparative evidence.

The consumption of food that is adequate in quantity and quality hangs in the first instance on the production of enough suitable food and on its efficient distribution to all sections of the population. If food was short, hunger endemic, and life a continuous struggle for survival, there are negative implications for the productivity of agriculture and/or the efficiency of trade and markets. Either not enough food was being grown, or it was not reaching non-producing consumers, or both. The problems might be endemic or episodic. In the former case, hunger was long-term and steady-state; in the latter, it occurred in short, sharp shocks through the agency of individual food crises. Food crises were certainly frequent occurrences in Mediterranean communities. What needs to be explored is the context from which they emerge, what constitutes the norm, and whether the norm includes endemic hunger.

In any case, an investigation of the place of food in both the economic and the political life of the societies in question is a desideratum. Two questions pose themselves under the heading of food and the economy: first, how far conditions were favourable for the production of food, that is to say, the physical environment, the state of agricultural technology, and the way ownership of and access to land and its resources were distributed among the population; and second, how far market mechanisms and institutions promoted the circulation of food between areas of surplus and areas of deficit.

Whatever the nature of the economic system, political factors might operate to obstruct the flow of food to those who needed it, to those of low 'entitlement' – to use Amartya Sen's term for access to, possession of, or control over food resources.[8] Under this head one looks in particular for indications of intervention by governments in the market and in extra-market distribution of food among consumers. If it turns out that the involvement of governments in the food supply was as a rule very limited, that commerce in foodstuffs was essentially unregulated and institutions for food distribution rudimentary, it would not necessarily follow that people often starved. For there would remain to be investigated the social as distinct from the political power of the rich, that is to say, the private mechanisms of redistribution. Did patronage and charity

---

[8] Sen (1981).

succeed where public institutions (controlled by the same people, to be sure) failed, or was the private redistribution of food resources too selective and on too small a scale to act as a socio-economic leveller? One way or another, by studying systems of redistribution we can hope to arrive at a deeper understanding of the ways in which inequalities of wealth and power were confirmed and preserved in Graeco-Roman society. For food is divisive. It is distributed and consumed in accordance with the differences and hierarchies that exist in the society. Are we what we eat, or what we are forced to eat?

That food separates and divides is true in existential, cultural, social and economic terms. In Greek myth, food plays a role in defining a hierarchy of being: there is food for gods, food for men, and food for animals. It was not so clear-cut when man shared the food of the gods at the Heavenly High Table. Prometheus' deceit, in stealing the fire and then in his division of the first sacrificial animal, introduced a more precisely differentiated hierarchy of diets.[9]

In Graeco-Roman society, food was a marker of ethnic and cultural difference. In the literature from antiquity, that is, in the perceptions of the literary spokesmen of the elite, Greeks were differentiated from barbarians, urban-dwellers from rustics, farmers from nomads, and so on, in terms of the food they ate, amongst other things. Within the family, the distribution of food might be expected to be an index of relative power and status, as between male and female, parents and children, young and old. Then, food reflected the vertical social and economic distinction between rich and poor. Greater purchasing power gave access to foods of superior quality and quantity, and of wider range. The conspicuous consumption of food by the elite advertised the social and economic distance between them and the mass of the population. *Nouveaux riches* aped the elite.

On the other hand, food involves 'commensality', that is, 'sharing a table', with 'companions', that is, 'sharers of bread'.[10] Food assembles and binds together those linked by blood (family), class (the symposiasts of archaic and later Greece), religion (the Passover Seder, the Eucharist) and citizenship (the civic banquet).

Food, then, stands as a pointer to distinctions of status, power and

---

[9] The god's share was the bones wrapped in fat, or the smoke that ascended from the altar as they burned; Prometheus reserved for man the edible portion of the animal.

[10] Augustine, *Serm.* 138.7: 'People are called companions, you see, because they eat together.' Augustine adds the conceit, that *sodales*, 'companions', means *quasi simul edales*, 'as if to say eating together'.

wealth, of group-separateness and -belonging, and of cultural differences in general. In saying this, we have already made the transition from food as food, as a biological necessity, to its non-food uses. In the classic formulation of the structuralist Claude Lévi-Strauss, food is 'bon(ne) à penser', 'good to think (with)'. Food and cuisine express fundamental human attitudes. Their meanings are written in code, and to decipher the code is to penetrate the 'deep structures' of a society: 'The cooking of a society is a language into which it unconsciously translates its structure – or else resigns itself, still unconsciously, to revealing its contradictions.'[11] Among those influenced by his work, Vernant, Detienne and Vidal-Naquet have applied the Lévi-Straussian paradigm, the raw/cooked/rotten triangle, and his technique of analysis, in particular, the search for contrast and correspondence (binary opposition and homology), in the study of Greek myth and ritual.[12]

The structuralist enterprise has received a mixed response. One can concede that oppositions and contrasts within the raw material of myth were seen by Greek authors as providing *a* clue to mythical meaning; also that food and its preparation form a significant element of that material. One can say this without wishing to endorse the model of the Greek mental universe created by structuralist ingenuity or 'bricolage'.[13] Further, it is noteworthy that Lévi-Strauss, though considering himself a semiologist, was preoccupied with investigating the patterns or organising principles of signs and symbols, rather than analysing their meaning – the primary concern of semiology as defined by its founder, Saussure.[14] Specifically, and with relevance to my own interests, while Lévi-Strauss proposes to move from food-relationships (as depicted in the culinary triangles) to social and economic relationships, this never achieves any other status than a programme of research. Meanwhile, one may question, as some have done, whether using the culinary procedures of a society to elucidate its social hierarchy or religious nature is the proper way to proceed, rather than vice versa.[15]

Roland Barthes also thought in terms of a 'code' (or 'grammar') of deep meanings underlying the food system of a society, but he was more intent on investigating the symbolic meaning of particular foods than on unveiling any pattern formed by such meanings. Any particular item of

---

[11] Lévi-Strauss (1966), 595. See also Lévi-Strauss (1969); (1978).

[12] See the essays in Gordon (1981), section 2.

[13] Here I echo Buxton (1994), 198–9; other gentle criticism in Gordon (1979), who talks of 'bricolage'. The word is used by Lévi-Strauss himself for mythical thought. See Sperber (1975), 71, on its significance.   [14] Cf. Sperber (1975), 68.   [15] Goody (1982), 14–29; Gellner (1985).

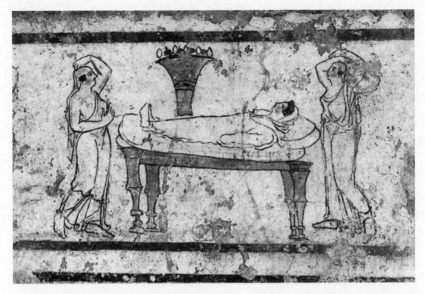

1. The laying out of the dead (*prothesis*). The basket (*kalathos*) is filled with eggs
and pomegranates. Customarily symbols of life and fertility, in the funerary context
they are food for the dead and carry hope for life beyond the grave. The pomegranate
is associated with Persephone, wife of Hades. Andriuolo, Paestum. Lucanian,
c. 350–340 BC.

food might carry a system of symbolic meaning. A simple example from
antiquity is foods such as eggs, apples, pomegranates, that represent life
and fertility and commonly make an appearance at marriages, or for
that matter, funeral ceremonies (Fig. 1). Sugar, for Barthes, 'is not just a
foodstuff, even when it is used in conjunction with other foods; it is, if
you will, an "attitude", bound to certain usages, certain "protocols", that
have to do with more than food'.[16] In a Chinese New Year dish as consumed in Singapore, the ingredients are carefully chosen 'auspicious'
foods, sugar among them, which combine to produce a potent message
of prosperity for the household and its guests:

Fish . . . is a compulsory New Year dish because the Chinese word for 'fish'
sounds the same as the word for 'financial surplus'. One particular dish consists
of raw fish ('raw' sounding the same as 'grow'), ginger (sounding the same as
'expand' – expanding wealth and family), sweet plum sauce (sugar sounds like
'home', and 'sweet' is synonymous with 'peace' and 'harmony'), sesame seeds
(they look like gold coins), and fired bits of batter (more gold). Each ingredient

---

[16] Barthes (1979), 166–7. For sugar as symbol see Mintz (1985), 74–96.

is added in layers, and the server recites the meaning of each layer with the prefix 'Wishing you . . .' Then we all have to get up and toss all the ingredients together, the term sounding like 'digging for happiness'. Then we eat it.[17]

Sugar was unknown in ancient Mediterranean societies. With bread, a staple food, Barthes finds an 'interesting difference': 'Bread does not as such constitute a signifying unit: in order to find these we must go further and look at its varieties.' Each variety of bread is a 'unit of signification'.[18] This calls to mind the 72 kinds of bread that Jack Goody found in the pages of Athenaeus. Some of these, in company with other foods listed by the same writer, 'marked out the social hierarchy, the emphasis being placed on riches, luxury and on difference itself'.[19]

Athenaeus' breads sometimes have distinctive shapes, for example, that of a sexual organ or of a flower, and carry an altogether simpler message. In general, food lends itself readily to use as a metaphor in other spheres of activity, and this reflects both the centrality of food and its emotion-evoking capacities. Some metaphorical usages have lost something of their earlier piquancy (e.g. ham, lemon), while others are ancient but still potent, for example, woman as food to be consumed or as prey.[20] Sex is a fertile field for food imagery, then as now. Food and sex were intimately linked in traditional agrarian societies, for they were seen as equally productive and reproductive. In such societies women were expected to devote themselves to the cause of social reproduction: in literature from Hesiod to Soranus (and beyond), woman is the field to be ploughed and sown, the cultivated furrow, or the oven in which the fruit of the man/earth is transformed into a finished product to be nurtured, or consumed. Thus the pursuit of virginity and chastity in the context of Christian asceticism was seen as challenging the inherited value system and as disruptive of the existing social order.[21] Nowadays, sex is less closely tied up with the propagation of the species, and interest in that end has declined. The association of food and sex lives on none the less in literary discourse and popular parlance.

Food operated as a powerful signifer in many different contexts and

---

[17] I am grateful to Tao Tao Huang for this information.   [18] Barthes (1979), 168–9.
[19] Goody (1982), 103.
[20] The hunting metaphor: Schnapp (1989); (1997). Food and sex: see e.g. McCartney (1925); Loraux (1990), 30–3 (gluttony and virility); Winkler (1990), 79–82 (aphrodisiacs); Henry (1992) (the theme in Athenaeus); and see next note. I am grateful to Sarah Currie for bibliographical advice.
[21] DuBois (1988); also Mason (1987); Olender (1990). Foucault (1988), 125–8, is a basic account of the relation between sex and diet, as seen by doctors. On Christian sexual abstinence (closely bound up with abstinence from food, see below pp. 95–8), see e.g. Brown (1988), e.g. chs. 13 and 18; Walker Bynum (1987), e.g. 33–48, 208–18.

throughout society. Literature provides most of the evidence, and it emanates from and is directed at the upper classes. But literature was sometimes aimed at a wider audience. Drama in democratic Athens was a civic event, open to all citizens. In this context, Aristophanes' suggestion that the ostentatious purchase of fresh sea-perch might be seen by the seller of humble sprats at the next stall as conveying undemocratic social and political attitudes may not be merely a figment of his comic imagination (Ar. *Wasps* 493–5).[22] Nor is it plausible that the food/sex link, which Aristophanes also exploited (and which was much more easily arrived at than the connection between food and politics), was made only in upper-class parlance.

Yet clearly the elite developed symbolic systems to which their social inferiors had little access. The subtleties of Horace's food imagery were not so much lost on, as unavailable to, the mass of Romans. That goes too for the whole theme of the dinner party, which is the focal point of a great deal of Latin literature, and a preferred setting for the critical evaluation of Roman society and culture, not to mention the creative activity of the authors themselves.[23] The role of food in moral discourse in Greece and in Rome was of little relevance to ordinary people, and was not intended to be. The charges of overindulgence in food and drink, a standard political weapon in late Republican and early Imperial Rome, and the creation and elaboration of the myth of archaic frugality, were intended for upper-class consumption.[24]

Barthes wrote that food's value as protocol 'becomes increasingly more important as soon as the basic needs are satisfied, as they are in France'.[25] It is likely enough that the value of food *as nutrition* received greater emphasis in the relatively poor societies of antiquity than it does in modern France. It does not follow that the metaphorical value of food was unimportant then, that food, or individual foods, carried little symbolic baggage among the many who were commonly hungry, as well as among the few. It is, however, entirely plausible that for the few the metaphorical rather than the nutritional aspect of food was paramount.

Each of the 'twofold values' of food, as nutrition and as protocol, merits discussion in a study of food in ancient societies. It is indeed difficult, and ultimately I suspect unnecessary, to make a rigid distinction between the two roles or 'values' of food. But what if they appear to be

[22] See Davidson (1993).

[23] Gowers (1993) argues that Roman poets when they talk food, cooking and eating are in fact making assertions about their own compositions.

[24] Goddard (1994a); (1994b); Edwards (1993). See below, pp. 77–9.   [25] Barthes (1979), 172.

in competition, and one is invited to take sides? How, for example, are we to explain the food taboos of the ancient Israelites or the Pythagoreans? For Lévi-Strauss and for Mary Douglas we are dealing with attitudes and world view (to be sought above all in myth, according to the structuralists), which are autonomous and 'float free'. Marvin Harris, Jack Goody or Ernest Gellner would favour a materialist or contextual explanation which reflects ecological and social realities. *Chacun à son goût.*

CHAPTER I

Diet

The Mediterranean diet is healthier than the diets of the affluent societies of the West. On this nutritionists and pathologists are in agreement. A writer for *The Times* (of 31.8.93), under the banner headline 'Switch to Mediterranean diet "can cut heart risk"', cites papers to a congress in Nice, a study on diet conducted at Lyon, and a consultant physician at Leicester Royal Infirmary, described as 'author of the latest study'. Mediterranean peoples have a lower incidence of heart disease, cancer and digestive disorders, and this can be attributed directly to diet and life-style in general. In the Mediterranean region (according to a survey conducted in South Italy in the 1960s) a high proportion of total energy is provided by cereals (more than 60%); a low proportion of total energy comes from lipids, that is, fats (less than 30%); a high contribution is made to total lipids from olive oil, so that the diet is low in saturated fatty acids; and there is a relatively high intake of fruit and vegetables, providing at least half the dietary fibre that is ingested. Then, nutritionists talk of the presence in plant foods of various non-nutrients with a health-protective function that are only beginning to be understood.[1] All this favourable publicity for the Mediterranean diet has served only to bolster the assumption already harboured by students of antiquity, that the ancient inhabitants of the region were well-off in terms of food and health.

Diet in the Mediterranean has not remained static. There have been intrusions, notably maize, potatoes, tomatoes, sugar from the New World. There have also been corrosions, in that traditional diets are being transformed before our eyes under affluent New and Old World influence. In consequence, eating habits have increasingly diversified, so that it might be thought inappropriate to talk in terms of a single

[1] Ferro-Luzzi and Sette (1989).

Mediterranean diet. More inappropriate than ever, one might be tempted to say. Still, in the ancient world Mediterranean diets, despite local variations, were by and large centred on cereals, the olive and the vine, and that is my justification for using the singular. It is also my impression that the same triad remains basic, if of somewhat diminished importance; in other words, that diets have not (or not yet) radically changed. However, the accuracy of this judgement is not crucial to my purpose.

There is another issue that concerns me more. It is one thing to assert that 'The Diet', then as now, was healthy, and another, that the ordinary inhabitants of the region enjoyed a good nutritional status. Scholars tend to give blandly optimistic summaries of the 'typical' Mediterranean diet, as exemplified by the following: 'The diet of ordinary people in Greece and Rome was derived from cereals, pulses, vegetables, fruit, olive oil, milk, cheese and a little fish and meat.'[2] The writer, a nutritionist, continues: 'This pattern fits well with what we would regard as a healthy diet.' He goes on to signal the 'remarkable feats' and 'stupendous works' of Greeks and Romans, specifically the temples, aqueducts, roads, ships and pots, and concludes: 'Surely such things could not have been achieved by people who were by and large malnourished, unless we remove all ideas of functional capacity from the definition of malnutrition.'

The question sidestepped concerns availability. It cannot be assumed that food was evenly distributed in the societies in question. One might equally propose, and with greater plausibility, that food distribution was anything but even. Let us at least recognise that the question, whether the ordinary people of the Mediterranean were well-nourished, is a fair one, which needs to be asked. We cannot hope to frame an answer to it, however, until the wider context has been considered, in particular the systems of production and distribution and the character of political life. The answer that is ultimately arrived at may still be *non liquet*, essentially because the evidence that might decide the matter is lacking; but the ambiguity of this answer will at least be informed.

THE MEDITERRANEAN TRIAD

Cereals, vines and olives, what Braudel called the 'eternal trinity', provided the basis of the traditional agricultural and dietary regime. This

---

[2] Waterlow (1989), 3, 11; cf. White (1976), 147; André (1981).

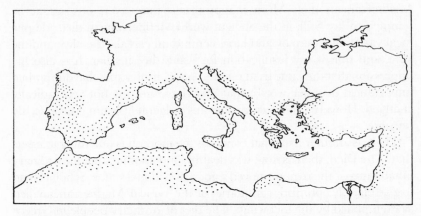

2. Olive distribution in the Mediterranean region. From Renfrew (1973), 132, fig. 82.

statement seems unexceptionable, but some analysis and interpretation are required.

First, the triad was not everywhere in place. Only cereals were truly ubiquitous, wine was not grown everywhere or with equal success, and the range of the olive was definitely circumscribed.[3] Sesame oil competed with olive oil in Egypt and parts of the Near East. More crucially, the olive does well only in the regions of true Mediterranean climate (and there are many transitional climates in the region). It needs a dry season in which to develop its oil content, and a cool winter in which to rest. It does not tolerate frost, and is normally unsuccessful above about 800 m. In the northern regions of the Mediterranean, the olive line follows the sea coast, penetrating little inland except in Italy and Spain. In the Balkan peninsula, the olive is not found further north than the Macedonian plain, Chalcidice and southern Thrace. In Italy, it grows on the foothills of the Central Apennines, but no higher or further north, except in Venetia at the head of the Adriatic. In Spain it reaches the southern edge of the Central Cordillera and penetrates the Ebro valley. In short, away from the coast and river valleys, and in upland regions, olive oil was an item of import, one therefore that had to be paid for or exchanged – in so far as it was not displaced by animal products which served similar functions and were more readily available (see Fig. 2).

Second, within the triad, the product-range was much wider than is

---

[3] On the olive, see e.g. Forbes and Foxhall (1978); Loussert and Brousse (1978); Amouretti (1986); Mattingly (1988a); Sallares (1991), 304–90, 474–6. For the vine, see e.g. Billiard (1913); Dion (1959); Purcell (1985); Tchernia (1986).

often assumed. 'Cereals' must be taken as shorthand for a whole group of seed-crops.[4] To begin with the most important cultigens, wheat and barley, each of these is a family name for a number of varieties, some of more recent appearance and of higher status, like the two naked wheats which became more prevalent in the course of antiquity, namely, *Triticum durum* wheat, which is hard, and *T. aestivum*, soft and best for bread. Other varieties were more primitive and less fashionable, but they nevertheless persisted and coexisted to some extent with the other varieties. I refer to the various husked grains, like emmer and einkorn. There were other less important crops (millets, oats, rye, and so on), not to mention cereals of more local significance, such as the various cold-region cereals (from Bithynia, Phrygia, Thrace and Macedonia) to which reference is made in Galen's treatise *On the Properties of Foodstuffs* (VI 515). If we adopt a top-down perspective, focusing on the food preferences of the urban elites, we will miss many of these 'lesser' cereals.

Not only were there numerous kinds of cereals, and for many consumers alternatives from which to choose, but in addition cereal products took a number of different forms, which can be grouped together under headings such as porridge, flat-cakes and bread.

Third, there is a strong case for expanding the triad to accommodate dry legumes or pulses, which as 'the poor man's meat' have traditionally played a considerable role in the diet of Mediterranean peoples. The most significant of these for human consumption were broad beans, chickpeas, lentils and peas. They supplied vital nutrients in which cereals are deficient (see below). The relative neglect of pulses in modern accounts of ancient diets is difficult to understand, considering the frequent reference that is made to them in a wide span of sources. Only the most determined sceptic would discount the numerous allusions in Greek comedy (accessible especially in the form of citations in Athenaeus) to the consumption and anti-social effects of broad beans and lentils, however wary we may be of using comic drama as historical evidence. In any case, the descriptive/prescriptive works of Theophrastus, the Roman agronomists and Galen in his *On the Properties of Foodstuffs*, are in a different class as evidence. These authors all give pulses ample coverage next to cereals (and do not always distinguish clearly between the two), and show that in many parts of the Greece and Italy of their respective days pulses were a regular field crop, and were not simply grown on a small scale in garden-plots.[5]

---

[4] See below, ch. 8, on varieties of cereals.
[5] See Garnsey (1998), chs. 12–13, with the evidence cited there from epigraphy and archaeology.

The case for classing fish or meat as staple foods is weaker. The argument against fish as a staple starts from the fact that most people were
farmers, not fishermen. According to a more sophisticated line of argument, the backward state of the technology of the industry and the
rarity of fish in large shoals in the area limited the size of catches and
the capacity of fish to serve as a staple, certainly among ordinary people,
who would have had to purchase their fish in the market. Fish supplemented staple foods in the case of fishermen and the residents of certain
cities – the copious references in Athenaeus to a flourishing market for
small-fry in Athens are relevant here.[6] Salting extended the life of fish
and the range of the fish-trade in Greece. In the Roman period, fermented and salted fish products were prepared in quantity, especially in
the Spanish (later the African) provinces, and extensively transported
and traded, especially among urban consumers. These sauces or pastes
(*garum, liquamen, allex*) were popular in the Roman army, too. They were
of course no substitute for bread, rather a relish that made bread more
palatable.[7]

As for meat and other animal products: in the context of the agricultural economy of the Mediterranean region (as distinct from central and
northern Europe), meat and other foods of animal origin were relatively
speaking in short supply, and therefore of minor importance in the diets
of the mass of the population. This is a matter of physical geography.
The growing season for plant life in the Mediterranean is short. After
the spring, drought quickly dries out the natural pastures, at any rate in
the semi-arid regions. Grass and fodder were not plentiful there; nor for
that matter was arable, especially where population was relatively dense
and land scarce, as for example in Italy in the classical period. Under
these circumstances, only the largest landowners could contemplate
reducing their arable in order to raise livestock on meadowland.
Moreover, livestock-raising is an uneconomical use of land; plants
produce far more food per unit area than animals do. Animals turn
plants into meat, but a lot of energy is lost in the process. It makes more
sense for humans themselves to eat the plants. Under these conditions,
then, cattle-raising on a large-scale was ruled out. There were oxen, but
they were work animals, kept neither for meat nor for dairy products.
Sheep and goats were numerous, but were raised primarily for wool (or

---

[6] Fish: Gallant (1985); Purcell (1995). Small-fry are a valuable source of calcium and phosphorus
    just because they are bony. Fish in general is a good protein source; it happens to be high in lysine,
    a vital amino acid in which cereals are short. See Heen and Kreutzer (1962).

[7] On fish-sauce, see Curtis (1991). On meat, see below, ch. 8.

hair), secondarily for cheese (and skins); in any case, according to the traditional picture, they were essentially transhumant, forsaking the lowlands during the hot summer months for mountain pastures. Pigs alone were kept basically for meat.

One can make small adjustments to the traditional view. A close reading of the Roman agronomists from Cato to Columella (who cover the period from the mid-second century BC to the mid-first century AD) shows that, in Italy at least, it was standard practice to keep sheep on the farm. So Columella says that up to 100 goats or 1,000 sheep could be housed in the same fold within the estate (7.6.5). There are implications for consumption, in particular of cheese, but also of meat, in the case of the owners of such estates and their dependants. Of greater significance for meat consumption is the prevalence of pig-raising. In Greece, the pig(let) was the preferred sacrificial animal for private cult. In Italy, the rhetorical question of Varro (writing in the 30s BC), 'Who of our people cultivate a farm without keeping swine?' (2.4.3), carries the suggestion of ubiquity.[8] Finally, the Roman army consumed large quantities of meat, whether freshly slaughtered (as in Britain), or salted and dried (in Egypt).

It remains the case that there was no mass meat production and no mass meat consumption. Meat was never the staple then that it is in the West today. It was not synonymous with food. What is 'meat and drink' to us, was 'bread and drink' to them. The elite had access to meat of all kinds, but were still not heavy meat-eaters.[9]

THE CENTRALITY OF CEREALS

In an engaging story of Herodotus, an Egyptian king, Psammetichus, 'discovered' that the Phrygians not the Egyptians were the original race of mankind, by means of an experiment in behavioural psychology. The first word uttered by two infants, isolated from birth, was interpreted as the Phrygian word for bread, 'becos' (Herodotus 2.2). In undermining Egyptian claims to primacy among the peoples of the world, Herodotus was tacitly accepting a parallel claim for cereals among foods. The reference to bread is anachronistic, for it was relatively speaking a latecomer in the catalogue of cereals and their products; rather, it reflects the 'primacy' (in another sense) of bread within contemporary diets,

---

[8] The popularity of pork is reflected in an inscription from the Piraeus (early first century BC), which places it above goat, mutton, and finally, beef. See Steinhauer (1994). For a similar hierarchy, see the Price Edict of Diocletian (AD 301), ch. 4. See Lauffer (1971).
[9] See below, pp. 122–7, on meat.

specifically no doubt the diet of Egyptians, notorious bread-lovers. More indirectly, the prominence of cereals in religion and mythology is a pointer to the crucial role they played in the material and spiritual life of ancient societies: one could cite, for example, the alimentary aspects of the myth of Prometheus, the singular role in Greek religion of Demeter as Grain Goddess, the use of cereals in sacrifices of ancient origin and in religious ceremonial – traditionally older grains, barley in Greece and *far*, emmer wheat, in Rome, were employed – and the central involvement of *puls*-consumption (*puls* is a porridge made from *far*) in the archaising, moralistic myths of Rome. Or one could point to ritual practice and symbolism within the new religion of Christianity. The Eucharist was at one level simply a meal of bread and wine. At a deeper level it involved the spiritual consumption of the flesh and blood of Christ (cf. John 6:53–8, 1 Cor. 2:23–6). The Eucharist was a reinterpretation of the traditional Jewish Passover meal, and a redefinition of existing notions of sacrifice. The sacrificial animal marked out for consumption was not a year-old sheep or goat 'without blemish' (Exodus 12:3–6), as stipulated in the Code of Holiness (Leviticus 22:22–5), but Christ himself. This was radical enough at the symbolic level, even before the medieval church identified the consecrated host as heavenly flesh.[10] Christians from the first, following the example of Christ in the Last Supper, chose for this 'most common of human functions' the food that was at once ordinary and fundamental.

There are a number of other indications that the peoples of the Mediterranean were heavy cereal-eaters. To begin with, no rival staple comes into view, at least for the heartlands of Graeco-Roman civilisation. Not rice, nor any root-crop. Meat consumption was insignificant among ordinary people, or even among the rich, by modern, Western standards. Next, in all ancient discussions of food, notably the agricultural treatises and Galen's *On the Properties of Foodstuffs*, cereals and their products are put at the top of the list and surveyed first. Again, when food is given out as rations to soldiers and slaves, cereals are the main item. The amounts are sizeable. In general, the figures provided by ancient sources, such as they are (and they are not figures for the amount consumed), suggest that substantial amounts of grain were eaten. Further, when food is handed out to urban residents, it is usually in the form of cereals. We note too that when political authorities intervene in the area of food-supply, it is usually grain that is at issue. Athenians

---

[10] Rubin (1991), 26; cf. Feeley-Harnik (1981).

under the democracy regularly debated the supply of grain and no other food, and were much more interested in controlling the movement and marketing of grain than of any other commodity. Finally, cereals held their place at the centre of diets over a long period of time in which kinds of cereal, methods of food processing, and patterns of consumption changed. Barley lost ground to wheat, husked grains to naked grains, porridge to bread, and other forms of wheat to that which made the best bread, *Triticum aestivum*. A hierarchy among cereal products emerged, with white wheat bread at the top. Throughout this long process of evolution, the rich never abandoned cereals – though their diets were always more varied than those of the poor. On the contrary, the rich were able to signal their superiority over social and economic inferiors in their consumption of cereals as of other foods.

Cereals, then, were central. This said, one cannot hope to arrive at actual rates of cereal consumption, in respect of ancient as of other pre-modern societies. Certainly, a serious attempt has recently been made to reach such a figure – 70–75% of total consumption has been suggested for cereals – but this, however plausible, is a conjecture.[11] We can establish (by means of the kind of arguments that are used above) only that a lot of cereals were consumed. This is a not insignificant finding, carrying implications for nutritional status (see below). The other key question with consequences for health is, how far diets incorporated other foods capable of supplying nutrients that cereals lacked. The estimate of 70–75% of total food energy might actually be too low in the case of members of the lower classes. It would make a difference if other foods were cheap and in plentiful supply. A post-war survey in modern Crete showed that olive oil contributed around 29% of total calories.[12] In general, substantial variations in dietary regimes are to be expected, reflecting differences in wealth, locality and taste.

A HEALTHY DIET?

The staple food was a good one, as staples go. The wheats and barleys have a number of nutritional advantages. They are not associated with any particular deficiency disease, as are maize and rice with pellagra and beri-beri, respectively. They are an adequate source of food energy. Taking minimum calories at 1,625–2,012 kcals per day, and 1 kg of soft

---

[11] Foxhall and Forbes (1982). On cereals, see also Amouretti (1986), 113–31; Sallares (1991), III. Agriculture.   [12] Allbaugh (1953).

wheat as providing 3,330 kcals, the basic requirement could be satisfied by around 490–600 gm of wheat, or, at a high extraction rate, around 650–800 gm of wholemeal bread (2–2.4 Roman pounds). I am talking of minimum requirements, that is, enough to keep life going, not to ensure good health. Then, cereals are higher in protein than most other staples, in particular the root crops to which many contemporary Africans are wedded, such as yams or sweet potatoes, or the 'false banana plant', *Ensete ventricosum*, of the Ethiopian Gurage tribe, which supplies a mere 12 gm of protein per 1,000 calories. This amounts to about a third of the protein value of plain white household wheat flour.[13] Again, cereals have a good proportion of most vital nutrients, including the B vitamins thiamin and niacin, and vitamin E, and are adequate sources of calcium and iron. Wholemeal wheat will provide per 100-gm edible portion 36 mg of calcium (72–90% of the requirements of a moderately active man) and 4 mg of iron (44–80% of requirements).

Cereals are less than perfect in several respects. They are low in the amino acid lysine (and to a lesser extent threonine); in general, animal proteins have advantages over plant proteins. Again, while a good source of the B vitamins thiamin and niacin and of E vitamin, they are low in B2 (riboflavin) and deficient in A, C and D. Those nutrients could in principle be supplied from other plant foods, notably pulses, vegetables and fruit (and ultraviolet radiation is an important source of vitamin D).

Cereals if consumed in quantity will give one most of what one needs. But the way they are taken in makes a difference. High consumption of unleavened breads made with a high bran content is associated in the Middle East and elsewhere, including the British Isles, with various serious pathological conditions, such as iron-deficiency anaemia, dwarfism and rickets. The reason is the presence of phytate acid in cereals, especially in the bran and the germ, which impedes the absorption of vital minerals such as iron and calcium – both of which are present in wheat and barley in adequate quantities. Thus one might expect serious health problems in ancient societies to the extent that flat-cakes, chappatis, and so on made from high-extraction (under-sieved) flour, without leavening, were consumed in quantity – and especially where not much else was eaten. Today there are some Mediterranean peoples who are much more heavily dependent on cereals than others are: the North Africans eat more cereal than the Southern Europeans of Greece or Italy or the former Yugoslavia. Regional differences are also

---

[13] Shack (1981), and see p. 142, below.

likely to have been significant in antiquity. So too were class differences. The poorer one was, the less good-quality flour one could buy, and the less efficiently that flour was sieved. Flour inefficiently sieved would have a high phytate content; and the higher the phytate content, the more deprived of vital minerals the body was likely to be. Galen's survey of breads encompasses four classes, which range from 'extra dirty' bran-bread to 'clean', fine-ground bread (vi 480–6). The passage should be read with an eye to the class differences that were a feature of Graeco-Roman society.

To conclude, although wheat and barley as staples score relatively well, some doubts are raised. The first doubt concerns quantity. Did ancient populations get enough of the staple to serve their basic food-energy and protein requirements? In particular we might wonder about the situation of two vulnerable groups, children in periods of most rapid growth, and pregnant and lactating women. A similar problem arises in the matter of minerals. A moderately active woman requires about three times as much iron as a man, a pregnant or lactating woman more than twice as much calcium. How far were these needs supplied by higher intake of the staple? Or from other sources?

The second question concerns dietary balance. Were the deficiencies of wheat/barley in certain vital proteins made up by the consumption of foods with a complementary amino acid pattern, in particular, dry legumes? Did ancient populations suffer from vitamin deficiency of one kind or another through over-concentration on a cereal diet?

As indicated at the outset, these questions cannot be answered directly through recourse to figures of actual consumption, for there are none. Our plan of action is rather to approach the problem of the availability of food via an exploration of production and distribution. We shall be in a better position to assess the nutritional status of the population once an evaluation has been made of the success or otherwise of farmers in growing enough food, of traders in carrying it from areas of surplus to areas of deficit, and of the social and political elite in facilitating its distribution through all levels of society.

CHAPTER 2

Food and the economy

PRELIMINARIES

People can consume only such food as is available. Availability is determined by the physical environment and the economic, social and political structures. It is not a straightforward matter to separate out the economic factor. By one influential view associated especially with Moses Finley, the economy of early or simple societies was embedded in society and politics. Economic relations were an extension of social and political relations; they were governed by the value system of *homo politicus* rather than *homo economicus*. The dependence of the economy on the *polis* or state structures is symbolised in a lacuna in the works of Aristotle. Aristotle was a prolific writer, but he did not write a book about economics. If he *had* composed a book with the title *Oikonomia* (or following Xenophon, *Oikonomikos*), it would have been about household management, for that is what *oikonomia* means. In the absence of 'an enormous conglomeration of interdependent markets'[1] and the spirit of economic rationality that such a market system engenders, ancient thinkers simply had not conceptualised the economy.

The problems involved in disentangling economics from politics are exemplified in the area of distribution and trade. The essence of trade is market exchange. One can easily misclassify as trade a lot of commodity movement and transference which is *politically* directed and controlled, and does not involve exchange in the market. Yet market exchange did exist in antiquity, even if it was less important than it is today, and the distribution of surplus food does have an economic dimension. It can certainly be legitimately talked about, alongside the production and processing of food, in a discussion of the economic aspects of food.

---

[1] Finley (1985), 22.

PRODUCTION: THE GOAL OF SELF-SUFFICIENCY

What we are discussing, food and the economy, is of central importance. Food made up the major part of surplus production, the land being the most important source of wealth, and food being the most significant product of the land. The distribution of the product to the consumer, whether in raw or finished form, was also of significance, but not to the same degree as production. This is because in antiquity most people consumed food they had themselves produced; in our society, most people do not. What was crucial then was harvest performance and the storage of the surplus of a good year against the deficit of a poor year. We on the other hand are overwhelmingly non-producing consumers. We do not put our hand to the plough, and we find enough food, and more than enough, in the shops. In many countries of the contemporary world the picture is not so rosy. Nevertheless it appears that in the world community as a whole, enough food is grown – the difficulty is how to distribute it, to move it from areas of surplus to areas of deficit. Famine and malnutrition are ultimately problems of distribution.

Producers in ancient societies aimed at self-sufficiency. However, self-sufficiency was an unattainable goal. Small farmers could not avoid looking outside the farm for some of their required food resources, regularly, or occasionally: *regularly*, if the environment of the farm was permanently unsuitable for the production of some desired or vitally needed commodity, like salt, in the case of inland districts, or olive oil in cold or mountainous regions; *occasionally*, to make up deficits left by bad harvests, which were recurring and inevitable, if not precisely predictable, in the context of Mediterranean rain-fed agriculture.

Self-sufficiency was not the goal only of the small producer. It was also an important element of the traditional value system of the aristocratic elite. Finley writes: 'Relishing independence from the market as buyers, from reliance on others for their own necessities, the landowners of antiquity operated by tradition, habit and rule-of-thumb, and one such rule was that "a paterfamilias should be a seller, not a buyer".'[2] The maxim runs through writings on agriculture: it is the elder Cato's (mid-second century BC), picked up by Varro a century later, and by Pliny the elder a century later than Varro (Varro 1.22.1; Pliny, *Naturalis Historia* 18.40). Finley gives some attention to the mentality of Cato, but the example he uses in developing the point about self-sufficiency is

[2] Finley (1985), 110.

Trimalchio, the imaginary freedman of Petronius' *Satyricon*. He writes:
'In two respects Trimalchio was expressing perfectly good doctrine,
which he merely exaggerated: he was openly delighted with his wealth
and boastful about it, and he was equally pleased with his self-sufficiency,
with his possession of estates capable of producing everything he
needed, no matter how expanded the needs and extended the desires.'[3]
The doctrine of self-sufficiency obviously fits badly with 'expanded
needs and extended desires', and that is why the following words are
funny, put in the mouth of one of Trimalchio's dinner-guests:

You must not suppose either that he buys anything. Everything is home-grown:
wool, citrons, pepper; you can have cock's milk for the asking. Why, his wool was
not growing of fine enough quality. He bought rams from Tarentum and sent
them into his flocks with a smack behind. He had bees brought from Athens to
give him Attic honey on the premises; the Roman-born bees incidentally will be
improved by the Greeks. Within the last few days, I may say, he has written for
a cargo of mushroom spawn from India. (Petr. *Sat.* 38; cf. 48)

This is of course a travesty of the ethic of self-sufficiency, which essentially enjoins the farmer or landowner to avoid the purchase of basic
commodities and equipment that could actually be grown or made on
the estate. What Trimalchio is doing is importing items like the spawn of
mushrooms from India and Attic bees, so that he can produce Indian
mushrooms and Attic honey on his estate, and representing this not as
conspicuous consumption, which it was, but self-sufficiency, which it was
not. The main point is that self-sufficiency was quite impossible of
attainment even for conservative Roman senators like the elder Cato, for
practical reasons, let alone for the average member of the elite, who was
committed to an extravagant lifestyle.

In short, small and large landowners alike did have to buy, and so they
also had to sell. Necessity aside, large landowners in particular stood to
gain from the sale of a proportion of their surplus. There is no doubt
that they did appreciate this fact, and that they realised at least some of
the profit which their land was capable of generating. The crucial issue
is, what was the size of the agricultural surplus?

THE SIZE OF THE SURPLUS

The size of the surplus mattered because there was a large number of
non-producing consumers, inhabiting cities and lesser agglomerations,

---

[3] Finley (1985), 36.

who depended upon food produced by others for their survival. Some 10% of the total population of the Mediterranean basin may have been city-dwellers – in Italy a higher percentage because of the inordinate size of the city of Rome – most of whom had no direct access to the land.

There is a dilemma here, and it can be put in these terms: the farming goals and mentality of peasants, and the technology at their disposal, were not conducive to the generation of a large surplus. Hence the live-lihood of millions of urban consumers was perpetually at risk. Peasant agricultural production aimed primarily at minimising the risk of sub-sistence failure and maximising the opportunities for survival.[4] For present purposes, we are interested in the implication of the goal of risk minimisation that it is antipathetic to the goal of profit-seeking, let alone profit maximisation. Instead of concentrating on the growing of one or two cash crops for sale in the market, the peasant diversifies his crops in order to spread his risks. As the peasants of modern Methana in the Peloponnesos told the ethnoarchaeologist Hamish Forbes, 'We have a little of everything.'[5] Crop diversification combined with land frag-mentation makes very good sense in the broken, hilly landscape of Greece and Italy, with their great variety of topographies and micro-climates. The farmer is extremely unlikely to experience a low return in any particular year in respect of all his various crops in all his scattered pockets of land; but the cost of risk minimisation is low net production – a smaller surplus.

Peasants nevertheless do expect to produce a 'normal surplus'.[6] Forbes found that in present-day Kosona on the Methana peninsula peasants aim to set aside two years' supply of wheat and four years' supply of olive oil (since olive trees produce a respectable crop only in every second year).[7] The question therefore is, how successful were peas-ants in holding onto their 'normal surplus', always supposing that they were successful in producing it? I say 'holding on to it', because by definition the surplus was regarded as a survival resource: it was not ear-marked for sale.

Peasants did have to give up a portion of their surplus in exchange for necessities which they did not themselves produce. They might even have to devote some of their property to the systematic production of goods for the market. If we turn to Italy and the peasant of the pseudo-Virgilian poem *Moretum*, we find that the vegetables in Simulus' 'kitchen-garden' were destined not for his own ploughman's lunch, but

---

[4] Gallant (1991).   [5] See Forbes (1976).   [6] Halstead (1989).   [7] Forbes (1982).

for sale in the local urban market. A powerful case can be made for the routine involvement of small producers in the market, on an empire-wide scale.[8]

In addition, a peasant might have to give up a proportion of his product to a creditor, landlord or tax-official. The larger the demands from outside, the smaller his chances were of maintaining his farming strategy and surviving in the long term. The kind of demands imposed from outside, not just their scale, was important. So, the requirement to pay rents or taxes *in cash* would force him to grow crops that he could sell, and so would undercut his subsistence base, while exposing him to the vagaries of the market. The peasant economy could, in principle, tolerate and absorb demands from outside up to a certain level without major structural changes and adaptation. Beyond that level, it would have to transform itself or decline. It is worth asking how capable the peasant economy was of self-transformation.

In so far as scholars have addressed the issue, they divide into pessimists and optimists. The pessimists are those who have a low opinion of the productivity and efficiency of ancient farming, especially as undertaken by subsistence peasants. It is a matter of limited objectives (as outlined above), primitive technology, and a particular mentality – classically exposed by the Russian peasant theorist, Chayanov. Peasants have a keen sense of the drudgery of work and the desirability of leisure, and will simply put down their hoes or pitchforks at the point when they think the benefits of work are outweighed by its burdens.[9]

New arguments for low productivity have recently been advanced by Robert Sallares[10]. Farming in antiquity must have been low-yielding, it couldn't have been otherwise, because seed-selection had not proceeded far enough, seeds were too small and too light in weight. His second point concerns the way farmers conceptualised yield: they (it is argued) thought in terms of yield per plant rather than (as we do) yield per unit area, and the consequence of that was lower net product. Guided by this approach to farming, a farmer might produce some superb individual specimens, but the cost would be fewer plants and fewer bags of wheat.

The optimists are those who say that smallholders, and especially those who lived on their land rather than in some urban centre some distance away, had the capacity to increase productivity, and did so in certain circumstances.

---

[8] De Ligt (1993).   [9] Chayanov (1986).   [10] Sallares (1991), 335–8, 341–4.

The arguments of the pessimists take one only so far. What is at issue is not an agricultural revolution, but rather the generation of modest additional income such as could be achieved by crop changes, more manuring and weeding, and in general a greater input of labour. If agricultural technology in the Mediterranean region was primitive, it remained so right through to the early twentieth century. As for concepts of yield, one should be wary of getting too close to the world of the agricultural writers, who were rich men writing for people of their class and level of wealth. It was rich landowners with land to spare who manifested the 'prize marrow syndrome', looking for an impressive yield per plant rather than a higher yield per unit area. It is quite implausible to suggest that small landowners operating close to the level of subsistence did not make careful calculation as to how to use their limited resources of land to best advantage.

It can be accepted that when peasants did raise their sights and seek more out of their land, it was usually because they were forced to do it. This was recognised by Chayanov, who focused on the internal constraints associated with higher food needs within the family.[11] Alternatively, the constraints might come in the form of demographic pressure from the community as a whole. Peasants in fourth-century BC Attica and Argos responded to population growth by introducing more intensive methods of production on their properties. More people, less land per head, perhaps also a reduction in food imports following the collapse of the Athenian empire, forced farmers to squeeze more out of their land than they had done previously.[12]

Finally, the peasant might face an increase in financial and other burdens imposed from outside. It has been argued[13] that something like this happened to peasants on a global scale as a consequence of the expansion of the Roman state. The hypothesis is that conquest and the imposition of tribute by the Romans forced farmers in the provinces to raise productivity.

In all these cases increased productivity did not necessarily work to the benefit of the producer. Some peasants at least would have found themselves running faster to stay still, their higher surplus creamed off by others. And there was always the risk that the burden would prove too great, that the peasant economy would be depressed rather than stimulated. Most commentators, following A. H. M. Jones, believe this

[11] Gallant (1991), 60.
[12] Jameson (1978); Jameson et al. (1994). Pessimists include Isager and Skydsgaard (1992).
[13] Hopkins (1980).

happened in the late Roman Empire, often seen as a period of rising taxation and progressive land abandonment.[14]

It is not so simple. Let us consider Greece. Archaeological land-survey (in areas as diverse as Aetolia, the Argolid, south-west Boeotia, southern Euboea, northern Keos, Lakonia, Megalopolis, Melos, Messenia, Nemea and Panakton) indicates that the countryside of Greece was actually repopulated from about AD 300.[15] The pattern is repeating and unmistakable. Site numbers gradually returned, over three or more centuries, to something like their former count in the Classical and early Hellenistic eras, signalling more intensive land-use and a demographic upturn – or (more attractive to potential sceptics, but a less probable alternative) the redistribution of population to the benefit of the countryside. Nor does this necessarily support the theory that taxation (its introduction or increase) stimulated production and raised productivity. For on the basis of this theory, the rural landscape of Greece would have filled up under the early Principate following the population decrease of the last two centuries BC and the introduction of a modest tribute under Augustus. In fact the countryside stayed empty for around three centuries.

It is impossible to generalise about the state of the rural economy over the whole period of antiquity. It is similarly a tall order to assess the condition of the peasantry, either in detail or in potted summary, in terms of the burden of taxes and rents, involvement in the market, and survival chances. There was no typical ancient peasant. Some ancient societies were more successful than others in extracting the surplus from their farmers without jeopardising their survival, or they were more successful in some periods than in others. On the other side, it is clear that the ancient world never lost its dependence on small-scale production. Even the large estates of the rich were frequently divided up into parcels and worked by small tenant-farmers. Peasant farming survived – so it must have been viable. If there was a long-term trend, and now we are talking of developments gathering pace from the turn of the third century AD, it involved the depression of the legal condition and the social and political status of the small farmer.[16] But that is a statement about political and social relationships, not economics. The ancient political authorities could not afford to kill the peasant goose that laid them golden eggs. Free-range geese were transformed into battery geese, perhaps.

---

[14] For general surveys of the situation on the land in the Late Empire, see Whittaker and Garnsey (1998); Garnsey (1996a).   [15] Alcock (1993).

[16] The reference is to the late Roman colonate. See Whittaker and Garnsey (1998), 287–303.

DISTRIBUTION

With distribution, attention switches from the farmers and countrymen of antiquity, the vast majority of the population, to those resident in cities and not themselves engaged in agriculture, in other words to those consumers who were not themselves producers. (I do not mean to deny that some urban dwellers worked on farms in the vicinity of cities.) What was the likelihood that they would get the food that they needed, and by what mechanisms did this food arrive?

Every *polis* and *civitas* lived off its territory: *polis* and *chora*, *urbs* and *territorium*, were each a single legal and economic unit. Small farmers brought in for sale what they could not avoid selling in order to raise money to buy necessities they lacked, or to pay off debts, rents and taxes. Large landowners, typically urban grandees, had a proportion of their surplus brought in for marketing in the city, for consumption in their large households and distribution among clients.

What happened if the city outgrew its hinterland? The historic solution was for a community to reproduce itself in a distant part of the world. It is cheaper to move men than commodities. Colonisation was a movement of men. It was not designed as a way of bringing agricultural produce back to the mother city over long distances – even if the one did lead to the other in particular cases. In fact it might be fruitful to view emigration, the siphoning-off of surplus population, as an alternative to the development of long-term exchange or trade relationships, and of a network of institutions to monitor or administer these relations.

When the era of colonisation on some scale was over (in Greek history in the seventh and sixth centuries BC, though there was another flurry of activity in the fourth century BC), the cities that emerged had no tradition of intervention in trade, and had not developed a network of institutions to monitor or administer such matters. It was not that imported goods did not reach their markets. This happened, but private initiative was responsible. The cities on the whole (imperial Athens was a partial exception in the fifth and fourth centuries BC) did not trade, run monopolies, found trading stations, own ships or employ sailors. This situation did not change significantly until late antiquity. For example, late-fourth-century BC Clazomenai, a Greek city off the Anatolian coast, did not own ships (as a passage in Aristotle tells us).[17] In 129 BC Thessaly did not have ships, as the Roman magistrate Metellus discovered, when he

[17] For references and fuller discussion, see Garnsey (1988), 70ff.

wanted to transport a large quantity of Thessalian wheat to Rome in an emergency. The Ptolemies of Egypt, whose state functionaries were legion, did not have ships. Rome of the Republic and Early Empire did not own merchant ships. In the late Roman empire, the state secured its vital supplies for the capital cities through private merchants and ship-owners – who, to be sure, were bound to this service (the so-called *annona*), as were their heirs.

The traffic in foodstuffs, then, was essentially in the hands of private traders. Its scale was huge. The end of colonisation did not mean that cities had invariably reached an equilibrium between population and the food resources of their own territory. Some cities no doubt had done so. Others most certainly had not. There were some big cities in antiquity, especially in the Roman period. Rome had around a million inhabitants; Alexandria, Carthage, Ephesus, Antioch, among other cities, were well into six figures. Their inhabitants were dependent for their survival on the ceaseless activity of traders. Even those communities that were not in permanent deficit had to turn to traders when local harvests were poor. In effect, climate and geography (that is, the inevitability of harvest fluctuations in a semi-arid zone where rain-fed agriculture was the norm), in combination with social and political conditions (man-made shortages), ensured that there would be a substantial medium-range movement of staple foodstuffs.[18]

This may seem puzzling in the light of the older argument, associated in particular with A. H. M. Jones and M. I. Finley, that trade was insignificant in the ancient world, both in quantitative and qualitative terms. Traders were 'small fry', transport facilities were primitive and costly, the market undeveloped; wealth was in land, and landowners aimed at self-sufficiency and minimal involvement in the market, in consumption not profit-maximisation. There is a lot to be said for the argument. At one level, it is about the nature of the operations that took place when commodities were moved from producer to consumer. Finley wanted to say that those so-called trading operations were usually not trade at all, that is, not free market exchange. What else could they have been? The chief possibilities are two, gift exchange or reciprocity, and administered trade, sometimes called redistribution.

Gift exchange was a structural element of the peasant economy. The capacity to exchange with kinsmen, near neighbours or the farmer over the hill was vital to the survival of small-unit farming. Peasants were

---

[18] On climatic variability, see Garnsey (1988), 8–18.

aware of the risks involved in over-dependence on the market. Gift exchange between *aristocratic* households is well-established as early as Homeric Greece, and there are traces in all periods. It is an aspect of the ritualised friendship, *xenia*, which Gabriel Herman found to have been alive and well in classical Greece. Ritualised friendship he defines as: 'a bond of solidarity manifesting itself in an exchange of goods and services between individuals originating from separate social units'. In a section discussing the exchange of natural products, he posits the existence of ties of such a kind between eminent Athenians and the royal leaders of the grain-rich Pontic kingdom in the north of the Black Sea in the fourth century BC.[19] For Romans, the counterpart of *xenia* was the patronage networks that bound together Roman nobles and distinguished foreigners.[20] But the Roman state developed a different way of dealing with foreign parts that were rich in primary resources, namely, imperial expansion and at times annexation. By this means they gained freer access to, in particular, the grain stocks of what were now dependent states. A consequence is that as the empire expanded, administered trade, the movement of goods by direction of political authorities, grew at the expense of gift-exchange or reciprocity. In the context of the command economy established by the Romans, and particularly by the Roman emperors, vast amounts of grain were systematically shipped from Sicily, Sardinia, Egypt and Africa in the form of taxes in kind and rents in kind (in the latter case, where the grain came from land confiscated and converted into public land, *ager publicus*, or imperial property, *res privata*.)

Consideration of empires, and in particular the Roman empire, should not be allowed to distract our attention from the basic rhythm of exchange as practised all over the Mediterranean, as it involved producers, large and small, merchants, large and small, and the very numerous urban communities. There is very little sign that governments of the ordinary cities of the Mediterranean world, or even the larger cities, with the exception of imperial Athens and imperial Rome, intervened in a systematic way in the regular procurement of food supplies. This should mean that the market was active, and that it had to be.

One might say that where reciprocity, resting on the exploitation of long-established traditional links, and administered trade, proceeding in the context of relationships of superiority and dependence, were insufficient to furnish essential supplies, there was no alternative to establishing a corn-fund and buying at the market rate. This is just what

[19] Herman (1987), 10, 82ff.   [20] Badian (1958); Ferrary (1997a); (1997b).

the evidence, especially the inscriptional evidence, shows cities doing. There was a market rate for wheat and barley, just as there was a market rate for slaves and other commodities. In any individual case, it was a rate which fluctuated according to supply and demand. We find, for example, that there were seasonal fluctuations in prices – so wheat was cheaper after the harvest than before the harvest, for example, in Sicily in the time of Cicero, or in Egypt in the Ptolemaic and Roman periods. We find again, not surprisingly, that prices at Rome were higher than elsewhere – perhaps twice the Sicilian norm – and that wheat was usually twice the price of barley.[21]

So there was a food market: what does not seem plausible is the kind of reconstruction that Heichelheim attempted.[22] Heichelheim thought in terms of global price-fluctuations, with, for example, wheat prices soaring all over the Mediterranean at the same time in response to some imagined general shortage (notably in the period leading into the Gracchan crisis). Finley's dissatisfaction with this kind of economic history, built on an assumption of a world market, and based on the flimsiest of evidence, was justified.

CONCLUSION: THE ECONOMY – AND POLITICS

How did the common people get the food that they needed if they were not themselves engaged in farming? It was in cities that sizeable numbers of non-producing consumers congregated. The cities happened to be the power-base of the ruling class, who doubled up as landowners and politicians.

Economic processes help to explain how city-dwellers were fed. Market forces brought food to the cities, ensuring that *some* people could buy what they needed much of the time. The mass of ordinary urban residents, however, had little purchasing power. Their resources of wealth were minimal, and there was no guarantee of regular, lucrative employment in a city. An additional problem lay in the variability of supply, and the large fluctuations in price that inevitably followed even small fluctuations in the quantity of available foods in a pre-industrial society.

Enter politics.[23] A political solution had to be found. Public interven-

---

[21] Cic. *2 Verr.* 2.3.72, 84, 90, 173–5, 188–9, 194; Duncan-Jones (1976); (1982), App. 8.
[22] Heichelheim (1954–55).
[23] For an extended treatment of the 'politics of food', see Garnsey (1996b). Additional bibliography includes Sirks (1991); Virlouvet (1995); Garnsey (1991a); 1996); (1998), ch. 11 with addendum; Garnsey and van Nijf (forthcoming).

tion was inevitable. But in what form and how extensive was it to be? There were two main, and contrasting, ways of dealing with the food issue: a network of permanent institutions set up and monitored by governments, and generosity displayed for the benefit of the civic community by members of the elite acting as individuals – euergetism.

In the matter of institutions, my position is as sketched out above. There is very little sign that governments of the ordinary cities of the Graeco-Roman world, even of the larger cities, intervened in a systematic way in the regular procurement and distribution of supplies. Imperial capitals are exceptions. Rome and, from AD 330, Constantinople operated elaborate systems of supply and distribution for the benefit of a select group of their residents. Centuries earlier, classical Athens in its imperial prime was able to use its sizeable navy to direct grain traffic towards the Piraeus. And Athenian democratic governments, by instituting payment for the performance of political, administrative and judicial office, put ordinary citizens in a position to purchase the grain and other supplies that they needed. In the great mass of cities, however, then and later, the standard, accepted response to the food supply problem was euergetism. The problem was that typical euergetists were two-faced, looking for both financial profit and popular gratitude. In times of inflated food prices, they did not abandon speculative activities, but rather reduced their scale – or redirected them. The balance was a delicate one. The urban populace, which was essentially employed in servicing a conspicuously consuming elite, could become restless and resentful if its own basic requirements were not met, and might question the authority of the elite and the legitimacy of their rule. In general, it seems that the local elites showed just enough concern for the welfare of the masses to keep the peace. They worked the rudimentary food supply system which they controlled as landowners and politicians, and ensured through their periodic acts of euergetism that food crises did not degenerate into famines. In antiquity, food was power.

CHAPTER 3

Food crisis

The Father of Famine Theory, Thomas Malthus, asserted that a violent remedy was needed to adjust galloping population levels to existing food resources, and that was provided (along with war) by famine.[1] His principle of population, and even more so his prescribed remedies for checking demographic growth, have always aroused controversy. The strong definition of famine with which he was working is, however, less vulnerable to criticism, and that concerns me more at present. Famine is, as he implied, catastrophic; it is a food crisis of devastating proportions, bringing in its train a sharp rise in the death rate and social, political and moral dislocation. As such it should be distinguished from, on the one hand, lesser food crises, and on the other, endemic, long-term hunger and malnutrition. These distinctions are not always carefully made. In many historical discussions, 'famine' and 'shortage' (*la famine / la disette*) are more or less interchangeable.[2]

One thing at stake in the proper definition of famine is its incidence. When Fernand Braudel, the eminent historian of early modern Europe and the Mediterranean world, wrote that famine 'recurred so consistently for centuries on end that it became incorporated into man's biological regime and built into his daily life',[3] he must have had food shortage, not famine, in mind. Shortages were frequent in antiquity. The precipitating cause was often one or more bad harvests. A high degree of variability of crop from year to year, in reaction to low and variable rainfall and fluctuating interannual temperatures, were basic features of the Mediterranean region. Then, difficulties of distribution could independently provoke food crisis or compound the problem, having themselves been brought on by administrative inefficiency, political

---

[1] On Malthus and his *History of Population* of 1798, see e.g. Petersen (1979).
[2] See, more fully, Garnsey (1988); (1992a).   [3] Braudel (1973), 38.

corruption, transport breakdown, or speculation by producers or traders. Finally, foreign and civil wars, as much a feature of life in antiquity as unfavourable and changeable weather conditions, were disruptive of both the production and the distribution of food.

If shortages were frequent, famines were infrequent. While ancient communities did not have the capacity to ward off shortages, they were able, on the whole, to prevent shortages from degenerating into famines. There are two dimensions to famine-prevention, covering the attitude and behaviour of the political authorities and of the peasantry. The former had the responsibility of attracting food surpluses and distributing them among a sizeable body of non-producing consumers. We have already seen that, in so far as local governments were able to achieve this end and maintain civic peace (and on the whole they were remarkably successful), this was through informal means, in particular, the judicious use of euergetism, rather than through the operation of a comprehensive supply-and-distribution network. The urban elites, large landowners to a man, were also in a strong position to influence the fate of the rural population, the producers of much of the surplus that had to be tapped to feed the urban populations.

In this chapter my interest is primarily in the peasantry, and specifically the way their patterns of consumption changed under the impact of shortage. This is an aspect of the broader theme of the survival strategy of the peasantry, a theme treated in detail elsewhere by myself and others, but with rather less attention to consumption than to production and patterns of exchange. We happen to have a superb source for these matters in Galen, the doctor from Pergamum who flourished in the second half of the second century AD, and I base my discussion on him without apology. There are of course gaps in his coverage, and in that of the ancient sources in general. In particular, little is said of the psychological effect of food crisis on those who suffered. Even the most detailed 'famine narratives' describe the behavioural responses of victims only at a superficial level.[4] The medical writers allude to some of the physiological effects of food contamination, but fail to explore the psychological dimension. There are no diaries or reminiscences of participants, such as were composed, for example, by inhabitants of Leningrad during the siege of the city by the German Sixth Army in 1941–42, revealing the physical and

---

[4] See e.g. *Chronicle of Joshua the Stylite*, transl. W. Wright (1882), chs. 38–45, with Garnsey (1988), 3–39; *Chronique de Denys de Tell-Mahré*, J.-B. Chabot, ed. (1895).

moral disintegration of a population at a time of extreme hardship and distress.[5]

FAMINE FOODS

Chuckling, the Collector went downstairs. On his way he spotted a large black beetle on the stairs; he caught it between finger and thumb and took it out with him to the ramparts. There he generously offered it to the Magistrate, who was busy carrying cartridges to the firing-step. The Magistrate hesitated.

'No thanks', he said, though with a note of envy in his voice.

The Collector popped it into his mouth, let himself savour the sensation of it wriggling on his tongue for a moment, then crunched it with as much pleasure as if it had been a chocolate truffle. (J. G. Farrell, *The Siege of Krishnapur* (London, 1974), 301–2)

People in antiquity, including countryfolk, when times were normal ate mainly foods produced from cultivated crops (cereals and dry legumes, a vital source of vegetable protein) and domesticated animals. A second category of foods was obtained by hunting (wild animals) and gathering (wild plants). The evidence from antiquity for this is plentiful enough in aggregate, though scattered. We can complement it with comparative evidence for the habitual collecting of greens and other wild plants and fruits by peasants while they move around the country-side on standard farming tasks.[6] Nutritionally speaking, greens, berries, fungi, and so on, are useful for the minerals and vitamins they add to the diet. In terms of food energy they are an inadequate substitute for cereals, unless consumed in prodigious amounts. Galen knew this, while remaining in ignorance of calories: 'The fruit of the cornel-tree and the plum and the blackberry and white rose, sloe, arbutus, jujube, nettletree, winter cherry, terebinth and wild pear, and so on, give meagre nourish-ment' (Galen VI 621). He was right, if by nourishment he meant energy.[7] Wild plants are not and cannot be a staple food. A diet consisting of wild plants in combination with wild meats is another matter. That was the diet characteristic of the hunter/gatherer societies which preceded sedentary agricultural societies. The populations of the Mediterranean had made the transition to sedentary farming well before the classical period of Greek and Roman history, but the hunting/gathering

[5] See e.g. Elena Iosifovna Kochina, 'Blockage Diary', *Parniat: Istoricheskii Sbornik* 4 (Paris, 1981). I am extremely grateful to Irina Levinskaya for obtaining this document for me, and to Daphne Dorrell for translating it.

[6] Frayn (1979), ch. 4 (=*JRS* 65 (1975), 32–9); Evans (1981). The classic work is Maurizio (1932).

[7] See Halstead (1981), 315, table 11.1.

economy survived on the margins, as long as uncultivated land remained within range and accessible. To the poor, wild foods offered variety in what would otherwise have been a monotonous diet. The rich were not averse to tapping the resources of land beyond the cultivated zone, much of which they effectively controlled. But they (and they only) increasingly turned to another source of dietary diversification, in the form of costly spices imported from the Orient. Apicius' recipes point to extensive use of spices in the Roman *haute cuisine*.[8]

A third group of foods (after cultivated plants and wild foods) consists of items that were not normally human food, but were nevertheless eaten in emergencies. These are the true 'famine foods', and they covered a very wide range. In a severe food crisis, almost anything might be eaten, including human flesh. In Egypt during the famine of AD 1065:

Dogs and cats were eaten, though dogs were almost impossible to come by: they were sold as food for 5 dinars. The shortage worsened to such an extent that people ate each other. The population kept careful watch on themselves, for there were men in hiding on house-terraces with ropes furnished with hooks, who latched onto passers-by, hoisted them up in a flash, carved up their flesh and ate them.[9]

The category of famine foods comes into sharp focus in the writings of Galen (but he deals almost exclusively with plants) chiefly in *On the Properties of Foodstuffs*, but also in the briefer treatise *On the Wholesome and Unwholesome Properties of Foodstuffs*. The two works complement each other. In a passage from the second and shorter of the treatises, Galen envisages country people in periods of severe scarcity using up their pulses during the winter (in the absence of other grains), and being forced to turn to 'unhealthy foods' during the spring: 'They ate twigs and shoots of trees and bushes, and bulbs and roots of indigestible plants; they filled themselves with wild herbs, and cooked fresh grass' (Galen VI 749ff.).

Galen has jumped from pulses to non-foods, and it is in the longer work that this gap is filled with a whole group of what might be called

---

[8] Apicius' cook-book, as we have it, is a fourth- or fifth-century compilation, based on a first-century original usually thought to be by M. Gavius Apicius.

[9] Wiet (1962), chs. 24–5; also 26, 30–1. About a century earlier (early tenth century), rats and grass were eaten in Argos in the midst of a three-year famine induced by Arab incursions. See Jameson et al. (1994), 116. A preyed-upon cat plays a minor role in the Kochina Diary (n. 5, above), while cannibalism is hinted at but not dwelt upon. See however Figes (1996), 777–8, with pl. 100 (Russian Civil War). Examples of cannibalism in Garnsey (1988), 28–9 are mostly set in the context of a city under siege. Galen has a revealingly casual reference to cannibalism in a different setting. See below, pp. 83–4.

inferior foods. They are edible, but eaten by humans only when there
was no alternative. The rustics whom he talks about in the quoted
passage must have increasingly had recourse to such items as their
supply of pulses ran out. There are two broad categories of inferior
foods: animal foods which are fodder not food, and wild foods. Examples
of animal food in Galen include an inferior cereal (in a different category from the acceptable, though lesser cereals *tiphe* and *olyra*) and several
kinds of vetches (vi 522–3, 546, 551). Vetches occur as famine foods from
one end of antiquity to the other. Offered for sale in the market at
Athens in the early fourth century BC during a war with Sparta, they
were also consumed in villages of northern Mesopotamia at the height
of the famine at Edessa at the turn of the fifth century AD. Galen notes
the toxicity of vetch in another work, in connection with a food crisis in
the Thracian city of Ainos, described initially by a Hippocratic author.[10]
The symptoms point to lathyrism, a disease marked by muscular weakness and paralysis, and associated with consumption of *Lathyrus sativa*,
and vetches and pulses related to it.

So much for animal fodder which served in emergencies as human
food. Another category of 'famine foods' includes some found in the
wild. Manna is the classic wild famine food of the Mediterranean region,
or at least its hotter, dryer parts. This is the manna of the Wilderness of
Sin in Exodus 16 (cf. Numbers 11, Deut. 8), which God sent down to
sustain the Israelites as a favour to Moses. Neither the Israelites nor
anyone else in antiquity (nor the middle ages) knew where it came from.
The fact that it was often airborne, carried by the winds, added to the
confusion.[11]

The use of wild plants as famine foods is a recurring motif in Galen.
In an extended discussion in *On Diverse Kinds of Fevers*, they form one of
two categories of 'bad foods', those bad by nature, as distinct from naturally good foods (barley, wheat, and so on) that have been contaminated.[12] In *On the Properties of Foodstuffs* there is a fuzziness of boundaries
at both ends, between wild foods that are and are not regularly eaten,
and between wild foods and what are for us non-foods.

There is a special category of wild foods, which formed part of the
normal diet simply because the plants in question grew in the cultivated
area and could not be separated effectively from the regular crops. In
times of scarcity their contribution to the diet increased in significance,

---

[10] Dem. 22.15; *Chronicle of Joshua the Stylite*, ed. W. Wright, ch. 41; Gal., *Comm. on Hippocr. Epid. II*
(=*CMG* v 126, 4–6 L).   [11] See Donkin (1980); Nelson and Svanberg (1987).
[12] Gal. vii 285. See Lieber (1970), esp. 339–45, on contaminated foods in Galen.

and often with bad effects. Before the introduction of effective weedkill-
ers in the twentieth century, there was no such thing as a field of wheat
or barley, for multiple weeds grew and were harvested along with the
crop. (Major crops were often grown together, as *mesta*, but that was
deliberate, and is another story.) Galen has a heading (at VI 551): *On
sundry seeds that are found mixed with every grain.* Galen's father, a proto-agri-
cultural scientist, investigated the nature of the intrusive seeds. He was
especially intrigued by darnel and *aigilops*, and decided that they were
mutations. He recommended that they be selected out because of their
noxious qualities. Some people did not share his anxieties. They were
lazy or incompetent, and in any case, there was profit to be gained in not
sifting out the foreign matter when the harvest of the main crop was
poor. Both farmers and 'public bakers' indulged in this practice.

Galen was interested in such weeds for professional, medical reasons.
He noted that they induced headaches, ulcers and other skin-diseases,
but missed or passed over their 'stupefying' effects.[13] Mid-sixteenth
century Italian sources are explicit about darnel's properties: 'The bread
that has this [*sc.* darnel] in it, besides disturbing the mind by making
people act as if drunk, causes much weariness and nausea.'[14] A seven-
teenth-century writer referred to darnel-contaminated bread as 'dazed'
bread, which 'often causes people to beat their heads against walls'. One
may assume that the symptoms were not confined to the regions south
of the Alps (the French for 'darnel' is *ivraie*, from *ivre*, 'drunk'), or to the
early modern period. On the basis of Galen's discussion, Camporesi's
generalisation can be applied to ancient as much as to early modern societies:

One of the side-effects of famine which has not been paid its necessary due was
a surprising fall in the level of mental health, already organically precarious and
tottering, since even in times of 'normality' halfwits, idiots and cretins constituted a dense and omnipresent human fauna (every village or hamlet, even the
tiniest, had its fool). The poor sustenance aggravated a biological deficiency, and
psychological equilibrium, already profoundly compromised . . . visibly deteri-
orated.

In periods of scarcity, then, countrymen turned progressively towards
'famine foods'. Galen seems to have thought in terms of a hierarchy of
foods. There are, to be sure, no sharply delineated stages. Even the distinction between 'famine foods' and 'non-famine foods' is not clear-cut.

[13] Other references to darnel are no more informative on this point. They include Theophrastus,
Enquiry into Plants 8.4.6; Ovid, *Fasti* 1.691; Pliny, *Nat. Hist.* 18.156. Nor is the issue raised in Lieber
(1970), at 337–8.   [14] See Camporesi (1989), 122–3.

We should bear in mind that he was talking about a world relatively unfamiliar to him and his audience, who were prosperous urban dwellers. For all his interest in the dietary habits of peasants (and there is no extant source to match him in this), he had no personal experience of life on the 'famine food' / 'non-famine food' boundary. It is none the less clear that, as food crisis descended on the land, there was among ordinary people a pronounced movement down a hierarchy of foods, however ill-defined that hierarchy was. The process was a gradual one. In the first instance, the flour content of the bread (or flat cakes, or porridge, or whatever) was reduced, and extraneous matter (more so than normal) was introduced to make up the difference. The additives might be foodstuffs quite nutritious in their own right. Early Romans, as Pliny tells us, blended wheat and bean flour, while mountain-folk in the Mediterranean region have traditionally baked chestnut bread, or acorn bread, making a virtue of necessity. Chaff, straw, bark, earth are less desirable fillers, but nevertheless turn up in famine narratives through history. During the famine of 1867–68 in Norrbotten, Sweden, a provincial doctor made this comment on the use of emergency bread substances by the poor: 'The inner bark of birch and straw have been used for preference. They do not readily want to use lichens, although instruction in their use has not been lacking.' This probably refers to the campaign led by the pharmacist Jakob Widgren to promote famine breads made with various lichens, the roots of white and yellow pond lilies, mosses and mushrooms.[15]

In addition to the progressive dilution or adulteration of the main staple food, in periods of shortage stored foods are consumed prematurely. Storage is one of several strategies habitually employed by peasants in order to slow the descent down the food hierarchy.[16] It enabled them to linger at each stage rather longer than they would have been able to do, had they been completely dependent on the harvest from any particular year. Food-storage is a recurring theme of Galen, and in this he is a reliable witness of the strategies of peasants.[17] The slaughtering of animals is relevant here, in the first instance 'household animals' (pigs and, less significant in the Graeco-Roman world, poultry). Animals are the classic stored food: 'Acorns were previously food for swine, but when the pigs could not be maintained in the winter in the usual way, first they slaughtered them and used them as food, then they

---

[15] Nelson (1988), 156–60.   [16] For a full discussion, see Gallant (1991).
[17] Gallant (1991), 94–8.

opened up their storage pits and began to eat the acorns, preparing them as food in a variety of ways from place to place . . .' (Galen VI 620).

CITY AND COUNTRY

Thus far the countryside has been treated apart from the city, and there is some logic in this. Rural dwellers as a matter of course operated a complex system of survival strategies, which included exploiting the resources of the countryside more fully than they normally did. We can be sure that social networks came into the reckoning in times of short-age, both those within the peasant community itself, and also patronage or dependency relationships revolving around the larger landowners. The operation of such networks is not well documented, but that is not surprising, for we are talking about relationships which were personal and private and part of the warp and woof of rural life.

Urban dwellers were not necessarily cut off from the land, particularly the inhabitants of smaller townships that were closely integrated into the life of the countryside. But in general – and this would apply in partic-ular to the larger urban agglomerations – city-people did not have priv-ileged access to the land and its resources. There were compensations. They could fall back on rich benefactors (euergetists), who had both the motive to prevent the city sliding into genuine famine, namely, the main-tenance of their authority, and sufficient resources to stop this happen-ing. Such resources included ample food-surpluses in their own barns, and also the capacity to secure emergency supplies, through connec-tions, wealth, and coercion. Galen, an urbanite himself, was aware that city-dwellers helped themselves to the harvests of the farming popula-tion (VI 749).

City-dwellers had the upper hand. Euergetism was based in the city, as was, in due course, Christian charity. (Euergetists appear to have been rather more active than rural patrons, but this may be an accident of the sources.) And the forces of coercion were based in the city. It is to be noted that in the Edessa famine of the early sixth century, the country folk headed for the towns in numbers as a last resort. There were (too few) bakers in the city who baked bread, and the Edessenes were said to 'take good care of those who were in want' (*Chronicle of Joshua the Stylite*, chs 40, 43). But in the end one has to go beyond the city/country dichotomy to reach an understanding of the impact of food crisis on a population, rural plus urban. Shortage did not hit all members of the community with equal force. The rich would have escaped except in the most dire emergencies, but ordinary people were not exposed to the same degree. Occupation and social position and the strength of their support group both horizontal (relatives, friends, neighbours) and vertical (patrons) produced different levels of vulnerability. Amartya Sen's entitlement theory is an ingenious elaboration of this truth.[18] There were high-risk groups in *both* city and countryside, the unemployed or underemployed poor of the cities, the day-labourers of the countryside, and in both sectors, women and young children.

[18] Sen (1981).

CHAPTER 4

Malnutrition

The historiography of malnutrition in past societies is an undernourished plant. A striking exception to the general neglect of the subject is the massive investigation into nutrition and mortality from 1700 to the present day directed by Robert Fogel of Chicago, and the studies that have proceeded under the stimulus of this project or in parallel.[1] Otherwise, in so far as historians have been interested in problems of hunger and shortage, their attention has been captured by short-term setbacks or disasters in the historical record, while long-term deprivation and its effects on the health of the population have been little remarked upon. In short, historians have focused on famine or food crisis rather than malnutrition. In our own day, famine has evoked a world-wide response orchestrated by the media with the aid of relief agencies, statesmen, church leaders and pop stars – at least it did until the novelty wore off. Malnutrition in contrast is no news, though it is widespread and continuous in most developing countries, where it probably constitutes the greater threat to life.[2] Malnutrition has of course been studied extensively by biological and social scientists, especially in connection with contemporary developing countries. Historians who are unaware of their findings are in danger of harbouring overoptimistic assumptions regarding the health and nutritional status of populations in antiquity and other pre-industrial societies. Among students of the ancient world, such assumptions are usually associated with a positive evaluation of 'the Mediterranean diet', one, however, which characteristically avoids the issue of availability, across the social spectrum, of an adequate supply of food-energy and necessary nutrients, and which leaves out of consideration deficiency diseases,

---

[1] See Fogel (1991); (1992); (1993); Komlos (1989); Floud et al. (1990); etc. For critiques of Fogel's approach, see n. 23, below. For malnutrition in antiquity, see Garnsey (1991a), 88–93; cf. Sippel (1988).   [2] See Whitehead (1989), 83; cf. Sen (1989).

although they certainly existed and significantly undermined the health
of the population. Such accounts, in other words, pass over the phenomenon of malnutrition in all its aspects.[3]

I know of only one scholarly discussion that asks whether diets were
healthy and nutritional status good across the population – only to
dismiss the question as hardly worth asking. The writer stakes all on the
'functional capacity' of Greeks and Romans, as shown in their construction of aqueducts, roads, bridges, and so on:

> It is difficult to conceive how the Greeks and Romans could have achieved such
> remarkable feats, which involved far more than a small elite, if they had not in
> general had an adequate and nourishing diet. . . . Surely such things could not
> have been achieved by people who were by and large malnourished, unless we
> remove all ideas of functional capacity from the definition of malnutrition.[4]

This argument, if valid, would equally rule out chronic malnutrition
within the populations of early modern France and England (a hypothesis clashing with the research findings of Fogel and others, see below),
because of the conspicuous monumental achievements that mark these
societies. But it was not the undernourished poor who built the roads,
bridges and aqueducts of the Roman empire, or the railways of England
and France. It is well-known that the Roman army in peacetime was put
to good use in the provinces, building the infrastructure by which supplies
and men could be moved around the empire, and that this was a privileged
group in terms of diet (among other things). Otherwise, various classes of
dependent workers did the job, often under duress, as in the case of slaves.
Such workers were presumably chosen for their fitness for the task and
were adequately fed, at least while they were required for the job in hand
– just as Cato's agricultural slaves (on the testimony of their owner, at least)
were stuffed with cereals, among other foods. English railway navvies,
according to Terry Coleman, 'ate and drank enormously'. One employer
'mentions quite casually that his navvies consumed on average two pounds
of meat, two pounds of bread and five quarts of ale a day.' A newly
recruited navvy might have been 'an indifferent specimen of a labourer',
but after a year or so of solid work, good pay and ample food and drink,
'he was about as strong as he would ever be.'[5]

---

[3] E.g. Corvisier (1985), 43–4.   [4] Waterlow (1989).
[5] Coleman (1968), 25–6, 85–6; cf. 204–5, for the inferiority of French navvies who worked side by
side with English navvies on the Paris–Rouen railway in 1841–3. The French were paid less (and
complained about it) 'simply because they could not do anything like the same amount of work.
They ate lightly, bread and an apple or pear, compared with the Englishman's beef and bacon
and beer.'

The argument for the good health of Greeks and Romans, just considered, comes from a nutritionist – hence his attention to the issue of malnutrition. How is the lack of interest in malnutrition among *historians* to be explained? To some extent this is a reflection of a lack of interest on the part of the literary sources from antiquity. Many Greek and Latin authors mention *limos* and *fames*. However, these terms, which are ambiguous as between famine and hunger, usually refer to an *event* rather than a *condition*, or, if they refer to hunger at all, it is to *episodic* rather than *endemic* hunger. The reference, in other words, is to the hunger that strikes people in a food crisis, rather than the hunger and malnourishment that are always there, a chronic condition of the undernourished, poor and deprived.

We might expect informed comment on these matters from the medical writers of antiquity. But their preoccupation was with the health of the upper classes, whose members they serviced and from which they themselves came. They saw their business as recommending a daily regimen to follow that would preserve bodily health. The rules they laid down invariably covered, amongst other things, food and drink. Food was thought of as medicine. Food maintained the health of their clients, and staved off diseases and cured any afflictions to which they had succumbed. But their patients are more likely to have looked to them for advice about slimming diets than for help in recovering from long-term food-deprivation.[6] There is little sign that Galen, Soranus and their like saw chronic malnutrition as a medical or a social problem, if they had conceptualised it at all.

One can nevertheless find malnutrition in the texts if one looks hard enough and knows what one is looking for. The markers tend to be specific maladies which point to malnutrition but were not recognised as having that origin.

DEFICIENCY DISEASES

There is a kind of malnutrition that doctors would have witnessed but probably not recognised as such: malnutrition as deficiency disease, that is, a pathological state caused by the lack of specific nutrients, vitamins or trace elements. Deficiency diseases in a pre-scientific society affected all social classes, including the propertied classes. I discuss briefly here bladder-stone, rickets, and certain eye diseases.

---

[6] The 'morbid gluttony' of a wealthy woman is cured by Macedonius, a holy man, in Theodoret, *Historia Religiosa* (=*History of the Monks of Syria*) 13.9 (tr. R. M. Price, 1985).

(i) Bladder-stone (strangury, calculi)

This malady is given a lot of attention by medical writers and others like Pliny the elder, polymath rather than medical expert. Pliny regarded it as the most painful of all afflictions and hence a leading cause of suicide (*Nat. Hist.* 25.7.23), and he returns to it obsessively, offering bizarre remedies from mouse dung rubbed on the belly to the ash of wild wood-pigeon feathers in oxymel (*Nat. Hist.* 30.21.65–8). No ancient author improves on the diagnosis of the Hippocratic writer that bladder-stone was caused by bad milk and bad water (*Airs, Water, Places* 9). Certainly no one attributed the trouble to early weaning, the too speedy abandonment (or the non-adoption) of an all-milk diet. But then bladder-stone was more or less endemic in Europe until the turn of the nineteenth century, counting among its better-known victims Samuel Pepys and Napoleon I and III.[7]

(ii) Eye diseases

As with bladder- (and kidney-) stone, so with certain eye diseases, including (in order of development) night-blindness, xerophthalmia (dry, wrinkled cornea), keratomalacia (softened, perforated cornea) and blindness, ancient writers spotted the symptoms but missed the cause. These ailments are to be associated with Vitamin A deficiency,[8] a consequence of underconsumption of animal-derived food (especially milk, butter, eggs, liver and kidney, but fish liver oils are also a good source), and of vegetable products such as green leaves of plants, cabbage, lettuce and carrots, which provide the carotene that is converted to vitamin A in the intestinal wall during absorption. The disorders are endemic among the poor of South and East Asia today, and are also prevalent in large cities in the Near East, Latin America and Africa.[9] They were widespread in ancient societies also, to judge from the space given in medical and other writings to the description of symptoms and the prescription of cures. Among the cures prescribed there happens to be a genuine one, liver. This is recommended with some regularity by authors from a Hippocratic writer (fourth century BC) to Aetius Amidenus (sixth century AD), and beyond. It is usually found in company with bogus remedies. An example is in Aetius, citing Herophilus, a famous physician from Alexandria of the early third century BC. The text reflects a common

---

[7] Ellis (1969); van Reen (1977); Makler (1980).   [8] Wing and Brown (1979), 60.
[9] Thylefors (1987).

confusion between two kinds of blindness, but I quote it for the remedies:

Herophilus says the reverse in his work *On Eyes*. For those who cannot see in the day-time, twice daily rub on an ointment [composed of] gum, the manure of a land-crocodile, vitriolic copper, and the bile of a hyena made smooth with honey; and give the patient goat-liver to eat on an empty stomach. But my guess is that one should rather do this to people who cannot see at night.[10]

Just as the therapeutic powers of goat-liver were not lost sight of through the centuries of antiquity, so the disabilities under consideration did not go away, but continued to plague those with restricted access to sources of vitamin A and carotene, especially, one might imagine, city residents. The rich were not immune, despite their capacity to command a wide range of foodstuffs. Doctors could have shortened the queues of patients had they prescribed eggs as food rather than as eye-salve, and had they recommended the yolk of egg, rich in vitamin A, rather than the white.[11]

(iii) Rickets

This condition, of which the most familiar and telltale symptom is limb-deformity, is a product in the first instance of vitamin D deficiency.[12] Unlike the preceding disabilities, rickets was not identified as a specific ailment in antiquity, indeed not before the middle of the sixteenth century. A passage of the early second-century medical writer Soranus graphically illustrates this point; it also shows that the affliction was no respecter of social class, and that it flourished in big cities:

When the infant attempts to sit and to stand, one should help it in its movements. For if it is eager to sit up too early and for too long a period, it usually becomes hunchbacked (the spine bending because the little body has as yet no strength). If moreover it is too prone to stand up, and desirous of walking, the legs may become distorted in the region of the thighs. This is observed to happen particularly in Rome: as some people assume, because cold waters flow beneath the city and the bodies are easily chilled all over; as others say, because of the frequent sexual intercourse the women have or because they have intercourse after getting drunk – but in truth it is because they do not make themselves fully acquainted with child rearing. For the women in this city do not possess sufficient devotion to look after everything as the purely Greek women

---

[10] Herophilus, *On Eyes*, frg. 260, H. von Staden, ed., who suggests Demosthenes the famous eye-doctor of the age of Nero as an intermediary; see p. 421 for some references to liver. See Gourevitch (1980), e.g., on the confusion in the sources between day-blindness and night-blindness. [11] Oribasius, *Synopsis* 8.35–42 (drawn from Galen and others).
[12] See e.g. Ortner and Putschar (1981), 273–83; Stuart-Macadam (1989), 206–12.

do. Now if nobody looks after the movements of the infant, the limbs of the majority become distorted, as the whole weight of the body rests on the legs, while the ground is solid and hard, being paved in most cases with stone. And whenever the ground upon which the child walks is rigid, the imposed weight heavy, and that which carries it tender – then of necessity the limbs give in a little, since the bones have not yet become strong. (*Gynaikeia* 2.43ff.).

Babies who were swaddled and confined indoors might well have a proclivity to develop rickets, even before dietary factors are brought into the reckoning. A sentence in Galen about women, and by implication, mothers, has relevance here. He complains that they 'stay indoors, neither engaging in strenuous labour nor exposing themselves to direct sunlight' (Gal. xi 164). But rickets arising out of dietary deficiencies, along with a number of other disorders including iron-deficiency anaemia, hepatosplenomegaly (enlargement of liver and spleen), hypogonadism (impaired function of sexual organs), dwarfism and geophagia or pica (consumption of earth and other non-food items) is more likely to have developed among people who ate little apart from cereals, and those cereals composed of high-extraction, phytate-rich flour which inhibited the absorption of key minerals. This kind of consumer would have belonged lower down the social scale than the clients of Soranus.

Hypovitaminosis, that is, vitamin deficiency, was not in itself a killer, at least in the short term. It could however point to other diet-related health problems and to a deeper level of deprivation which spelled an early death. As we saw, rickets can indicate a malabsorption of key minerals, not just vitamin D deficiency, while the absorption and utilisation of the carotenes from which vitamin A is derived are hindered by inadequate levels of both dietary fat and protein.[13] But premature death was much more likely to follow the onset of infectious diseases.

INFECTIOUS DISEASES AND NUTRITIONAL STATUS:
COMPARATIVE EVIDENCE

Infectious diseases have a message to convey about malnutrition too, but of a different kind. While deficiency diseases for the most part reflect specific dietary inadequacies, infectious diseases could reduce the patient to a poor nutritional status overall, thus producing a similar effect to lack of food. This has interesting implications. Deficiency diseases

[13] Wing and Brown (1979), 29.

struck right across society; so, clearly, did infectious diseases. The rich as well as the poor were vulnerable to malnutrition from both sources, and this despite the privileged access of the former to food. A satisfactory diet was no protection against infection.

Early studies of the interaction of nutrition and infection, beginning with the seminal paper of Scrimshaw and others of 1968, emphasised the combined and interactive ('synergistic') effects of malnutrition and infection. If malnutrition was already present, infectious diseases were likely to have a significant impact on the sufferer and hasten the decline into acute malnutrition and early death. (Scrimshaw was also aware that a reduction or limitation of food intake could have the paradoxical effect of increasing resistance to certain diseases, like malaria.[14]) If the 'already malnourished' were primarily drawn from the poorer sections of society, then it might seem to follow that the rich by and large avoided the downward spiral. However, in the view of Scrimshaw and many other observers since, those most at risk to infection and aggravated malnutrition have had in common not social class but age and gender, being predominantly infants and pregnant and lactating women. Diarrhoea is the major killer in large parts of the developing world, especially of infants, and has maximum impact in the weaning period – hence the term 'weanling diarrhoea'.[15] In so far as feeding practices cross class lines in modern developing societies, the diseases that characteristically arise at the time of the delicate transition to adult diet affect a cross-section of the community.

After the peak period of mortality was passed, the rich might be expected to achieve better health than the poor, because of their superior diet and lower work-load. The level of health attained, however, would vary in individual cases with the impact of infectious diseases, and the higher the incidence of disease, the greater the risk of malnutrition.

At this point I move from the contemporary third world, the prime concern of Scrimshaw and many other nutritionists and epidemiologists, to eighteenth- and nineteenth-century France, Britain and the USA, the focus of the investigations of Robert Fogel and others. A summary of their argument might run like this. Chronic malnutrition was severe in France and in England throughout the eighteenth century. This was the product of exceedingly poor diets (diets of low calorific value) and of excessive claims made on diets by disease and work. There was an impact on functional capacity. In the eighteenth century, a

---

[14] Scrimshaw et al. (1968); Scrimshaw (1975).   [15] Rowland (1986).

significant number of households in both countries (a higher proportion in France than in England) lacked the energy to participate regularly in the labour force, or had only enough energy for a little light work or a few hours of light work per day.[16] Although these estimates relate to the condition of the poorer sections of society, the better-off were also to some degree vulnerable to malnutrition, because of the high incidence of disease. Fogel writes: 'There can be little doubt that the high disease rates prevalent during the early modern era would have caused malnutrition even with extraordinary diets, that is, with diets high in calories, proteins and most other critical nutrients.'[17] Chronic malnutrition continued in France and Britain (and the USA) in the nineteenth century. Although diets had improved qualitatively and quantitatively, distribution problems and increased exposure to diseases relating to modernisation limited or prevented better health and nutritional status. This finding applies just as much to the USA as to the two European countries in question. The explanation for the retarding or reversing of improvements in nutritional status and health is to be sought in rapid urbanisation. Cities with 50,000 or more inhabitants had at least double the mortality rates of rural areas. This was a consequence of over-crowding, poor sanitation, adulterated food, polluted water, vulnerability to epidemic disease – not to mention lack of dietary variety and reduced access to certain nourishing foods.

In reaching their grim conclusion about chronic malnutrition in early modern societies, Fogel and his associates were influenced by data on stature and body-mass. These data are relevant because height and weight-for-height measure aspects of malnutrition and health. Height 'is determined by the cumulative nutritional status during an entire developmental age span', weight-for-height reflects primarily 'the current nutritional status', and 'fluctuates with the current balance between nutrient intakes and energy demands'.[18] However, anthropometric data do have a degree of relevance for current nutritional status at a given age. Short and light people, where stunting has occurred during developmental ages, especially infancy, are more likely to catch disease and die than tall and heavy people. Fogel writes: 'Extensive clinical and epidemiological studies over the past two decades have shown that height at given ages, weight at given ages, and weight-for-height (a

---

[16] Fogel calculated that 10% of French families in the late eighteenth century lacked the energy for any work, and the next 10% were capable only of 6 hours of light work daily or one hour of heavy work. His figures for English families in the same period were 3% and 15% respectively. For some critical responses, see n. 23, below.   [17] Fogel (1993), 11.   [18] Fogel (1993), 13.

body-mass index, or BMI) are effective predictors of the risk of morbidity and mortality.'[19]

Stunting would have been most marked among the poor and particularly among those living in cities. The relatively low stature of the urban poor of Britain, especially London, in the early twentieth century is a familiar truth.[20] But Western Europeans and North Americans in general have become between 10 and 20 cm taller over the past two centuries.[21] French adult males, according to Fogel, measured around 163 cm on average in the late eighteenth century, the English about 168 cm. The higher of these figures happens to equal Fogel's absolute measure of shortness. This is an arbitrary figure, but it is not without value. Many Europeans of the eighteenth and nineteenth century fell below the line.[22]

What use can be made of the comparative evidence by a student of ancient (or for that matter, medieval) society? We have to cut our coat according to our cloth. We do not have the volume or the quality of information that is available for early modern and, in particular, for modern societies. At the very least, we can use the work of nutritionists, developmental economists and physical anthropologists to ask pertinent questions of the ancient evidence. But the comparative evidence also helps us establish some probabilities. We can, for example, hypothesise that the groups most vulnerable to malnutrition were the same in ancient societies as in developing countries today. Fogel's arguments too give us some pointers, even if they are not utilisable as a package. Of the three factors around which his account revolves, caloric intake, claims made on this from disease and work, and stature and body-mass, only the first is of no use to us, because we lack data on the basis of which to estimate food-energy intake. But that is in any case the weakest and most contested part of his analysis.[23]

THE PREVALENCE OF MALNUTRITION IN ANTIQUITY

The prevalence in ancient societies of malnutrition associated with inadequate intake of specific vitamins or minerals has been established (pp. 45–8). In addition, on the basis of the comparative evidence, including

---

[19] Fogel (1993), 13.   [20] See Floud et al. (1990).
[21] Fogel (1993), 14. This cannot be attributed to natural selection or genetic drift, since these processes require much longer time spans.   [22] Fogel (1993), 20, table 5.
[23] The labour productivity figures for England in particular are criticised by Voth (1996), and the general methodology is disputed by Riley (1994). Nor do we have information on body-mass. There is a covert attack on Fogel in Johansson (1994), see 106 and nn. 9–10.

that just now adduced, the following hypotheses can be advanced for discussion concerning the presence of malnutrition in the broader sense of inadequate nutritional status.

First, there was a high incidence of undernourishment, disease and death among the under-five population of the Graeco-Roman world at all levels of society, among children of rich families as among children of poor families. Secondly, mature adults who had survived the dangers of early life and endured the dietary regime imposed on infants were likely to have been relatively short in stature and correspondingly prone to disease and malnutrition. Again, this statement is applicable to all social classes. Final heights reflect nutritional status during infancy and childhood, disease was a major determinant of nutritional level, and it did not discriminate as between rich and poor, high and low. Thirdly, mature adults who were members of the upper classes are likely to have been less stunted than their social inferiors, and their nutritional status at a given age would probably have been higher. Although disease was a social leveller, diet and the energy demands of work would have discriminated against the poorer, labouring classes. Finally, there are negative implications for the work-capacity of the population and for the productivity of agriculture.

In what follows I explore ways of testing some of these hypotheses. An exhaustive discussion is not appropriate at this time, essentially because of the continual emergence of new evidence and the constant refinement of scientific techniques for its analysis. In general, we can say more about the health of children than of adults, and about the accumulated past nutritional experience of adults than about their 'current' nutritional status.

Malnutrition must have been prevalent among the under-fives. Children of the rich did not escape. The acute perils facing the newborn were familiar to parents of all social classes. Aristotle wrote: 'Most are carried off before the seventh day, and that is why they give the child its name then from the belief that it has now a better chance of survival' (*Historia Animalium* 588a5). We can trace a stage further the fortunes of the lucky ones, those who had survived birth and the associated *rites de passage*, by studying through the literary evidence, predominantly medical treatises, the feeding practices and other aspects of the treatment of infants, and by analysing the stress marks on deciduous teeth – as the team working on the skeletal material from the Isola Sacra skeletal near Portus is doing in an inventive way (Fig. 3). The close connection between infant feeding practices and infant malnutrition, morbidity and mortality is proved by the experience of contemporary developing

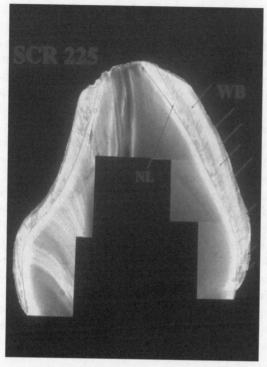

3. Digital reconstruction of a cross-section of a deciduous lower incisor, × 40. Necropolis of Isola Sacra, near Ostia. Specimen no. 225. By this technique an individual's history of stress or 'disturbance' can be read from a tooth with precision and in detail. The 'neo-natal line' (=NL) is, predictably, distinctive. A Wilson Band (=WB) is an unspecific stress indicator.

countries. Many parents in antiquity followed child-rearing methods which undermined the health and survival prospects of their children. In the world of the Roman empire, at least in the circles in which doctors such as Soranus and Galen moved, babies were frequently denied colostrum (protein-rich and protective against infections), were regularly given to a wet-nurse (although in principle mother's milk is best), were standardly subjected to swaddling (which might contribute to bone deformation if coupled with confinement and a poor diet), were liable to be weaned dangerously early or dangerously late, and were weaned onto foods that were often nutritionally inadequate.[24]

The determined sceptic might question any reconstruction based on

---

[24] See below, pp. 106–7.

Malnutrition

the medical writers, on the grounds that their works are prescriptive rather than descriptive, ideological rather than informative as to real conditions. In fact, these authors are operating at several different levels, and their discussion includes what are apparently comments on current practice, often of a critical nature. Furthermore, it is improbable that the advice of men who were practising doctors was completely ignored, even if there is no way of measuring its impact. In any case, the argument presented here does not depend entirely on a few tendentious medical works, let alone on the prescriptive elements therein. I will illustrate with reference to a particular kind of archaeological evidence.

Ancient cemeteries contain a vast amount of relevant data, in the skeletal remains of populations. The richness of this resource is only beginning to be recognised. If only archaeologists were interested and the funds were available, we could put together a detailed if inevitably incomplete picture of the diet, nutrition and health of large numbers of people. Skeletons contain a number of indices of nutritional status. I single out for brief treatment enamel hypoplasia, a condition of the teeth, porotic hyperostosis, affecting the skull, and stature, an index of long-term nutritional status.[25] Robert Fogel and his associates have made heavy use of the last of these indices, stature, but on the basis of records of living not dead subjects.

(i) Enamel hypoplasia

This term refers to defects in the dental enamel that occur when enamel formation is arrested or reduced, itself a consequence of the impact of disease or nutritional stress. The record of stress registered in this way on the teeth is a permanent one, since enamel once formed is not remodelled or restored. Moreover, the enamel is formed according to a strict chronological sequence which runs through the whole period of enamel-formation, namely, from three months *in utero* to about eleven years. This means that it is in principle possible to read from the teeth a history of foetal, neonatal, weanling and older childhood stress.[26] Hypoplasia is common in skeletal samples (see Fig. 5). For example, at Herculaneum 27% of both men (N = 51) and women (N = 43) were affected, at Roman Jerusalem and Ein Gedi 50% of a sample of 63.[27]

---

[25] Other commonly considered indicators of health status include sexual dimorphism, cortical thickness, oral health and bone minerals.

[26] E.g. Rose et al. (1985); Smith, Bar-Yosef and Sillen (1984); Smith and Peretz (1986).

[27] Bisel (1988), table 1; Smith, Bar-Yosef and Sillen (1984), 123, table 5.7.

Dying
seemed
the
least of life's
afflictions and when
death came he smiled,
at the sweet ease of
unshouldering the
body's burden,
old age, infirmity,
and slow disease.
Centuries later,
white skull
uncovered,
he lies still
smiling,
but the
trowel
fails to
locate
the
source
of his
good
humour
among the
long bones
and the   coffin nails.

4. 'Excavated Skeleton', by Conant Brodribb.

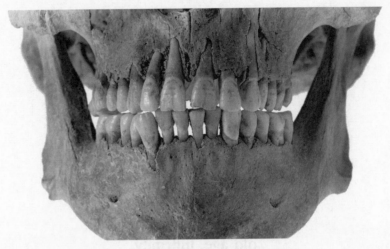

5. Enamel hypoplasia, from Barrington, Cambridgeshire. Sixth to seventh century,
Anglo-Saxon. Stress lines on the teeth preserve a record of arrested growth caused by
episodes of disease or food deprivation.

(ii) Porotic hyperostosis

This, a pathological bone condition affecting the skull, also has negative
implications for the health status of children. The name was coined by
the physical anthopologist Lawrence Angel, founding father of the study
of the skeletal remains of the ancient Greek world, to describe lesions
affecting the outer dense compact bone of the skull and the middle layer,
or diploe. The bone, mainly in the orbital roof and skull vault, is pierced
by small holes of varying size and frequency. The condition points to
anaemia, that is a reduction below normal in concentration of haemo-
globin or red blood cells.[28] Over a hundred years or so of scientific
examination and speculation have produced widely different explanations of the phenomenon. The current wisdom is that the condition
signals iron deficiency anaemia much more frequently than genetic
anaemia, and that it is to be associated not with low dietary intake of
iron (as has frequently been suggested), but with the impact of infection
on body iron stores. It was a product therefore not of nutritional stress,
but of exposure to high levels of pathogenicity. It must be emphasised
that iron deficiency is both common and part of the body's protective
shield against infection. It is *chronic* iron deficiency which is dangerous,

[28] E.g. Ortner and Putschar (1981), 251–63; Stuart-Macadam (1989), 212–19.

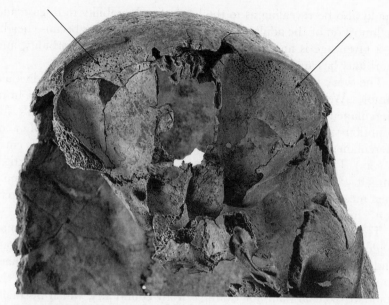

6. *Cribra orbitalia*, from Barrington, Cambridgeshire. Sixth to seventh century, Anglo-Saxon. The porous condition of the eye-sockets points to chronic anaemia.

and a pointer to low nutritional status. Children prone to, for example, weanling diarrhoea, and women under attack from disease and experiencing heavy blood loss (through natural causes and the commonly prescribed venesection), were particularly at risk. At Herculaneum, 41% of the women in the skeletal sample bear the marks of porotic hyperostosis (see Fig. 6) as opposed to 29% of men. At Poundbury in Dorset, in a large sample (457), the condition is present in all age groups, but is severe only among juveniles (6 months – 14 years in the case of orbital lesions, 6 months – 6 years for vault lesions). More than half of those afflicted also had enamel hypoplasia – another sign of the primarily pathogenic origin of the condition.[29]

(iii) Stature

How short and light were Greeks and Romans? As already indicated, the answer, if available, would be directly relevant to nutritional levels experienced during infancy and childhood rather than during adulthood. It

---

[29] Bisel (1988), table 2; Stuart-Macadam (1985), tables 1, 2, and 4.

would also be revealing as to the level of vulnerability to disease and malnutrition of the adult population concerned. This is because height at a given age is an effective predictor of the risk of morbidity, and morbidity has an impact on current nutritional status.

The work has begun. We have some information, some individual samples. We have, for example, Sarah Bisel's study of skeletal data from Herculaneum, Estelle Lazer's for Pompeii, Theya Molleson's for Poundbury, and a number of other smaller samples. Men of Herculaneum average in height 169.1 cm (5 ft 6½ in.), women 155.2 cm (5 ft 1 in.). The stature data for Pompeii give the following figures: 167.6 cm (5 ft 5½ in.) for men and 154.7 cm (5 ft 1 in.) for women. At Poundbury, men measure 162–172 cm (5 ft 4 in. – 5 ft 8 in.) and women 158–164cm (5 ft 2 in. – 5 ft 5 in.).[30]

The data from Herculaneum and Pompeii are as comparable as such evidence can be, because they represent a slice of two populations at one and the same moment of time. In this respect (but only in this), they have something in common with modern data, and form a contrast with the standard skeletal data, for example from Poundbury, which normally cover an extended period of time.

In the present state of the evidence, no general synthesis is possible. If the data show anything, it is that there was substantial variation over time and from place to place, a likely enough hypothesis in any case. The data fall for the most part within the range 162–170 cm for men and 152–157 cm for women.[31] The figure from Herculaneum falls near the top of this range, and incidentally just beats Fogel's absolute measure of shortness of 168 cm.[32] I would expect average height of residents of the city of Rome and other major cities in antiquity to fall near the bottom of the range. We may compare figures from a survey of some suburban parts of the city of Naples in the early 1960s. Males averaged 164 cm and females 152.6 cm.[33] Towns in the Bay of Naples were perhaps somewhat healthier places to live in during the early Roman Empire than a generation ago. Other data from Italian sites cluster either at the top of the range (Tarquinia, Tuscany, sixth to second centuries BC) or at the bottom (sundry Tuscan, Late Iron age; Cagliari, Sardinia, second to first centuries).

Finally, a stray figure from the late Empire carries a hint of a low

[30] Bisel (1988), 64, table 2; Lazer (1995), 203; Molleson (1993), 168.
[31] Other sundry data in Garnsey (1989), 80, table 12. At Isola Sacra adult males were 163.5 cm (N = 85) and adult females 152.4 cm (N = 85) on average. I owe this information to Roberto Macchiarelli and Alessandra Sperduti. [32] Fogel (1993), 14. [33] Bisel (1988), 63.

figure for the stature of farmworkers in this period. The emperor Valentinian in AD 367 legislated a minimum height of the equivalent of 5 ft 5 in. or *c.* 165 cm for army recruits, at least in Italy.[34] The military formed a privileged group in society, for reasons that need not be spelled out here, and new recruits would be chosen from those in good physical condition (if there was any choice in the matter). I infer that Valentinian's minimum figure lay near the *top* of the range for the rural population from which the Roman army was traditionally drawn. It does not follow that army recruiters were able to enforce Valentinian's initiative.[35]

A further point concerns labour productivity. If malnutrition and disease are synergistic, so are malnutrition and work-capacity (and, for that matter, disease and capacity for work). If the energy required for work makes demands on food resources which cannot be adequately met, nutritional status is undermined, with the consequence that productive ability is reduced. It takes no great imagination to suppose that in ancient societies labour productivity was significantly reduced among the workforce. There is no temptation to try to arrive at figures, as Fogel did, controversially, for France and England, on the basis of food-consumption estimates. There are no such figures for antiquity. The argument, rather, rests on other indicators of impaired nutritional status. It runs, in summary, as follows. Literary and skeletal evidence, backed up by comparative data, suggests that malnutrition, traceable to, on the one hand, deficiency of specific nutrients and, on the other, to the impact of infectious diseases, was rife in antiquity. Evidence from skeletal populations, for the most part, indicates that stature was low. Because adult stature is proxy for cumulative net nutritional status, the inference is that low nutritional status was widespread among the population from conception to young adulthood, say, 18–25. At this point it is worth reminding ourselves that life expectancy at birth in ancient societies is universally accepted as lying between 20 and 30. The nutritional status of mature adults would have varied with food-energy intake, incidence

---

[34] See *Codex Theodosianus* 7.13.3 (AD 367). Cf. 7.22.8 (AD 372): a lower height standard was required for frontier troops (*ripenses*) than for the field army (*comitatenses*).

[35] If Valentinian was optimistic, Vegetius was more so. In a book on military matters composed towards the end of the fourth century AD, he says that a height of (in our terms) 173 cm was desirable and 178 cm ideal in an army recruit. Among contemporary Western populations surveyed by Fogel and others, only Norwegians and North Americans attain 178 cm in height on average. Vegetius appears to have had in mind (dreamed of?) a corps of strapping young men, *florentiorem . . . iuventutem.* See Vegetius, *Epitome* 1.5.

of disease, and burden of work. But the health history of individuals in their childhood and youth would have affected their condition in later adulthood, if they survived. I conclude that nutritional status was low among a significant (though undeterminable) proportion of the population of ancient societies.

Accounts of the diet and health of ancient classical societies have generally been unrealistically favourable. The Mediterranean diet was certainly in principle a relatively healthy one. Even those people whose diet was monotonously cereal-dominated had in cereals a relatively nutritious staple food. If they were to suffer severe malnutrition, they would be less likely to be victims of kwashiorkor ('wet' malnutrition) – caused by a diet low in protein, characteristic of Africans dependent on certain root-crops – than of marasmus ('dry' malnutrition), literally, a wasting away, as of someone starving from an absolute shortage of food and therefore food energy.

We should be thinking not just of the quality of the diet, but also of the way it was distributed as between rich and poor, patrons and clients, masters and slaves and so on, and from one region to another – for today some (e.g. North Africans) are more heavily dependent on cereals than others (e.g. Greeks and Italians). Another consideration, especially relevant to those who ate mainly cereals, is the way they were processed, and in particular, how far the poorer consumers, especially in the countryside, were exposed to mineral malabsorption.

Further, we have to go beyond diet to consider the prevalence of disease, which is corrosive of health status. Thus, we can look for, and expect to find, malnutrition caused by or aggravated by disease: to begin with, diarrhoea and dysentery, products of the social environment, poor sanitation and public health facilities and so on. Because disease would have been in large part non-discriminatory in its impact, and malnutrition and premature death were not just functions of dietary intake (or gross nutrition), we should not expect to find a precise correspondence between the hierarchy of health and the hierarchy of social and economic circumstances. Case-histories of individual members of the elite, if known, would reveal striking contrasts, as would case-histories of individual members of particular occupational groups further down the social scale, reflecting especially the uneven impact of pathogens.

Nevertheless, certain broad social divisions are very relevant to our subject, as reflecting a combination of environmental conditions and social/cultural customs and attitudes – such as, the different situations of men and women, and of city and country residents. One can predict that malnutrition and morbidity would have been more widespread and more serious among women, especially those of child-bearing age, than among men, and among inhabitants of large urban agglomerations than among rural populations. And one would expect to find, as in developing countries today, that malnutrition was predominantly an affliction of children.

CHAPTER 5

Otherness

PRELIMINARIES

The literary sources of antiquity depict the inhabited world as culturally heterogeneous, and regard food as one or the more significant markers of divergence.[1] Most obviously, they contrast the food choices and eating customs of the urban elite, to which they themselves belong, and those of societies at the farthest reaches of the Graeco-Roman world or beyond its limits: the Scythians of Herodotus' *History*, the Mossynoeci of Xenophon's *Anabasis*, the various Celtic peoples of Strabo's *Geography*, the northern tribes of Tacitus' *Germania*, and so on. The construction is ideological, the details inaccurate or imaginary, and the purpose of the exercise is to emphasise the identity, singularity and superiority of the dominant cultures of Greece and Rome over those of sundry 'barbarians'.[2]

The fragility of the edifice constructed by our sources is transparent. Discrepant versions are offered of the diets of the same peoples. Contradictions and implausibilities occur in the treatment of major cultures like the Egyptians – for although their level of civilisation was in fact comparable with that of the Greeks, they too were seen by the Greeks as barbarians, simply by virtue of being non-Greek. Then, the inclusion of particular 'barbarian' tribes such as the Celts within the expanding Roman empire, and the cultural advancement that they were making in the view of their Roman overlords, created a particular problem for authors like Strabo, well-practised at imposing pre-fabricated cultural dichotomies. In the assessment of the Celts, a spectrum of civilisation or barbarity might have been a more apposite image to apply than a polarity of opposites.

---

[1] See especially Rosellini and Saïd (1978), who stress the connection between food and cuisine, on the one hand, and sexual *mores* and the treatment of women, on the other. See also Hartog (1988). On otherness ('alterity') in general, see Nippel (1990); (1996b); Cartledge (1997).

[2] 'Barbarian' was originally used in a descriptive sense for non-Greek speaker, as in Homer's *barbarophonoi*, or 'bar-bar speakers'.

Mountain-dwellers were traditionally viewed askance by the 'higher' civilisation, for example, the Ligurians of north-western Italy who came to the notice of Strabo. In his account they are not unambiguously 'barbarian'. For an objective treatment of such 'others', however, one turns not to ethnographers and historians, but to Galen, the physician from Pergamum. Self-consciously adopting a 'scientific' approach to his subject of foodstuffs and their properties, Galen writes with relative detachment of the Macedonian and Thracian use of coarse, smelly, black breads, merely pointing out that these peoples, living in a cold, mountainous environment, had no choice but to grow and eat inferior cereals. There is no hint of the suggestion made routinely by other writers, typically in discussing barbarians at the edge of the inhabited world, that a hostile environment nurtures a savage culture.

Countrymen were regarded as cultural opposites of the civilised, urban elites. In both Greek and Roman literature, they appear as rude, boorish and ignorant.[3] Galen is matter-of-fact in depicting their eating habits, displaying patronising interest in rather than distaste for them, and he avoids stereotypes. These people ate badly – inferior cereals or worse, sometimes boiled wheat instead of bread – but in the main only when forced to do so by food shortage, which was aggravated, we are permitted to infer, by the demands of city-dwellers.

Another contrast familiar from Latin literature, and present though less conspicuous, in Greek, is that between their own affluent and decadent society, and a mythical, ancestral one, built on simple, peasant values. The Roman elite were equivocal about the peasantry. On the one hand, they were conscious of the social and cultural distance between themselves and the rustics of their own world, on the other, they kept alive in their moralising rhetoric the myth of the yeoman farmers who had provided the leaders and the rank-and-file of Rome's victorious armies. Rome's pious and patriotic heroes practised frugality and simplicity in their diet and mode of life in general. Athenaeus has Homeric heroes play a similar role: they are champions of a simple fare and life-style, avoiding luxuries and delicacies. Precautions have to be taken in approaching such accounts, which are self-evidently not descriptive. They are composed by moralising writers intent on framing a critique of social practices and values in their own worlds on the basis of idealised portraits of earlier societies.[4]

---

[3] MacMullen (1974), ch. 2; Gallo (1989).
[4] Whether the social critique in Athenaeus is aimed at his own world is, however, problematic. See below.

7. An ox is led to the sacrifice. The context is funerary. A man has a sacrificial
axe in his left hand, a woman carries an offering-table laden with loaves of bread,
and a small girl bears a dish of eggs and pomegranates. Andriuolo, Paestum.
Lucanian, *c.* 350 BC.

A thorough treatment of cultural differences reflected in food and
foodways would embrace also contrasts between urban communities
themselves. Rivalry between Greeks was a more present reality than
Greek/barbarian opposition, and this rivalry went deeper than politics.
Athenians, Spartans, Cretans, Thebans and so on were considered
different, in character and institutions – and food and foodways formed
part of the picture.[5]

There remains the most basic of all distinctions, that which is revealed
by the act of ritual sacrifice (Fig. 7). In sacrifice, the (normatively domestic) beast is prepared for killing, is killed, its flesh is divided, the meat is
cooked and eaten. The sequence of acts marks out the hierarchy of existence: gods, humans, animals. The gods are fed first as a sign of their

---

[5] *Athenians*: see Athen. 43bc, 47bc, 50e, 74de, 130e, 131f–132b, 134a–138b; Sallares (1991), ch. 3, esp.
294–313; Long (1986), 69 ff.; etc. *Spartans*: Hdt. 9.82; Athen. 138b–143a; Xen., *Lac. Pol.* 5; Plut.
Luc. 12; Cartledge (1979), 170–5, cf. (1987), 32–3, 107–8; Figueira (1984); Fisher (1989). *Cretans*:
Arist. *Pol.* 1263b30–1264a11; 1271a27–37; 1271b20–1272b24; Plato, *Laws* 625d–e; Strabo C 480–4;
Athen. 143; Huxley (1971); Willetts (1955), 139–40, 153ff.; Morrow (1960), 17–35. *Thebans*: Athen.
148d; cf. Hdt. 9.16. *Arcadians*: Athen. 148f–149d. *Macedonians*: Athen. 129de, 126e, 128–130d, cf.
157e.; Tomlinson (1970). *Greeks in general*: Hdt. 1.133.

pre-eminence. Their share of the meal goes up in smoke; it consists of the internal organs, the heart, lungs, liver, bile duct, peritoneum, not to mention the blood. In short, those parts of the animal in which its life resides are for the gods. Humans take the choice portions. As for the animal, its lot is to be burned, cooked, eaten.[6]

Portrayals of otherness have in common the perception of distance, spatial, social and moral. They are essentially self-referential, in that their function is to define the cultural identity of the core-group by reference to another community, so as to represent the latter as the opposite of or at least significantly different from the former, and to the former's advantage, except where the writer concerned is fashioning a critique of contemporary society. I focus below on the Greek–Roman (civilized) / barbarian (uncivilized) and the archaic (pure) / contemporary (corrupt) polarities, with special reference to diet and eating practices.

BARBARIANS

In the *Politics* Aristotle sets out a number of modes of life (*Pol.* 1256a40–b1). Most people are sedentary farmers and live off the land and domesticated plants. They also have to work hardest to survive, which is an index of their moral superiority. The idlest are the nomads, who cultivate mobile, 'living fields'. Hunters who live off the fruits of the chase, and others who live off banditry or fishing, make up the list. Several ways of life might be blended: specifically, pastoralism and banditry, and farming and hunting/gathering (but agriculture and pastoralism are not paired).

Authors from all periods of antiquity exploit a dichotomy between civilised, sedentary farmers who live off the land and domesticated plants, and uncivilised, pastoral nomads who are 'eaters of meat and drinkers of milk'.[7] The tradition goes back as far as Homer. In Homer, the meat in question is regularly taken from the herd, but it might include the flesh of wild animals or even human beings, as with Polyphemus the Cyclops. The Cyclopes as a whole approached a civilised diet only in so far as they made cheese, but this they did infrequently and with crude results. The irony is that they might actually have adopted a predominantly vegetarian diet had not laziness stood in the

---

[6] Detienne (1977); Vernant (1981a); (1981b). Between sacrifices, as it were, the divine food is ambrosia and nectar. It was this alimentary regime that Prometheus abandoned when he stole the fire from heaven.   [7] Shaw (1982–83).

way, for their land was capable of producing wheat, barley and grapes in profusion.[8]

Herodotus' digression on the Scythians and other peoples of the North is a more elaborate version of the same theme. The Scythian nomads consume meat and milk, eating their own or wild animals. Their neighbours include cannibals. Herodotus alludes (6.84) to the proverbial Scythian weakness for wine. Wine is a civilised drink, but it is the mark of a savage to drink it 'in a Scythian fashion', that is, in excess, and neat. Scythians were more inclined to mix wine with blood than with water, as in their oath-swearing ceremonies.

Yet overtly in Herodotus, and hinted at in Homer, there is a suggestion of levels of civilisation, a spectrum or continuum of barbarity. There are 'good' as well as 'bad' Scythians. Herodotus remarks upon Scythian good order (*eunomia*) and courage (*andreia*) and the rewards for courage include ceremonial, controlled wine-drinking. The Scythians include farmers who 'sow and eat grain, onions, garlic, lentils and millet', as well as others who grow grain but only for sale. Herodotus is prepared, it seems, to admit elements of civilisation among barbaric peoples, even if this is incompatible with, and undermines, a strict dichotomy between the (civilised, Greek) sedentary farmer and (uncivilised, barbaric) pastoral nomad.

For the late Republican and early Imperial periods of Roman history, the counterpart to Herodotus on the Scythians is Strabo on the Celts and other barbarians of north-west and central Europe.[9] Strabo, writing about the Gauls after Caesar's conquest, is torn between the urge to pass on the picture of the Gauls taken over from earlier, traditional accounts, and the need to praise the Romans under Augustus for converting a nation of soldiers into farmers and turning them away from barbarity towards the civic life:

The Gallic or Galatic race is war-mad . . . if coaxed, they so easily yield to considerations of utility that they lay hold not only of training (*paideia*) but also of language (*logoi*) . . . At the present time they are all at peace, since they have been enslaved and are living in accordance with the commands of the Romans who captured them, but it is from the early times that I am taking this account

---

[8] The Cyclopes were unaccustomed to drinking wine – another mark of their barbarity. When inveigled into drinking it by the civilised outsider Odysseus, Polyphemus lost control of his senses. Against Kirk (1970), who thought that the Cyclopes were vegetarians, I follow Shaw (1982–83).

[9] Strabo also deals with the Scythians, transmitting the standard account with variations, see C 300–3, 311; see Briant (1982), ch. 1.

of them, and also from the customs that hold fast to this day among the Germans. (C 195)[10]

Strabo's description of *present-day* Gauls *à table* turns out to be completely traditional and anachronistic. Only the reference to a Gallic export trade in pork to Rome and Italy has a contemporary ring about it:

Most or them, even to the present time, sleep on the ground and eat their meals seated on beds of straw. Food they have in plenty, along with milk and flesh of all sorts, but especially the flesh of hogs, both fresh and salted. Their hogs run wild . . . Flocks of sheep and herds of swine are so very large that they supply an abundance of cloaks and salt meat, not only to Rome but to most parts of Italy as well. (C 197)

Strabo's Gauls are if anything more primitive even than Posidonius' Gauls of two or three generations earlier (Athen. 151c), when the only part of Gaul controlled by Rome was Narbonensis, basically modern Provence. The food of the Gallic Celts of Posidonius 'consists of a few loaves of bread, but of large quantities of meat prepared in water or roasted over coals or on spits'. This at least implies an agricultural sector of the economy, even if overshadowed by pastoralism. However, their manner of eating is uncivilised: though not messy eaters, they attack the meat 'like lions', 'grasping whole joints with both hands and biting them off the bone'. Other dietary details touched on by Posidonius are confirmed and filled out by other authors: the Gallic preference for butter over olive oil, the weakness of their chieftains for wine, which they drink unmixed, and the prevalence of beer among the common people.

We have to turn back from Strabo to Caesar's *Gallic War* to make contact with the reality of a Gallic nation heavily committed to grain production, and not just with a view to brewing beer. The Gauls were farmers, not nomads. It was only in Germany that Caesar was inhibited from campaigning because 'Germans are not keen on agriculture' (6.29), and simply did not grow enough grain to feed his army. For Caesar, it was Germans (and Britons), not Gauls, 'who live on milk and flesh' (4.1; cf. 5.14).

The Germans themselves are not without redeeming features. Tacitus, notoriously, attributed to them practices and values which were

---

[10] Strabo C 178, 180, 186. Cf. Thuc. 7.27–30 on the Thracians. For the Celts as warlike, see Athen. 154 a–c (gladiatorial bouts at dinner: Posidonius), with Mauss (1925). On the Celts in general, see Feuvrier-Prévotat (1978).

regrettably absent in the corrupt Rome of his day – like liberty. In the realm of food, we note that German mothers breast-fed their babies (*Germania* 20.1), and that the race as a whole was content with a simple diet: 'they banish hunger without great preparation or appetising sauces' (23.1). Caesar also noted that they were averse to importing wine, 'believing that men are thereby rendered soft and womanish for the endurance of hardship' (4.2). The Gauls on the other hand 'import items of use or luxury, and have gradually got used to defeat' (6.24).

These writers, then, are working with a stereotype of barbarians as nomadic pastoralists who eat meat and drink milk. However, the same writers find it convenient to admit degrees of barbarity or civilisation within the barbaric world, as indicated by choice of food and eating customs, among other things. Extreme barbarity is represented by the Irish for Strabo, by the Fenni in the furthest reaches of northern Europe for Tacitus, and by the Huns for the late fourth-century historian, Ammianus Marcellinus. Tacitus on the Fenni:

> So hardy is their way of life that they have no need of fire nor of savoury foods but eat the roots of wild plants and the half-raw flesh of any kind of animal whatever, which they put between their thighs and the backs of their horses and thus warm it a little. They all feed upon game and an abundance of milk, which is their main sustenance, on a variety of plants, as well as on such birds as they can take by fowling; and I have seen many of them who are wholly unacquainted with grain and wine. (*Ger.* 31.2.3; cf. 46.3)

At the opposite end of the spectrum, there are peoples who live close to the Graeco-Roman world, or are actually incorporated in it, and who are involved in regular economic relationships with the superior culture. In Strabo, Celtic peoples who are neighbours to the Romanised Turdetanians of Southern Spain are said to have civilised qualities (C 151). The same goes for the mountaineers of Cantabria in the north of the Iberian peninsula, though the toughness of their women, who, among other things, work in the fields (C 165), is definitely not a mark of civilisation.

In Strabo and in this literary genre as a whole, clear, unambiguous criteria of civilisation, and consistency of analysis, are not to be expected. On the one hand, the Ligurian mountaineers of north-western Italy according to Strabo make civilised purchases of olive oil and Italian wine at Genoa in exchange for flocks, hides and honey; on the other hand, they are represented as 'living on sheep for the most part, and milk, and a drink made of barley', and as governed by an equestrian prefect 'like other peoples who are perfect barbarians' (C 202–3). The approach of the various writers varies significantly: we need only juxta-pose Strabo and Caesar on the Gauls.

We are dealing with ideological constructs, as has been seen. Their artificiality is amply demonstrated when we come to consider how Greeks, and Romans, dealt with other cultures which were old and sophisticated. Egypt was 'other', lacking defining features of the 'core' cultures, and so technically barbaric. But one could still take up different stances in relation to Egypt. Herodotus pushes the idea of cultural opposition to the limits of absurdity, while Diodorus Siculus, writing around four centuries later, takes a more realistic and pragmatic line.[11]

The Egyptians, Herodotus says, did the opposite of 'mankind' in just about everything, and refused to change their ways (2.91.1). In support of this contention Herodotus claims that 'they eat their food out of doors in the streets'(2.35.3), and that, while 'others make barley and wheat their food, it is a disgrace to do so in Egypt, where the grain they live on is olyra, which some call zea' (2.36.2). He might just as well have added that Greeks when drunk (with wine) lie on their faces, whereas Egyptians when drunk (with beer) lie on their backs (as a comic poet jokes). Unlike Pliny the elder, Herodotus did not appreciate that Egyptian olyra was a variety of emmer wheat that 'gave a good yield and was easy [*sc.* to thresh]'(*Nat. Hist.* 18.92). It also made acceptable or good bread, and the Egyptians were known as bread-eaters as early as Hecataeus (Athen. 418e; 447c–d). Hecataeus died less than a generation before Herodotus was born.

Egyptian culture is given a different appraisal by Diodorus. The Egyptians are still barbarians, but Diodorus is on the whole prepared to let Egyptian myths about the origin of cereal, vine and olive cultivation speak for themselves, and to point to the singularities of Egypt without imposing artificial polarities. Egypt's main claim to uniqueness is the Nile, ultimately the source of a richly varied and abundant diet. The people of the Delta are particularly well-served, says Diodorus. The rich, alluvial soil 'produces many crops of every kind'; in the marshes, 'tubers of every flavour grow . . . and fruits and vegetables which grow on stalks of a nature peculiar to the country, supplying an abundance sufficient to render the poor and the sick . . . self-sustaining (1.34). Diodorus also attempted to provide rational explanations of Egyptian food-avoidances. Herodotus makes merry at their expense, but the result is confusion (Diod. 1.87–9; Hdt. 2.37, 47).

[11] On the Egyptian diet, see Darby et al. (1977); Morcos and Morcos (1977); Crawford (1979).

We have been exploring the way contrasts are drawn, in the area of food and foodways, between the world of the Graeco-Roman city and the barbarian world, or rather, worlds. The spokesmen of the urban elite operate with a stereotype of the nomadic pastoralist who eats meat and drinks milk. The stereotype changes little from one generation to another (there are variants and elaborations), although the societies to which it is considered applicable do. So, the Romans in the eyes of the Greeks once belonged to the barbarian sphere. However, there is a second strand to the analysis. Coexisting with the generalisations about barbarian diet, it is tacitly recognised that there existed a variety of combinations of foods and ways of consuming them, not all of them equally barbaric. Moreover, those who came under the influence of a higher culture, notably that of Rome, were seen to be in the process of evolving into something that could almost be called civilised. And there were advanced societies like Egypt and Persia to whom the label 'barbarian' hardly applied, except in the technical sense that they were non-Greek.

As for the principles of differentiation, the level of civilisation of a people or a group was a function of its distance from the core society and culture. Distance is a multi-dimensional measure, encompassing culture, economy, politics, geography and time. In the conceptualisation of barbarian societies at the edge of the Graeco-Roman world, all except the last of the various aspects of distance come into play. Geography, or spatial distance, evaluated in terms of remoteness, severity of climate or high altitudes, always compared with the supreme advantages of the Mediterranean region, is notably prominent. Take the Scythians, this time as portrayed in the Hippocratic treatise on *Airs, Waters, Places*. Its main theme is that the physical and mental character of a people, and their manner of life, are a product of the nature of the climate and terrain. The Scythians appear as the representative people of the north, stunted, infertile, moist, feminine and diseased, owing to the severity of the climate and the barrenness of the land. Predictably we are told that 'they themselves eat boiled meats and drink mares' milk'. They also drink water from ice and snow, which is uniformly 'bad' (8.52–3; 19.32–3).[12] In Strabo's Thule and Tacitus' land of the Fenni, too, an inhospitable climate and barbarity, including uncivilised food customs, come together. These places also are set at the limits of the

---

[12] Cf. Arist. *Pol.* 1327b23: 'Those who live in a cold climate and in Europe are full of spirit, but wanting in intelligence and skill; and therefore they retain comparative freedom, but have no political organisation, and are incapable of ruling over others . . .'; cf. *Ethics* 3.7.7 on the Celts, without reference to diet.

inhabited world. We have seen already that although Galen sees himself in general as writing in the Hippocratic tradition, his discussion of agriculture in Macedonia and Bithynia does not offer a parallel to the Hippocratic portrayal of Scythia, for he is interested in making, without prejudice, what is to us the obvious point, that cold climate and lofty terrain will favour the production of some varieties of cereal over others. Cassius Dio's exaggerated talk of the Pannonians as if they were a barbarous tribe living in miserable conditions at the perimeter of the world tells us more about his own political attitudes and cultural bias than the true nature of the people of the lower Danubian provinces in his day, the late second and early third centuries:

The Pannonians dwell near Dalmatia along the bank of the Danube from Noricum to Moesia, and live of all men the most wretchedly. Both their soil and climate are poor; they cultivate no olives and produce no wine except to a very slight extent and of a very poor quality, since the climate is mostly extremely harsh. They not only eat barley and millet, but drink liquids made from them. For having nothing to make a civilised life worthwhile, they are extremely fierce and bloodthirsty. (49.36.4)[13]

In discussions of less remote or more obviously advanced peoples, the physical environment forms a backdrop at most. The Egyptian climate, says Herodotus, was 'different from that of the rest of the world' (2.35.2), but the peculiarities of Egyptians are not explained thereby.[14] The absence or unimportance of farming in, say, Gaul or Germany is not apparently to be explained in terms of the climate. After all, as Tacitus concedes, 'Germany is fertile in cereals (*Ger.* 5.1–2). Caesar had written of Germans, that they did not allow private ownership of land 'through fear that they might be tempted by continuous association to substitute agriculture for warrior zeal' (*BC* 6.22). Georges Duby, the historian of medieval France, thought of societies as constrained by their cultures rather than able to change them by choice:

It is unnecessary to believe that a society is sustained by whatever is most successfully produced by the land where it is located. Rather, a society is the prisoner of customs that are handed down from generation to generation, and are changed only with difficulty. In other words, it harnesses its resources to break down the resistance of soil and climate in order to procure for itself to the best of its ability the foodstuffs that social custom and religious rite compel it to consume.[15]

---

[13] Cf. Garnsey and Saller (1987), 16–17.
[14] The Hippocratic writer's treatment of Egypt and Libya, signalled retrospectively at ch. 13, is lost.
[15] Duby (1974), 26.

None of these authors was inclined to embrace the doctrine of environmental determinism.

We now turn to an opposition which involves not spatial but temporal distance, between earlier and later stages in the development of the culture, morality and diet of the same society.

HEROIC OR ARCHAIC SOCIETIES

Criticism of the misuse of wealth by the rich is a leitmotiv of Greek and Latin literature. Literary tradition attributes sumptuary laws to Greek tyrants and reforming lawgivers such as Solon and Lycurgus, who are represented as promoters of a communitarian spirit against the socially divisive and political disruptive behaviour of contemporary aristocrats.[16] A 'specifically Hellenistic debate' about luxury focused on conspicuous expenditure at the courts of Alexander the Great and the successor kings, and in the households of the rich.[17] The Roman interest in or obsession with the themes of luxury and moral decline showed itself in laws against extravagance from the early second century BC, and in a stream of moralising literature.[18]

A number of strategies were available to critics of contemporary society. One that is often thought of as characteristically Roman involved conjuring up a picture of an idealised past society rooted in the values of frugality and self-sufficiency – namely, the Rome of legendary peasant/generals such as Quinctius Cincinnatus – as the moral opposite of contemporary society marked by extravagance and idleness. Was this not just characteristically but also exclusively Roman? Greek interest in luxury (*truphē*), especially in a political context, surfaces in Plato and other fourth-century writers such as Isocrates and Xenophon and continues into the Hellenistic age.[19] Some authors, particularly in the fourth century, looked sideways at Sparta as a living example of a state falling apart because of moral weakness (though Sparta even in decline had its admirers); others looked to the past for examples of city-states destroyed by luxury and the resultant social strife – so Phylarchus writing in the third century BC about Sybaris (Athen. 521c). But there are also traces of

---

[16] Gallo (1993).   [17] Schmitt-Pantel (1992), 439–66; (1997).
[18] On Roman sumptuary laws, see Gell. 2.24; Macr. 3.17.11ff.; Tac. *Ann.* 3.52–5; Dio 61.10.3; Suet. *Div. Aug.* 34. For (standard) complaints about luxury, see e.g. Pliny, *Nat. Hist.* 33.150; Juv. 10.72–81 ('bread and circuses'). See Toner (1995), ch. 7.
[19] See e.g. Plato, *Rep.* 403dff.; 564ff.; Isocr. *Philipp.* 107c; Xen. *Cyroped.*, passim; Passerini (1934); Bordes (1982).

a 'Roman' line of thought in the advancement of Homeric, heroic society as an ideal against which to measure the decadent present. If the scale and nature of the phenomenon are harder to assess in the Greek than in the Roman context, this is because much of the evidence comes to us second-hand, in fragments, and through the agency of Athenaeus, a Greek in culture and sentiment but a citizen of the Roman empire.

(i) Greece

Homer saw that moderation is the first and most appropriate virtue of the young, harmoniously joining together and enhancing all that is fair; and since he wished to implant it anew from beginning to end so that his heroes might spend their leisure and their endeavour on noble deeds and be helpful to each other and share their goods with one another, he made their way of living frugal and self-sufficient. For he considered that passions and pleasures become very strong, and that foremost among them and innate are the desires for eating and drinking, and that they who abide resolutely in frugality are well-disciplined and self-controlled in all the exigencies of life. (Athen. 8e–9b)

The Homeric heroes, according to Athenaeus, practised frugality and self-sufficiency, virtues that are linked with moderation, generosity and sharing. Their cereal and meat diet was good for the body and the soul, keeping the passions in check. Women and young boys are safe, in Homer. The heroes did drink wine, but in moderation, mixed and consumed with the food. Each hero had his own cup, and could thus control his drinking; he did not swill his wine from a common bowl. There was music and dancing at the heroic symposium, but singers and dancers were self-restrained. The heroes prepared their own meal, it took place without chaplets, unguents and incense, and the meat was divided equally. Athenaeus contrasts the behaviour of Homer's heroes with the primitive 'first men', who behaved like animals. Food was short, everyone grabbed what he could, violence was endemic. Eating was originally the setting for crime. Such was the state of the world before Demeter ushered in the civilising cereal. This contrast is made only in passing. In general, Athenaeus is intent on confronting the idealised world of the heroes with a degenerate present.

But which present? Not apparently Athenaeus' own present, but rather that of his principal sources, the comic poets, philosophers and sundry 'technical' writers of an earlier era, namely, the Greek late classical and early Hellenistic world. Athenaeus shows an almost total lack of interest in Roman sources and Roman history. If his 'then' is emphatically Greek, his 'now' also lacks any clear Roman reference or resonance. Athenaeus seems to have thought of the period from classical and Hellenistic Greece to his own day as a continuum, and the literature of that period as relevant equally to the late second century AD and to the fourth century BC. It does not necessarily follow that his account of Homeric society was completely derivative. In particular, it is not impossible that he was himself the source of the claim that recurs in his account of the heroic age, that Homer was himself a critic of contemporary *mores*.

The late classical and early Hellenistic period witnessed a major transformation of the diet and food preparation and consumption habits of Greeks everywhere. An *haute cuisine* developed, marked by elaborate, specialist cooking, imported foods (and cooks), conspicuous consumption by the rich and an explosion of a wide range of 'technical literature' on food and cookery and ancillary subjects such as farming and health.[20] The 'food revolution' and its impact on Greek culture and opinion at the time merit a thorough assessment. For the moment the issue that concerns us is whether the response of Greek writers and thinkers of the period to these developments involved a confrontation between heroic past and contemporary present at the expense of the latter.

It is possible to establish the existence of such a discourse, but not its importance. Too much literature is lost, and we depend too heavily on Athenaeus, a deeply problematic source. He cites texts, which are very often otherwise unknown, in a casual and haphazard way. Some of them have only a loose connection to the subject (they are there to demonstrate the speaker's erudition), others are apparently cited to support a case (they often fail to do so), but certainly not as parts of a logically structured argument. And they are decontextualised, so that the purpose of the author in question cannot be recovered. The technique can be studied in the case of excerpts from surviving works (a tiny minority of the dozens that are cited). If we were dependent on Athenaeus for our knowledge of Plato's *Republic*, we would possess only a minor part of an intriguing exchange between Glaucon and Socrates, in the course of which Socrates presents two dietary regimes for his new citizens, one frugal, labelled by Glaucon a pig's dinner, and one luxurious, a civilised

---

[20] A long list of works, many of them known only by name, can be recovered from the pages of Athenaeus. The considerable number devoted to food and eating were of course, directly or indirectly, celebrating the new art of gastronomy. See Degani (1990); (1991). Among the more colourful and famous of these works was the *Hedupatheia* or the *Life of Luxury* of the Sicilian Archestratus, of which work Athenaeus preserves 61 fragments. See Wilkins and Hill (1994).

dinner, to meet Glaucon's requirements (*Rep.* 372a). As it is, Athenaeus fails to quote a highly relevant text in which Plato prescribes a regime for warrior athletes, which follows Homer's prescriptions for his heroes:

You know that when his heroes are campaigning he doesn't give them fish to feast on, even though they are by the sea in the Hellespont, nor boiled meat either. Instead he gives them only roasted meat, which is the kind most easily available to soldiers, for it's easier nearly everywhere to use fire alone than to carry pots and pans. . . . Nor I believe does Homer mention sauces anywhere. Indeed, aren't even the other athletes aware that if one's body is to be kept in good condition, one must abstain from all such things? (*Rep.* 404b–5a)

This is I believe the first comment on the Homeric diet in a moralistic context in extant Greek literature, though it presumably had predecessors. Athenaeus does make use, though in a tantalisingly oblique and abrupt way, of a lost philosophical work, *On the Pleasure and the Good* by the third-century Stoic philosopher Chrysippus. One fragment conveys the message that philosophical schools, specifically the Academy and Lyceum, were hostile to culinary pretensions and tricks (137e–f), and others suggest that Chrysippus was prone to making comparisons with the regime of the Homeric heroes in a moralistic mode (9c, 18b). His work may well have followed up Plato's charge in the *Gorgias* that cooking, like rhetoric, pursues pleasure rather than virtue.

What of the comic poets, much cited by Athenaeus? It is hardly to be expected that comic poets would make common cause with philosophers. Yet one of Athenaeus' learned diners, Plutarch, is given these words:

Whoever wrote *Beggars*, generally attributed to Chionides, says that when the Athenians set before the Dioscuri a collation in the prytaneion, they place upon the tables 'cheese and a barley-puff, ripe olives, and leeks' in memory of their ancient discipline . . . Solon prescribes that a barley-cake be served to all who dine at the prytaneion, but that a wheat loaf may be added on feast days, thus following Homer. (Athen. 137e)

The connection between Solon and Homer, however, is made by Athenaeus' spokesman, Plutarch, not by the poet.[21] In general, it would be rash to ascribe to comic poets, on the basis of isolated fragments in Athenaeus, a sustained attack on their contemporaries for substituting luxury and extravagance for antique frugality and self-control. Satire of absurdly pretentious cooks, gourmands and food-experts, and of

[21] In case we were tempted to read Plutarch as an old-fashioned moralist, elsewhere in the same speech he is given the role of mocking the poverty of the Athenian diet, with the aid of selected passages of comedy. (See Athen. 137c–d.)

ostentatious rich men, and occasional references to the diet or behaviour of Homer's heroes, as once in a fragment of Eubulus,[22] comes to rather less than this. Comedy can be didactic,[23] but it is full of crosscurrents and its messages are hard to pin down. What for example is to be made of the frequently voiced criticism in Athenaeus of exiguous Athenian diets? The Athenians may have learned refinement, but they still ate small and cheap. So say observers. Who is the object of satire here? Who scores highest in comparisons between 'small-tabled, leaf-eating' Greeks, meat-eating Macedonians and Thracians, extravagant Romans and magnificent and luxurious Persians? Other comic fragments appear to be highlighting a growing divide between rich and poor, visible in the different foods they buy and consume, but this seems to fit more naturally into a democratic rather than an oligarchic/aristocratic social critique, and does not imply an appeal to the high authority of a Homer or Solon.

Thus far we have seen some evidence that Greek writers and thinkers moralised on the subject of food and eating through making adverse comparisons between their own society and an idealised heroic age, but little to suggest that they did this on a grand scale, at a level comparable with the Romans. We have still to ask where Athenaeus' description and assessment of Homeric society come from. This is obscure, but he did provide one clue, in citing by name a discussion by Dioscurides, introduced simply as a pupil of Isocrates, the celebrated teacher of rhetoric at Athens in the mid-fourth century.[24] The reference to Dioscurides is intriguing, because it seems to involve Homer himself in a critique of drunkenness. It is a feature of Athenaeus' account of heroic society that Homer is presented as a social critic of his age, promoting an idealised image of the heroes at dinner with the aim of influencing the behaviour of his contemporaries. There is an alternative to the assumption that Athenaeus' discussion is completely derivative, namely, that he himself made a contribution, including this crucial ingredient. Turning Homer into a Roman-style moralist was, one might say, Athenaeus' solution to the riddle that exercised various Hellenistic scholars, of the conflicting

---

[22] Athen. 25c, from Eubulus; see Hunter (1983), 219–20, with bibl.   [23] Cf. Hunter (1985).

[24] Athen. 11a–b. The identity of Dioscurides is disputed, as is the authorship of the treatise 'On the life of the Heroes in Homer' from which Athenaeus is held to have drawn his discussion with the same title. See Schwartz, *RE* 5.1128–9; Jacoby on *FGrH* 594 F 8. Athenaeus may have drawn some details of his account from the early third-century BC historian Dicaearchus, a pupil of Aristotle. See Porph. *De Abst.* 4.2, with Athen. 12d–13a. But Dicaearchus appears to been interested in the reign of Kronos. For Alciphron, *On the Truphe of the Ancients* (second century AD) as a source for Athenaeus, see Athenaeus, Loeb edn. 5, p. 333.

versions of the heroic diet in Homer. The heroes of the *Iliad* eat only plain and noble fare, roast meat and bread, whereas in the *Odyssey* their diet is more varied, including vegetables, fruit, fish, birds and boiled meat. Homer is represented as trying to protect heroes engaged in active warfare from the charge of gourmandise:

But the poet is silent about the eating of vegetables, fish and birds because that is a mark of greed, and also because it would be unseemly for the heroes to spend time in preparing them for the table, since he judges it beneath the level of heroic and godlike deeds. (Athen. 25d)[25]

The question whether Athenaeus or one of his sources foisted on Homer the role of social critic remains problematic. The general point seems secure, that moralistic attitudes that were characteristically Roman were already circulating in late classical and Hellenistic Greece.

(ii) Rome

Men's bodies were still sound and strong; their food was light and not spoiled by art and luxury, whereas when they began to seek dishes not for the sake of removing but of rousing the appetite, and devised countless sauces to whet their gluttony – then what before was nourishment to a hungry man became a burden to the full stomach. (Seneca, *Epistles* 95.15)

When I am reminded by the records of many writers that it was a matter of pride with our forefathers to give their attention to farming, from which pursuit came Quinctius Cincinnatus, summoned from the plough to the dictatorship to be the deliverer of a beleaguered consul and his army . . . from which pursuit came also Gaius Fabricius and Curius Dentatus, the one after his rout of Pyrrhus from the confines of Italy, the other after his conquest of the Sabines, tilling the captured land which they had received in the distribution of seven iugera to a man, with an energy not inferior to the bravery in arms with which they had gained it . . . I understand that yesterday's morals and strenuous manner of living are out of tune with our present extravagance and devotion to pleasure. All of us who are heads of families have quit the sickle and the plough and have crept within the city-walls: and we ply our hands in the circuses and theatres rather than in the grainfields and vineyards; and we gaze in astonished admiration at the posturings of effeminate males, because they counterfeit by their womanish motions a sex which nature has denied to men, and deceive the eyes of the spectators . . . (Columella, *De Agricultura* I, pref. 10–21, excerpts)

---

[25] For Hellenistic discussions of the Homeric diet, especially the question of fish, see Schmidt (1976), 182–7; Davidson (1997), 16–17. One commentator, Aristarchus, suggested that the diet of the heroes in the Iliad reflected Homer's interest in avoiding *to mikroprepes*, the demeaning, any suggestion of the plebeian.

Romans were determined critics of their own society. Their literature, here represented by two spokesmen from the mid-first century AD, one technical (Columella), the other philosophical (Seneca), has a pronounced moralistic tone, as writers routinely exposed the corrupt values of their society and sought to explain their origin. Between the age of the elder Cato (d. 150 BC) and the Augustan Principate (31 BC – AD 14), moralists formulated a myth of archaic Rome which was centred on the idea that their empire-building ancestors lived lives of extreme poverty and frugality, and they confronted this legendary world with their own society, decadent from top to bottom. The Romans were victims of their own success. Once the last major foreign foe, Carthage, was eliminated, the austere self-discipline of their ancestors was abandoned under the impact of the inflowing riches of empire, which fuelled the growth of avarice, ambition and the love of luxury.[26]

Frugality could be represented as a general virtue, as in Cicero's claim that, while being rooted in temperance, it encompassed the three other cardinal virtues of fortitude, justice and prudence (*Tusculan Disputations* 3.17). But its primary reference was to the individual's attitude to food, its nature and quantity, and the way in which it was produced and consumed (this last is the subject of the citation of Seneca above). As Valerius Maximus wrote (2.5.5): 'The great simplicity of the ancient Romans in eating is the clearest gauge of their civilisation and self-restraint.'

Frugality was an appropriate virtue in a people whose life was necessarily devoted to the raising of crops for their own consumption. Self-employment and self-sufficiency were of the essence. Food was grown to satisfy basic wants, and no more. For this purpose a small property would suffice: in the tradition, early Roman farmers worked properties of from two *iugera* (the *heredium* established by Romulus) to seven. The food too was basic: *puls*, a meal porridge made by boiling ground cereals, especially *far*, in water, supplemented by dry legumes. As befitted a pious people, their staple food accumulated religious functions. The roasted grains were beaten and ground. Salt was added to the flour, *farina*, thus obtained to make *mola salsa*, essential for sacrifices: *immolare*, 'to sacrifice', involved the sprinkling of the victim with *mola salsa*. *Far* gave its name to *confarreatio*, a solemn marriage ceremony celebrated by the pontifex maximus and not countenancing divorce: the bride was given a cake of

[26] Goddard (1994a); Toner (1995). For frugality, see Pliny, *Nat. Hist.* 18.6–15, 19–21, 24, 32, 35, 41–3, 83–4, 107; Athen. 274. And nn. 18, 27.

far. This way of life was practised by leaders as well as followers, by exemplary farmer/generals such as Columella's trio, Cincinnatus (worked four *iugera* of land, elected dictator twice), Manius Curius Dentatus (seven *iugera*, conqueror of the Sabines), and C. Fabricius (a humble shack, conqueror of Pyrrhus).[27] It did not matter that image did not match reality and could not have done. A stark contrast between past and present could be assumed. The achievement of past Romans and the decadence and corruption of the generations of the present and immediate past were only too visible. So were the consequences associated therewith – endemic political strife, repeated civil war, the collapse of the Republican order, the arrival of monarchy.

Nor did it matter- and this is more interesting – that the spokesmen for frugality and the traditional morality in general did not adopt the lifestyle of their celebrated ancestors or preach the desirability of its adoption. The gap between contemporary Romans and 'the other', in this case the legendary heroes of early Rome, was not to be bridged. A life of poverty and full-time farming was not contemplated by the elite of the late Republic and early Principate. Thus, for example, Columella, a champion of frugality, as we saw, has limited objectives. In the preface to his work on agriculture, he can be seen fashioning an 'honourable compromise' between the polar opposites of a legendary past of rustic simplicity, and a corrupt present marked by the extravagant urban living and the reckless disdain for agriculture of absentee landowners. Columella did not call upon the propertied classes to abandon their city-based political careers and to till minuscule farms, but rather to take an active and informed interest in their (ample) estates. Meanwhile frugality (as we saw in Cicero) was presented in certain contexts as a general virtue equivalent to moderation and self-restraint such as even a rich man could aspire to possess.

CONCLUSION

We gain access to ancient societies and cultures mainly through the mediation of a rather narrow range of literary spokesmen, drawn from the social and political elite of the cities. Consciously or not, they are busy constructing images of themselves, and contrasting them favourably in terms of civilisation and way of life with images of others. Food

---

[27] Val. Max. 4.4.11, with 4.3.5; 4.4.6–7; Pliny, *Nat. Hist.* 18.18. On the evolution of the Roman diet, see Pucci (1989).

is often at the centre of the confrontation, because the food we eat and the way we eat it are an integral part of social behaviour and cultural patterns, which themselves differ in ways small or large.

The factual base for these broad comparisons is often insecure, for there was ideology at work, sometimes in the service of practical political ends. Greek/barbarian polarity was more than a tool of foreign policy, but it was certainly exploited and popularised by Greeks anxious to rally support against the Persian invader.[28] Romans, once themselves classed as barbarians, and educated Greeks who found it advantageous to be friends of Rome, used the same polarity to explain and justify their conquest of the world away from the Mediterranean.

The Roman polity was more inclusive than the Greek, built to expand. This is the source of a problem facing writers such as Strabo, that of keeping the cultural stereotypes alive while the barbarian world was succumbing to 'Romanisation' before their eyes. A modern historian seeking to understand cultural transformation within the Roman empire may well find the image of spectrum or continuum more relevant than that of binary opposition.

In addition, the broad distinctions between Greeks/Romans and barbarians, civilised and uncivilised, were not the only ones that bulked large in their thinking, nor did they appeal to everyone. The Greeks in particular were first and foremost men of their own polis rather than ethnocentric. Like everyone else they preferred their own customs, as Herodotus put it (3.38). Few Greeks opposed the invading Persian king Xerxes with conviction, and some fought together with him. In fourth-century Greece, the 'Greek crusade' manufactured by the Macedonians against the Persian empire was a damp squib.

Finally, the image of alterity might be directed inwards, acting as a marker of social and moral change and conflict within a community, when, for example, the norms and hierarchies of a traditional aristocratic society were perceived to be under threat in a time of social and economic change. The creation of the myth of early Rome as a society marked by the stern morality and austere life-style of its citizenry was an aspect of the response of conservative Romans to the transformation of social practices and values, as the wealthy, from both old and new families, conspicuously consumed the riches of empire.

Moralistic archaising of this sort was a Roman speciality, but there was a Greek counterpart in the construction of a legendary heroic past

---

[28] Hall (1989).

where old-fashioned values prevailed. This is first visible in the extant literature in Plato – drawing presumably from an earlier source. In general, philosophers were the most conspicuous critics of luxury and extravagance, through their treatises, and, in the case of certain Cynics (most famously, Diogenes) and Pythagoreans (such as Diodorus of Aspendus) in their life-style. How far the then/now contrast coloured other literary genres is unclear. The case of comedy is especially problematic. If comedy had didactic purpose, the message is hard to identify, especially on the basis of fragments separated from their original context, or given a new context by the idiosyncratic later writer who preserved them. A more promising place to look for the source of Athenaeus' picture of the heroic age and the mind of Homer is in the attention given by late classical and early Hellenistic commentators, historians and grammarians to Homeric and archaic Greek society.

CHAPTER 6

Forbidden foods

PRELIMINARIES

Although humans are omnivores, some potential foods are in practice unavailable, while others that are available, edible and nutritious are rejected or not even considered as food, food for humans that is. Among edible things treated as unfoods, some are rejected for reasons of taste, but will be eaten if necessary, in emergencies – they are famine foods – whereas others are forbidden as food. They are taboo.[1] In this chapter I ask why it is that some social groups and communities impose food restrictions on their members, while others, the taboo against cannibalism excepted, do not. The Israelites of the Old Testament and beyond, and certain religious and philosophical groups within Greek and Roman pagan society, followed restrictive dietary rules, whereas Graeco-Roman society in general was 'tolerant' in this respect. Of course, food consumption is only one of the possible areas of restrictive regulation, and the range of prohibited practices will vary from society to society. As Freud observed, Greeks and Romans (as well as Jews) had their equivalents of the Polynesian taboo, in *agos, sacer* (compare the Jewish Kodaush),[2] and taboo restrictions did penetrate to some extent their social, political and legal structures, as well as regulating sexual relations. But this did not happen on anything like the Jewish scale. Nor did Graeco-Roman societies lack altogether the concept of physiological pollution, the belief that contact with certain physical products or the performing of certain physical functions – including eating particular foods – might be dangerous for the society and the individual. The normal response among such communities, however, was to regulate the behaviour of only a few individuals with

---

[1] On taboo, see Frazer (1911); Lévy-Bruhl (1922); Freud (1938); Simoons (1961); Douglas (1966); Farb and Armelagos (1980), ch. 6; Grant (1980); Harris (1986); Harris (1987). Additional literature, including specialist works, is cited below.   [2] Freud (1938), 37.

priestly functions.[3] They represented the people as a whole and on their conduct in office depended the safety of the community. The priest of Jupiter at Rome, the *flamen dialis*, and Egyptian priests are familiar examples.

Graeco-Roman societies, then, were relatively free from taboos and restrictive regulations regarding food. As for those communities that did bind themselves with rules, the effect and *raison d'être* of this self-regulation were to define the group or sub-group in question as different and apart from 'the other', the rest of the world, or the dominant culture. The origin of any particular taboo and the form that it takes are, however, not always easy to explain.

GREEKS AND ROMANS

The similarity of the flesh of man to that of the pig can be inferred from the fact that men have been known to eat human flesh served up to them as pork by rascally innkeepers and certain others, without the slightest suspicion, so like is it to pork in both taste and smell . . .[4] The flesh of the wild asses that are young and in good condition is like that of deer. Some people even eat the flesh of the tame donkey when it gets old, but this has unhealthy juices, and is very indigestible and ill-humoured as well as being very nasty to taste – like the meat of horse and camel, in fact. For people who are akin to donkey and camel in soul and body eat these too. Some eat bear and, what is worse, even lion and leopard, boiling it once, or twice . . . What shall I say about dogs? Many nations eat dogs when they are young and fat, and geld them for the table . . . Some people also eat the flesh of wild panther (just as they eat asses' meat when they are in good condition), a dish which is not only shared but even praised by some doctors. In my country the meat of fox is sometimes eaten by hunters in the autumn . . .[5] It would not be reasonable to omit them [*sc.* turtles and tortoises] from our list, like worms that live in trees, vipers or other snakes, which are in fact eaten in Egypt and by many other peoples. All Greeks eat tortoises every day, though they have hard flesh and therefore are difficult to digest, but if you can digest it, it gives a lot of nourishment . . .[6]

Galen goes on to discuss, among other things, parts of the pig, with sideglances at other animals: not only feet, snout and ears, but also lips,

---

[3] This is stated as a general principle in Porph., *Abst.* 2.3.2. Egypt provides his main example. See *Abst.* 4.6–8 (drawing on the first-century AD Stoic philosopher Chaeremon). I am most grateful to Gillian Clark for making available to me in advance of publication her translation of and commentary on Porphyry, *De Abstinentia*.

[4] Galen then discusses lamb, mutton, goat, ram, bull, hare, and deer.

[5] Next comes the turtle and/or tortoise. These, Galen says, cannot be classified either as birds or as fishes.

[6] Galen gives some tortoise recipes and then describes the different properties of the anatomical organs and tissues of edible animals.

chaps, tongues, and – described as delicacies – lymph nodes, thyrus gland, udders and testicles.[7]

Greeks and Romans were prepared to eat just about anything. Or, name something edible, and someone or other would not shrink from putting it into a recipe. This message is vividly conveyed by Galen's discussion of land animals as foods. The only sign of a taboo in the Galen passage involves cannibalism. People are sometimes fed human flesh, unknowingly, in a 'pub meal'. Galen tacitly recognises that 'eating people is wrong', but he is not upset about it. In fact, he does not address the issue, but simply goes on to say that it is natural that sucking pigs should produce more waste products, in so far as they are moister than full-grown pigs. Among the things named, there are a number that Galen was himself averse to eating, but then he belonged to a social and economic group which could choose what to put on the menu. As for his preferences, with Galen it is a matter of taste, and, at least on the surface, it is the character of the thing which seems to count, its taste, feel, what it does to the digestive system, and (virtually the same thing, for Galen) its perceived nutritional value. It is on such grounds that he implicitly condemns, for example, the eating of donkeys, horses and camels, though he is not above slipping in the snide remark that the sort of people who eat donkeys and camels (is the omission of horses significant here?) are themselves asinine and 'cameline'. In some societies horses and camels are not eaten because they are so close to man that they become quasi-human, but it is the reverse situation, the lowering of humans to the level of animals, that brings a hint of cannibalism into Galen's discussion. There is no sign that Galen has any aversion to the consumption of what we would call household pets.[8] We don't eat dogs and cats, which seem 'part of the family', and some would avoid eating pet rabbits or horses for the same reason. Not all modern societies feel these inhibitions. Dog and cat are eaten in China, and also in some western European countries.[9] Horse-meat shops do or have done busi-

---

[7] Galen also discusses brains – these induce vomiting, and greedy people take them during a meal – bone marrow, spinal marrow, fat, tallow, the viscera (liver, spleen, lungs, heart, the female reproductive organs, and intestines), and finally blood, that of hare and pig. For the whole discussion, see Galen vi 663–700, here excerpted.

[8] Porph., *Abst.* 1.14.3, says that 'we' (*sc.* Greeks) abstain from many animals which 'live with people', and adduces this as the reason that 'the Greeks' do not eat dogs or horses or donkeys. Porphyry was of course arguing the case for vegetarianism. He is contradicted by the Hippocratic writer (*c.* 400 BC) of *On Regimen* 2.46. For some Greek evidence for food avoidance, see Parker (1983), App. 4. See Simoons (1961), 86, 90, 114–5, 121 for horse and camel taboos. The motivations he discusses do not include the one advanced by Porphyry.

[9] Simoons (1991), 309ff. (eating of dogs, cats, snakes, rats, insects, in China and elsewhere).

Piatto del giorno 10.000

Secondi Piatti: Bollito assortito 12.000
Punta di vitello ripiena 12.000
Spalla cotta di S.Secondo calda con purea di patate 14.000
→ Cavallo pesto (macinato) anche scottato 12.000
→ Stracotto di cavallo 14.000
Trippa alla parmigiana 12.000
Spalla arrosto di vitello 14.000
Costine di maiale arrosto 12.000
Carpaccio di manzo rucola e grana o sedano e grana 10.000
Roastbeef di manzo 14.000
Filetto di manzo all'aceto balsamico 25.000
→ Vecchia (carne di cavallo e verdure) 12.000
Melanzane alla parmigiana 12.000
Formaggi assortiti 12.000

Alla griglia: Fettine di cavallo 12.000
Filetto di manzo 22.000
Nodino di maiale 10.000
Nodino di vitello 13.000

Contorni : Purea di patate 5.000
Patate al forno 5.000
Insalata mista 5.000
Verdure lessate 5.000

8. Horse on the menu, served raw and as stew. Parma, Italy.

ness in Belgium, France, Switzerland, Germany, Austria, Italy – in
Parma and Piacenza, horse is eaten raw with oil, lemon, salt and pepper
(*piccola di cavallo*) (Fig. 8). As for donkeys, *stufato d'asino* is commonly prepared in Novara and Asti according to an eighteenth-century recipe.
This involves cooking the meat for a long time in broth and tomato juice
to make it more digestible.[10] Greeks and Romans of antiquity, for the
most part, were similarly uninhibited. With the ancient Hebrews,
however, and a few fringe groups in the Graeco-Roman world, we have
to do not so much with delicate sensibilities or tastes, as rules or laws.

SAGES, PHILOSOPHERS AND PRIESTS

Abstention from particular foods, especially meat, was practised by
some individuals and sects with a philosophical or religious orientation
from the Greek archaic period to late antiquity. Our best source is the
Neoplatonist Porphyry of Tyre, a pupil of Plotinus, and himself an elo-
quent and effective advocate of vegetarianism, but the tradition of
writing on the subject, known to and used by Porphyry, goes back

[10] I am indebted for this information to Filippo Cavassini.

through Plutarch's *On Meat-Eating* to Theophrastus' *On Piety*, that is, to the early third century, at least. Right at the beginning of his treatise *On Abstinence* Porphyry identifies abstention from animal flesh as the 'philosophy' of Pythagoras and Empedocles, who flourished in the late sixth century and mid-fifth century respectively. To them we should add the Orphics and various other shadowy groups.[11] The absence of original or early source-material pertaining to Pythagoras – his disciples, notoriously, kept his teaching to themselves (cf. Porph. *Vita Pythagorae* 19) – means that there is much that is confused and problematic in the (later) tradition, not least the reputation that he developed, and perhaps cultivated, for unusual spiritual or magical powers. Despite Dodds' portrayal of Pythagoras as a sage on the model of Central Asian shamanistic cultures, the origins of the 'movement' remain a mystery.[12] Pythagoras believed in the immortality of the soul and its reincarnation in another body, which might be human but might also belong to another species of animal. For humans and animals are kin, breathing the same breath and being constituted out of the same elements. Therefore to kill an animal was murder, and to eat it, cannibalism. This doctrine had radical implications for the religious life of the Greeks, and must have provoked widespread criticism and opposition. Pythagoras was from early days a highly controversial figure.[13] Meat was the quintessential sacrificial food – indeed outside the religious context meat was hardly consumed at all – and the health and prosperity of the community hinged on the proper performance of the ritual sacrifices to the gods. An even more radical position that attributed souls to plants too did not apparently have dietary consequences for its advocates. Empedocles said that his soul had already been in 'a boy and a girl *and a bush* and a bird and a fish from the sea'. Pythagoras may have shared this view: according to Porphyry his teachings included 'not to destroy or harm a cultivated plant bearing fruit, or an animal that is not harmful to the human race'.[14] In the surviving literature the case for vegetarianism is best made by Porphyry himself (drawing on earlier

---

[11] Porphyry also composed a *Life of Pythagoras* (E. des Places, ed. Budé, 1982). For the Orphics and their relationship with Pythagoreans, see Kirk, Raven and Schofield (1983), ch. 1.4 & 7, and 220–2; West (1983); Gasparro (1987), 141–55; Laks and Most (1997). For vegetarianism in antiquity, see Haussleiter (1935); Dierauer (1977); Gasparro (1987); (1989); Sorabji (1993); Osborne (1995); in general, Spencer (1993).

[12] Dodds (1951); Guthrie (1962), 146–69; Burkert (1972); Kirk, Raven and Schofield (1983), 228–9.

[13] Kirk, Raven and Schofield (1983), 216–19.

[14] Porph., *Vit. Pyth.* 39. For Empedocles' saying, see Inwood (1992), frg. 111. See also Diog. Laert. 8.36 (from Xenophanes): the soul of a friend in a dog undergoing a whipping is recognised (?by Pythagoras).

sources, especially Theophrastus). Porphyry is moderate, rational, humane and sensitive to past criticisms of meat-avoidance. The doctrine of reincarnation (not surprisingly) makes no appearance. Animals have a soul. To kill an animal is to destroy something of value. To do this in an act of sacrifice is particularly unfitting, because sacrifice is holy (*Abst.* 2.12). In a second argument, Porphyry takes on the role of a historian of cult practice. Humans had traditionally sacrificed to the gods the wild and then cultivated produce of the earth. The sacrifice of animals and their consumption were late developments, forced on mankind by famine and war. Porphyry artfully interposes an intermediate stage, in which humans themselves were sacrificed and eaten, drawing the inference that to substitute animals for humans did not solve the moral problem: it did not mark a return to 'lawful' food (*Abst.* 2.27). A third argument develops the theme of holiness or piety in another direction. Meat-eating is not conducive to the health of either body or soul. In particular, it disturbs the soul, exposing it to the bodily passions and preventing us from drawing closer to god, preventing us, in the construction of Dicaearchus the Peripatetic, from recapturing the quality of life that mankind enjoyed in the age of Kronos:

Expounding the ancient way of life of Greece, he says that the men of old murdered no animate being: these men were born close to the gods, and being superior in nature and having lived the best kind of life are reckoned a race of gold in comparison with those of the present day, who are made from base and valueless matter. (*Abst.* 4.2)

To say that Pythagoreanism stands for vegetarianism and a belief in the kinship of all life is, however, an oversimplification. Pythagoras and his followers are credited with a number of specific taboos focused on particular animals and foods, which might be and were explained in a variety of ways. The discussion that is attributed to Aristotle on Pythagorean avoidance of the bean (*Vicia faba*, or broad bean) shows that we are in the presence of a complex phenomenon. The fragment of Aristotle begins in this way:

Aristotle says, in his work *On the Pythagoreans*, that Pythagoras enjoined abstention from beans either because they are like the privy parts, or because they are like the gates of Hades (for this is the only plant that has no joints), or because they are destructive, or because they are like the nature of the universe, or because of oligarchy (as they are used in the lot). (Diog. Laert. 8.34–5)

Aristotle does not suggest that abstention from beans was thought of as an extension of abstention from meat. Yet, according to the elder Pliny,

beans were to be avoided as food because they contain the souls of the
dead. This explains the use of beans 'in memorial services to dead relatives' (*Nat. Hist.* 18.119). In a citation in Athenaeus, eating beans is said
to 'amount to the same thing as eating the heads of one's parents'
(Athen. 65f). Porphyry's detailed and colourful explanation of the prohibition of beans goes along the same lines:

> The reason he proscribed them is as follows. In the beginning, the creation of
> the universe and the making of living things was in a state of disorder, and many
> seeds were brought together and sowed in the ground. They rotted together,
> and little by little birth resulted, and there came about the distinction between
> animals that were born and plants that were germinated. So, men were born
> from the same stock whence beans flourished. And he adduced irrefutable
> proof. Split a bean, and once you have broken it with your teeth, expose it for
> a while to the sun. If you go away and return a little later, you will discover a
> smell of human semen. Or, when a healthy bean has flowered, take a little of
> the flower when it is growing black. Place this in an earthenware pot, seal it and
> bury it for ninety days. When you dig the pot up again and open it, in place of
> the bean you will find either the well formed head of a child, or female geni-
> talia. (*Vita Pythag.* 44)[15]

'And he adduced irrefutable proof.' Porphyry's implicit claim of privileged access, from a distance of around eight hundred years, to
Pythagoras' 'scientific' analyses and the inferences he drew therefrom is
of doubtful worth. Pythagoras became a legendary figure and an object
of some speculation, not least among his later followers. Similarly, a
number of stories and bizarre associations clustered around the bean,
giving rise to rival explanations of its prohibited status.[16] Aristotle's
description of the bean as 'destructive' may be a reference to its physiological effects, ranging from flatulence through stupefaction to serious
illness (now known as favism). Pythagoras may have considered that the
legume was impure and unhealthy and reached his judgement on the
basis of his own experience.[17] Nor is a political explanation, also can-
vassed by Aristotle, to be dismissed out of hand, though it is surprisingly
associated in the text with oligarchy. The bean was a symbol of democracy. It was used in the allotment of offices, a key democratic institution.

[15] See Detienne (1977), 146–7. For Demeter as hostile to beans, see Paus. 8.15.
[16] Anthropologists who address the matter divide between those who put the symbolism of the
bean first and stress its autonomy, and those who favour a materialistic explanation of its rejection. For the bean, see Delatte (1930); Andrews (1949); Arie (1959); Chirassi Colombo (1968),
39–54; Detienne (1970); Detienne (1977), chs. 3–4; Grmek (1983); Katz (1987); Garnsey (1998), ch.
13.
[17] Was the bean bad for Pythagoras and he knew it? Did he suffer from a deficiency of the enzyme
G6PD? See Katz (1987). The anecdotal evidence is suggestive, but not conclusive.

Pythagoras' attempts to overhaul the civic life of his adopted city of Croton in southern Italy were not those of a democrat.[18]

The Pythagorean abstention from fish attracted a wide range of sometimes incompatible explanations, as a glance at the debate in Plutarch's *Table-Talk* (*Mor.* 728–30) reveals. It is not even clear that the taboo was applied to all fish, for Aristotle refers only to such fish as were sacred (Diog. Laert. 8.35). A wise remark is made by Lucius early on in Plutarch's discussion, which might have served as a conversation-stopper, but was not permitted to be one:

'Lucius said, quietly and simply, that *while the true reason is doubtless now as before secret and incommunicable,* no one would mind our seeing what plausible or probable answer we could find' (*Mor.* 728F). One of Plutarch's own suggestions brings us back to the principle underlying meat-avoidance: 'It is possible to conclude, both from the words and from the religious observances of the ancients, that they considered it an unholy and unlawful act not only to eat but even to kill a living being that did them no harm' (*Mor.* 729E).

If, however, only sacred fish were involved, then ideas about cleanliness and purity might be at work. No considerations of health and nutrition enter into any ancient discussion of fish taboos, nor any modern analysis that I have seen. Simoons's explanation of abstention from fish in the Middle East, that fish is unfamiliar to nomads and pastoralists and unsuited to be a food resource for them, is not applicable to the Pythagoreans.[19] While some doubt is legitimate over the origin of bean-avoidance, the dietary rules ascribed to the Pythagoreans appear in general to be explicable in terms of their religious and philosophical beliefs rather than nutritional, ecological or economic factors. In any case, their belief system and cultural attitudes are appropriate in a group which regarded themselves as a counter-culture, and stood aloof from the values and practices of normal urban and civic life.

Porphyry conceded that abstinence from meat was a discipline for 'philosophers' rather than the mass of humanity, and in the context of civic life, for priests rather than for lay people. In particular he acknowledged that meat was appropriate for athletes, soldiers, manual workers and those recovering from illness (*Abst.* 1.15; 2.4.3). Let us consider the case of priests.

---

[18] For Pythagoras in Croton, see Pomp. Trog. *Hist. Phil. epit.* 20.4.1–2, 5–8 (Justin); Porph. *Vit. Pyth.* 18 (Dicaearchus).

[19] Simoons (1961), 9, 113. Porph. *Abst.* 1.14.4 has a similar explanation of the abstention of Phoenicians and Jews from pork.

Frazer and others traced the regulation of the diet and life-style of priests to a general practice among primitive peoples to both guard and guard against their leader (sacred or secular) by encompassing him in a network of rules of taboo.[20] That the priests of Egypt were so restricted is well known, though the picture is confused. It is significant that there is a tradition linking them with Pythagoras. Plutarch has a professor of literature, one Theon, speak as follows:

> But it is fully agreed that he associated for a long while with the wise men of Egypt, and that he emulated them in many ways and considered them to be of very great authority in matters of priestly ritual. An example is abstention from beans; Herodotus says that the Egyptians neither plant nor eat beans, and cannot even bear to look at them; and we know that even now the priests abstain from fish. They also consider it a religious duty to avoid salt, so that neither cooked food nor bread seasoned with salt from the sea is served . . . (Plut. *Mor.* 729A)

Egyptian priests avoided pork. The pig was thought to be unclean, according to Plutarch, 'because it is reputed to be most inclined to mate at the waning of the moon, and because the bodies of those who drink its milk break out with leprosy and scabrous itching' (*Mor.* 353).[21] But if Herodotus is to be believed, the priests could not have been vegetarians, because 'a plentiful supply of beef and goose's flesh' was part of their daily food, in addition to bread 'of the sacred corn' and 'a portion of wine' (2.37). Nor were beans the only vegetable they did not accept. Onions, 'the only plant which naturally thrives and flourishes in the waning of the moon', were avoided, says Plutarch (*Mor.* 353E–F). Diodorus, who adds lentils to the list of forbidden foods (that is, to beans, onions and cheese), accounts for these prohibitions in terms of morality, ecology and politics, respectively, a self-denying ordinance, the need to conserve foodstuffs, and a decision by the early kings to keep communities at odds with one another by encouraging them to honour and despise different animals.[22] It is more likely that religious rules, in particular, ideas about sanctity, purity and cleanliness, dictated whether a food should or should not be eaten (cf. Plut. *Mor.* 352D–F).

Ceremonies in great number are imposed upon the priest of Jupiter and also many abstentions, of which we read in the books written *On the Public Priests*; and

---

[20] Frazer (1911), 132; cf. Freud (1938), 66.
[21] On pork, see e.g. Hdt. 2.47; Plut. *Mor.* 353F, 670F; Sext. Emp. 3.223; Darby et al. (1977), vol. I, 171–99; cf. 120–46, on beef. The crocodile was avoided as sacred (Diod. 1.35.6), as were various birds. See Darby et al. (1977), vol. I, 320 (falcon, ibis, vulture). The *testimonia* on fish are confusing. See Hdt. 2.37.4; Plut. *Mor.* 353C–E; Porph., *Abst.* 4.7; Griffiths (1970), 277–9; Darby et al. (1977), vol. I, 380–97.   [22] Diodorus 1.89.5 (not specifically of priests).

they are also recorded in the first book of Fabius Pictor. (Gellius, *Noctes Atticae* 10.15)

Non-food items dominate the discussion of the priest of Jupiter in Rome, the *flamen dialis*, by the miscellanist Aulus Gellius, who wrote under Hadrian, more than three centuries after Fabius Pictor. The priest must not ride horses, take an oath, wear knots in his clothing, have his hair cut by a slave, pass under an arbour of vines, go out without a cap, go to a funeral; and so on. The list of prohibitions includes the following: 'It is not customary for the Dialis to touch, or even name, a she-goat, raw flesh, ivy, and beans. . . . The priest of Jupiter must not touch any bread fermented with yeast.'

Plutarch asks why the priest did not touch flour or yeast, and speculates:

Is it because flour is an incomplete and crude food? For neither has it remained what it was, wheat, nor has it become what it must become, bread; but it has both lost the germinative power of the seed and at the same time it has not attained to the usefulness of food. Wherefore also the Poet by a metaphor applied to barley-meal the epithet *mylephatos*, as if it were being killed or destroyed in the grinding. Yeast is itself also the product of corruption, and produces corruption in the dough with which it is mixed; for the dough becomes flabby and inert, and altogether the process of leavening seems to be one of putrefaction; at any rate, if it goes too far, it utterly sours and spoils the flour. (*Mor.* 289E–F)

This account has a modern flavour, evoking both the binary polarities of Lévi-Strauss's culinary triangle and Mary Douglas's reading of the Jewish dietary prohibitions in terms of 'dirt', or 'matter out of place'.[23] Plutarch gives a parallel explanation for the avoidance of raw meat (*Mor.* 289F–90A).

Dogs and goats are to be shunned because impure in various ways, and in addition dogs, aggressive animals, might bar would-be suppliants from asylum at the altar of Jupiter. The vine and the ivy, symbols respectively of drunkenness and Bacchic revels and orgies, are both to be avoided by this 'as it were animate embodiment and sacred image of the god' (*Mor.* 290A–1B).

JEWISH DIETARY LAWS

The overall aim of the food regulations, as of the Mosaic code as a whole, is transparently the preservation of the holiness of a people

---

[23] Lévi-Strauss (1970); (1965); Vernant (1981b) 78; 244, n. 34: flour is 'a hybrid, a muddle, neither raw nor cooked, neither wild nor civilized'; Douglas (1966), etc. (see below).

chosen by God and separate from all other peoples. The internal logic and deeper meaning, however, are obscure. The forbidden animals are unclean 'for you', but in what does their uncleanness consist? The main texts, Leviticus 11 and Deuteronomy 14:1–21, do not offer any explanation. At most, the characteristics of clean animals are stated – so, of the land animals, 'every animal that parts the hoof and has the hoof cloven in two and chews the cud' – but sometimes just a list of the permitted or prohibited is given. George Foot Moore wrote: 'This is the logic of a revealed religion. Upon its premises, any other attitude is ipso facto a rejection of the religion and of God who is its author.'[24]

Speculation on the meaning of the laws began in ancient times. It surfaces in the Hellenistic period, in the circle of Hellenising Jews, as a response to the problems of maintaining the Jewish way of life while interacting actively with the world of the heathen. The Letter of Aristaeus[25], of perhaps the beginning of the second century BC, begins one section with a statement of the superiority of the Jewish religion in comparison with others, 'the Egyptians and the like, who have put their trust in wild beasts and most of the creeping things and vermin, and worship these and offer sacrifice to these whether alive or dead'. The lawgiver was fencing the Hebrews about 'with impregnable palisades and walls of iron . . . lest we should become perverted by sharing the pollutions of others or consorting with base persons' (139, 142). That is the general setting. When he comes down to details, the author favours explanation in terms of allegory (*semeion*, a sign or symbol, 150). When he rules out carnivores,

the lawgiver gave a sign that those for whom the laws were ordained must practise righteousness in their hearts and oppress no one, trusting in their own strength, nor rob one of anything, but must direct their lives by righteous motives, even as the tame birds . . . consume the pulse that grows on the earth and do not tyrannise to the destruction of their kin. (147)

The parting of the hoof and division of the foot 'symbolise discrimination in our every action with a view to what is right'; while 'chewing the cud' stands for the gift of memory, 'calling to mind life and existence', or 'what the Lord has wrought in you' (153ff.). Wild things, meanwhile, are clearly not models for human conduct. The weasel tribe, for example, is obviously defiled: it 'conceives through its ears and gives birth through its mouth' (165).

[24] Moore (1927), 1.77.
[25] Letter of Aristaeus to Philocrates, 120–81. For the text and Fr. tr., Pelletier (1962) = SC 89; Eng. tr. by Thackeray (1917).

The tradition of allegorical interpretation of the Jewish laws passes through Philo the Hellenised Jew from Alexandria[26] to patristic writers of the second and early third centuries, and beyond. It was a Christian idea that the hare represents homosexuality, a notion still alive or reborn in the early Middle Ages, when there was a revival of selected parts of the Mosaic prohibitions in the Christian Church. The prohibition on pork remained, as quintessentially Jewish.[27] Allegorizing apart, Christian writing on the laws was short of inventiveness. According to Origen and Eusebius, God wanted to prevent the Jews from worshipping animals which their neighbours, notably Egyptians, treated as gods. This is a less sympathetic version of an argument in the Letter of Aristaeus. Jerome stands alone in giving an interpretation which points forward to the arguments of modern cultural geographers and materialist anthropologists: the Mosaic prohibitions were appropriate to the culture and climate of the Near East.[28]

Modern debate on the origin and significance of the Mosaic laws divides sharply between symbolic and materialistic interpretations. Jean Soler[29] argued that the nature of the particular food items was irrelevant to their exclusion, and offered an explanation in terms of deep and complex structures. Mary Douglas explained the imposition of dietary and other rules in terms of a sequence of ideas revolving around dirt: 'Dirt is never a unique, isolated event. Where there is dirt there is system. Dirt is the by-product of a systematic ordering and classification of matter, in so far as ordering involves rejecting inappropriate elements.'[30] Dirt creates a situation of danger and encroachment, and prompts societies to take steps to defend their cultural system. As with the structuralists, the explanation is entirely in terms of mental attitudes. Douglas regards the irrationality of many food-avoidances as a point in her favour. It is culture, not nature, that determines what is dangerous and to be shunned. The Jewish dietary laws are her prime example.

According to the cultural materialist Marvin Harris, 'the selection of foods to convey meaning is not and cannot be an autonomous process', but must be understood with reference to 'the processes that are responsible for selecting foods for nourishment'.[31] His own preferred explanation of taboo is in terms of 'recurrent practical conditions', ecological and/or nutritional and sometimes economic. In the case of pork, he

---

[26] Philo, *On the Special Laws* 4.78–131, *On Agric.* 131–45.
[27] Laurioux (1988), 127–8. For the hare, see Clement of Alexandria, *Paid.* 2.10.83–5.
[28] Origen, *C. Cels.* 4.93 (SC 136); Eusebius of Emesa, *Fragm. Exeg. in Pent. PG* 86. 558; Jerome, *Adv. Jovin. PL* 23.294–5. [29] Soler (1979). [30] Douglas (1966), 35. [31] Harris (1986), 71.

decides that the source of the aversion lies in the environmental conditions of the Near East, and in the nomadic pastoral regime practised by
the Israelites in prehistoric times.[32] In this Harris is restating the preferred solution of the cultural geographer Simoons: 'It is logical to
suppose that pastoralists living in arid regions developed contempt for
the pig as an animal alien to their way of life and symbolic of the
despised sedentary folk, and came to avoid its flesh for food.'[33]

Harris rejects society-specific, cultural explanations in terms of religion, race and ethnicity.[34] However, unravelling the logic of the specific
dietary rules is one thing, explaining the existence of the rules, dietary
and non-dietary, as a package, quite another. The latter exercise can
hardly be done – as the introductory words of Deuteronomy 14 confirm
– without reference to the nature of the Jewish God, the special status of
the Jews as the chosen people, and their conception of themselves as a
race apart.

The way forward, it might be suggested, is to bring together Douglas'
general theory of purity with an analysis of the dietary laws which
reflects their complexity and relates them to the value system revealed in
the Pentateuch and the Prophets. In recent work Douglas has offered
such an account, which both is fine-grained and connects with the con-
ceptual scheme of the Israelites. The rejected animals fall into three categories: they are predators (and thus in breach of the laws against eating
blood); or they are preyed upon and need protection (in accordance with
Isaiah's prophecy of a city of justice and righteousness); or they lack
something which is needed, or have something superfluous (and thus
come under the rules of blemish). However, this is achieved at the cost
of the loss of the purity theory. Douglas abandons this mainly on the
grounds that the rules in question do not perform the function that rules
of purity and pollution characteristically do, namely, to establish and
maintain lines of social demarcation within a society.[35] There is no need

---

[32] Harris (1987), 59–60.
[33] Simoons (1961), 41. For the diet of Palestine in general in the Roman period, see Broshi (1986); Hamel (1990); Dar (1995).
[34] Harris (1986), 84–6; cf. Harris (1987), 61. He does grant that there can be a feed-back process: 'Religiously sanctioned foodways that have become established as the mark of conversion and as a measure of piety can also exert a force of their own back upon the ecological and economic conditions which gave rise to them' (1986: 86). Goody (1982), 146 made the same point with refer-ence to political relationships.
[35] Douglas (1993); (1993–94). She adds, implausibly, that in any case purity or cleanliness is too petty a concern to have served as the organising principle of the dietary laws. Soler (1996), in a restate-ment of his position (cf. n. 29), favours as a/the criterion for prohibition deviation from the dis-tinctions imposed on the animal world by the creator.

to follow Douglas in this. Sacral purity is characteristically demanded of priests, as we have seen, and in the Jewish context was required of the whole people. Porphyry saw the point. In other societies it was normal to make higher demands of leaders, be they philosophers or priests. The Jews were different, and in his experience unique, in that they were 'a race of philosophers' (*Abst.* 2.27).

CHRISTIAN ASCETICISM

In contrast with the Jews, the Christians were universalist, deliberately overriding all ethnic and political barriers. Former Jews and Judaisers made up the ranks of the first Christians, but the future lay with those concerned to mark off Christianity from Judaism. Both these factors militated against the prescription of a distinct dietary code and against the adoption of the Mosaic lawbook in particular.[36] That did not stop groups of Christians setting themselves apart from the main body of the Church, practising dietary and sexual asceticism in their retreats in desert, cave, mountain or tree, in pursuit of the lofty spiritual goal of holiness and a purer communion with God than was attainable in the world.

The ultimate source of the ascetic declaration of war on food and sex is the Judaeo-Christian foundation myth of the Garden of Eden. Forbidden fruit ushered sin into the world, sin of the gut, of the groin and of the soul (Genesis 3:1–7). As a result, Adam and Eve and their descendants were condemned to hard labour in the fields and travail in childbirth. These punitive consequences could be avoided only by the suppression of the appetites, specifically, sexual desires and the diet that fuelled them, in the first place meat and wine.[37] This was the ascetic enterprise, undertaken by fringe groups like the Encratites in the second century, becoming more prominent with the desert movement in Egypt and Syria from the late third century, and reaching a climax in the fourth and fifth centuries.

Tertullian, an African theologian who flourished around the turn of the second century, was an early apologist for a puritanical form of

---

[36] See the words of Jesus as reported in Matt. 15:11; Mk 7:19. The consumption of sacrificial meat divided Christians, not because it was meat, but because it originated in pagan sacrifice, i.e. in idolatry. Paul's view was that it should not be a stumbling-block to Christians. The main texts are 1 Cor. 8; 10:31–3; Rom. 14:13–23. Others disagreed: Rev. 2:14, 20; Acts 15:20, 29; 21:25. For discussion, see Segal (1990), 224–53.

[37] Brown (1988), 92ff. A more elaborate list of prohibitions might be imposed on monks. See Rousselle (1988), 172–3, for the 'drying' diet, including reduced water intake, that John Cassian following pagan medical theory laid down for his monastery.

Christianity. In his treatise on fasting, he criticises the laxity of 'Psychics' (by which he means Catholics) in alimentary and sexual matters. Tertullian forges an intimate link between gluttony and lust, using an argument from the proximity of the stomach to the genitals:

Look at the body: the region of these members is one and the same. In short, the order of the vices is proportionate to the arrangement of the members. First the belly, and then immediately the materials of all other species of lasciviousness are laid subordinately to daintiness: through love of eating, love of impurity finds passage. (*On Fasting* 1)[38]

Writing in the second half of the fourth century, Basil of Caesarea in *Ascetical Discourse* follows Tertullian in giving the palm to gluttony among bodily vices.[39] Using a metaphor from irrigation, he presents gluttony as the vice which leads on to all the rest, especially no doubt sexual desire, though little is said of that:

As the nature of water that is channelled along many furrows causes it to make verdant the whole area around the furrows, so also the vice of gluttony, if it issues from your heart, irrigates all your senses, raising a forest of evils within you and making your soul a lair of beasts. (ch. 6)

Basil moves to the ringing climax:

This vice of gluttony delivered Adam up to death; by the pleasure of the appetite, consummate evil was brought into the world. Through it, Noah was mocked, Cham was cursed, Esau was deprived of his birthright and married into a Canaanite family. Lot became both his own son-in-law and father-in-law by marrying his own daughters – the father was husband and the grandfather father, thus making a double mockery of the laws of nature. Gluttony also made the people of Israel worshippers of idols and strewed the desert with their bodies . . . To sum it all up, if you gain the mastery over your appetite, you will dwell in paradise; if you do not, you will go to your death. (ch. 7)

As the belly is the seat of bodily desires, so fasting is the trademark of the ascetic. Fasting usually involved the imposition of restrictions on an already limited diet. Symeon the Stylite's complete abstention from food for forty days was exceptional. Total fast was always temporary. The norm was to leave the stomach unfilled, to eat very little and as rarely as possible.[40]

---

[38] Clement of Alexandria, *Paid.* 2.1–2, takes a more moderate line on eating, arguing that while we are in the world we have to eat. He is concerned about the effects of wine, but does not outlaw any particular food.   [39] Basil, *Ascetic Discourse* 6 (=*PG* 31.639).

[40] Theodoret, *Hist. Relig.* 26.7 (Symeon); cf. Rufinus, *Hist. Mon. Eg.* 7.3: Elias 'in his old age ate three ounces of bread and 3 olives towards evening; but in his youth he ate only once a week'. On fasting see now Grimm (1995); (1996).

Was sex seen as the greater and more present evil and fasting a means of escaping it?[41] Or was hunger more painful than sexual deprivation, and food perceived to be the greater need? Augustine felt that he had put sexual temptation behind him when he became a Christian, but admitted to having been unable to free himself from the desire to indulge himself in eating and drinking.[42] 'Those who are used to fasting are not troubled by sexual inclinations', wrote Simplicius.[43] If indulgence in food and drink arouses the appetite for sex, undernutrition weakens the sexual drive, inducing impotence in men and amenorrhea in women. Of these, the latter condition was the more conspicuous and controversial. While for Christians of ascetic inclination the suspension of menstruation was a mark of purity, for traditionalists, Christian or pagan, it was a scandal, raising their hackles in the same way as the allied virtues of virginity (in the unmarried) and chastity (in the married). Asceticism entailed 'the boycott of the womb'.[44] By embracing it women were abandoning their natural and vital role of reproducing the community; or, from a different perspective, they were emancipating themselves from the grim cycle of child-bearing in the days before efficient means of contraception were available.

There was another central role played by women, that of controllers of food.[45] Moreover – and this is where the two roles come together – as mothers, women became food. This also touched on a sensitive spot. It was natural for Christian women to identify themselves with Mary, who by bearing Christ had salvaged the reputation of women after the disaster of Eve, prime temptress and consumer. Mary as virgin was a suitable model for ascetic women. But what of Mary as the food for Christ? One way of meeting the problem was to turn Christ into the feeder. Thus, in medieval art and literature a parallel is drawn between Christ's wound and Mary's breast. The parallel goes back earlier, to patristic writers. As Walker Bynum observes: 'Clement of Alexandria had already spoken of Christ as mother, drawing out the analogy between a God who feeds human kind with his own blood in the eucharist, and a human mother, whose blood becomes food for her child.'[46]

The ultimate rationalisation of female asceticism was the representation of the goal of women as the suppression of their femininity. Women who successfully practised the ascetic life were approaching the status of

[41] A theme of Brown (1988), esp. chs. 13, 18 and Rousselle (1988), chs. 9ff. Contrast Thélamon (1992). [42] Ferrari (1978). [43] Simplic. 33.8, ed. Dubner 117, cited by Musurillo (1956), 11. [44] Brown (1988), 27. [45] Cf. Walker Bynum (1987), 208. [46] Walker Bynum (1987), 270–1.

men. The ascetic Pelagius was discovered to be Pelagia, in former life a harlot, only after she was found dead, immured in her cell.[47]

CONCLUSION

Dietary rules are a predictable though not an invariable feature of religious and philosophical groups in antiquity which saw themselves as separate and distinct from the rest of the world. This perception was complemented in the Jewish case by a strong sense of their identity as a single nation, and a conviction of their privileged status in the sight of God. The Christians, in contrast, were a multiracial community and, after the early stages, concerned to mark themselves off from the Jews. They abandoned the Mosaic lawbook and did not contemplate a substitute.

Some Christians in late Antiquity sought perfection and greater proximity to God through shunning the world and its values and adopting a regime of extreme self-denial. This involved in the first instance the avoidance of foods that were thought to inflame desires rather than meet needs, and a reduced intake of 'safe' necessities. Ascetics attracted resentment and suspicion as well as admiration within the Church. In so far as they were not integrated within its institutional framework, they were an independent source of spiritual authority, by virtue of the ascetic feats they performed. They were visibly 'outsiders', and it was their style of life that made them so.

Few demands were made by pagan cults on their followers, and these were confined to the area of ritual, its proper conduct and maintenance. Dietary and other rules, imposed for the purpose of ensuring purity, order and the safety and prosperity of the community, were applied only to those who presided over the ritual, and that only selectively.

Paganism, like Christianity (and Judaism), had an ascetic fringe in its Pythagoreans, Orphics, Neoplatonist vegetarians and individual sages and wonder-workers such as Apollonius of Tyana,[48] and was similarly cross-cultural. But the parallel is not to be pressed. Christians formed a multiracial community open to all comers – *of believers*. It was their belief-system above all that made them a distinct and exclusive group, operating outside and undermining the existing religious framework, until, that is, Christianity became the prevailing religion. The Church did have

[47] Ward (1987), ch. 4, §15: 'When the fathers began to anoint the body with myrrh, they realised that it was a woman.'
[48] Apollonius is said to have kept alive on vegetables and dried fruits. See Philostratus, *Vita Ap.* 1.8.

an active interest in the life-style and social relations of its adherents, but in practice this stopped short of the imposition of detailed dietary and other regulations. Pagans lacked any motive whatsoever for elaborate self-regulation in this area.

CHAPTER 7

Food and the family

PRELIMINARIES

In antiquity men lived longer than women. This cannot be proved. But I am sure that this is what we would find, if the data were adequate to permit a demographic investigation of Graeco-Roman ancient societies. Where the two sexes are given equal treatment in the matter of nutrition and health care, women live appreciably longer than men. That is the case in Europe, North America and other affluent countries of the modern world. Women live longer than men because they are physiologically more efficient. They need a lower protein and calorie intake, and are more resistant to disease.

In the contemporary third world, men live longer than women. Instead of a female:male ratio of 1.05/1.06: 1, it is 0.94: 1, or worse. This means, as Amartya Sen put it, in the title of an article in the *New York Review of Books* (December 1990), that 'more than 100 million women are missing'. I think we would find, if we had comparable data, that there were a lot of missing women in ancient societies as well.

Sen blamed pro-male bias in two areas: division of food in the family, and access to medical and health facilities. Only the first variable is clearly relevant to us. In antiquity hospitals were hardly known, and doctors were in a complete fog about the nature of disease and how to cure it. Access to medical attention was not necessarily a benefit for the patient. Of course in antiquity the sick, or a proportion of them, did submit to medical or quasi-medical attention, and the condition of some of these perhaps improved in consequence, as it happened. Old-fashioned folk remedies sometimes hit the spot. But they might just as readily have worked the other way, undermining the health and nutritional status of the patient. The upshot is, that extra onus is put on the other variable, namely, discrimination in the distribution of food within the family.[1]

[1] Harriss (1990); (1993) to some extent provides a corrective to Sen's view. See n. 14, below.

To investigate food-allocation within the family, we need to explore the various principles that might have had an influence. The key words are needs, status and power.[2] There is, first, a functional/physiological explanation of food-distribution. I call this needs: the needs of the individual, the needs of the family. If the overall aim is to secure the survival and well-being of the family, then the larger share will go to the most productive members. At any rate, if there is a squeeze on food resources, and someone has to go hungry, it will not be the workers. The second factor is cultural – status. The guiding principle of this explanation is that food behaviour reflects the social hierarchy and social relationships. So the status of an individual in the household and in society at large will be crucial in food allocation. Thirdly, power, or control over resources. In this approach the focus is on material and power relations. Hierarchy rears its head again, but this time it is not a hierarchy of status so much as a hierarchy of power and control.

Under the heading of needs, men will score well; so will older children, especially boys, as making up the bulk of the productive workforce. Women of child-bearing age might logically be categorised as 'producers', in their role of social reproduction. Indeed an argument could be framed on behalf of young children, as representing the future hopes of the family. But at this point status, the cultural explanation of food allocation, might intrude, and its close ally power, or dominance and control both physical and political, and they characteristically do *not* act in the interests of women. It is likely enough that in patriarchal societies, as Graeco-Roman societies were, females would be given a less generous share of the family food resources than males.

Medical treatises from the first and second centuries AD, excerpted by the fourth-century physician Oribasius, nicely illustrate the joint operation of the three factors in the prescription of a regime appropriate for girls and women.[3] So Rufus of Ephesus, who lived in the early second century, wrote:

When they are older and growth has all but stopped, and when young girls out of modesty no longer want to play childish games to the full, then one must give much more continuous attention to their regimen, regulate and moderate their intake of food, and not let them touch meat at all, or other foods that are very nourishing. (Oribasius, *Liber Incertus* 18.10)

---

[2] Here I build on a framework of argument developed in Wheeler (1991).
[3] For the text of Oribasius, see L. Raeder, ed., *Oribasii Collectionum Medicarum Reliquiae*, vol. 4 (Leipzig and Berlin, 1933).

Rufus is very concerned about surfeit, which 'produces maladies'. He apparently has in mind the afflictions that beset girls who bear children at too young an age. He wants girls to marry early, that is, as soon as sexual desires are aroused, in order to control their appetites. His solution is to check those appetites by keeping food intake at a low or moderate level (and denying access to wine):

For the quicker she puts on weight, the quicker she becomes nubile, and the quicker her desire to have sexual relations and to produce children is aroused. It is because of this, more or less, that the law prescribes marrying young girls to older men. (18.2)

The ideal is for girls to marry 'at a more natural time' than the beginnings of puberty, namely, at around 18. The author, this time Athenaeus of Attaleia (mid-first century AD), sees his task as laying down a regimen of food, exercise and indeed 'work' that will postpone the 'dangerous period' of puberty. He engagingly advises 'mistresses of the house' to 'look at their servants':

In effect, women who lead a soft and delicate life would do well to watch those who earn their keep, to see what a difference there is between themselves and those women in the matter of health in general, and conception and ease of childbirth in particular, because their diet is simple and they exercise their bodies. (21.5)

He explains:

There is point therefore in a woman supervising her baker, admonishing her attendant and measuring out for him that which he needs, and doing the rounds, making sure that everything is where it should be, for this activity seems to me to be at once a cure for anxiety and good walking exercise. She can also get good exercise wetting the flour and kneading the dough, and making beds. If a woman takes this kind of exercise, she can eat with more pleasure and acquire a better colour. (21.6–8)

The 'simple diet' becomes in the mouth of another medical writer cited by Oribasius, Galen, 'the bare necessities'. He says, in a parallel passage, but this time with reference to the diet appropriate to pregnant women rather than young girls:

Pregnant women should above all else avoid repletion, and not be lazy at taking exercise. That is in effect why servant girls and other poor women reach their term easily, go into labour easily, and bring into the world a large and well-nourished baby, because they have not followed a delicate regime, the reason being that the necessity of doing their domestic jobs prevented them from leading such a life. Similarly, they are not stuffed beyond due measure with food, since they can scarcely get the bare necessity for themselves. Let that be a lesson to pregnant women. (22.13–15)

Doctors were concerned to limit the food consumption of females, whether rich or poor, young or mature. This discussion is about needs of women, but those needs are seen through the eyes of males and reflect the higher status and superior power of men. Women are judged to need less food than men, but their needs are defined by men and largely in the interests of men and of the male-dominated society as a whole. The desired ends are achieved through the systematic supervision and control of women from childhood to adulthood.

Before we proceed any further, there is a question to be faced about the ancient sources. We are heavily reliant on the treatises of medical writers. We have high-society doctors telling their male, upper-class clients what to do, what kind of regimen to put their children and their womenfolk through. There is no way of telling how far their prescriptions were put into practice. We have no idea how far their opinions were disseminated down through the social hierarchy.

A determined sceptic could have a field day here. Against him I would urge the following. In the first place, the doctors in question were practising doctors, not merely scholars sitting 'with a candle in a garret' producing their treatises. Galen often boasts about the satisfaction he brought to sundry clients, who included emperors and aristocrats. Medicine was a highly competitive profession at the top, because of the profits and prestige that it brought.

Secondly, in the medical writings one does come across what can only be descriptions or reflections of current phenomena and current practice. It is not clear, and it doesn't matter at present, for our limited purposes, whether doctors were the passive respondents, or whether they actively influenced and helped to frame the practices I have in mind. In either case we have here another indication that the writers concerned were in contact with the outside world. I am thinking of such practices as the hiring of wet-nurses, which we know from sundry sources was routine among the wealthier classes and is treated as such in the medical writings. In the same category might be listed the various health problems which the doctors mention with a view to prescribing remedies against them. Many of the diseases in question are completely compatible with the dietary prescriptions of the medical writers. I am thinking of baby sicknesses against which colostrum might have been a defence (but colostrum was distrusted, see below), various deficiency diseases, like bladder-stone, and certain eye-diseases that are diet-related. These disabilities are also alluded to by a number of writers who had no special medical expertise, like the elder Pliny, who was obsessed with bladder-stone, which strikes first in early child-hood.

Thirdly, within the field of literature, we are not completely depen-dent on the medical sources, and the other evidence is often clearly compatible with what the physicians say. Note for example these words of Xenophon in relation to the diet of girls elsewhere than in Sparta: 'In other states the girls who are destined to become mothers and are brought up in the approved fashion live on the very plainest fare, with a most meagre allowance of delicacies.' (Xen. *Lac. Pol.* 1.3).

A fourth point is that deficiency diseases which escaped the notice of the literary sources, partly no doubt because they were to some extent sub-clinical, are brought to light by the skeletal data – for example, iron-deficiency anaemia, which produces lesions on parts of the skeletons of women and small children. These problems too are compatible with the dietary prescriptions of the medical sources.

Finally, comparative evidence can be used with profit, in this area as in others, to raise questions that can be posed of the ancient evidence, and to confirm suspicions about the existence and prevalence of disease, food stress and malnourishment in vulnerable classes of the population in antiquity.

Let us now explore in more detail some of the implications of the three factors, needs, status and power, and the way they may have oper-ated in ancient societies.

NEEDS AND STATUS, 'SCIENCE' AND IDEOLOGY

There are various small indications that the medical and other sources in their descriptions or prescriptions about food both were not oblivi-ous to the needs of women and the society as a whole, and could make sensible judgements thereon. Xenophon, taking the Spartan side, points out that girls brought up (elsewhere) on an exiguous diet and the sedentary life could hardly be expected to produce fine specimens of children when they reached child-bearing age. The medical writers cited by Oribasius were aware that pregnant women required 'abun-dant nourishment' once the foetus was 'more solidly established' in the uterus, and that thereafter they should eat more and 'tire themselves more'.[4] Rufus is close to observing that because they do not and are not expected to work, women have reduced food-energy requirements, and

---

[4] Galen in Orib. *Lib. Incert.* 22.9.

should be fed less than physically active men. The writer is discussing the marriage age, which, as the wider context shows, is in his mind closely related to the quantity and quality of food that girls are allowed to eat:

So it is preferably at 18 that Hesiod wants girls to marry, and if anyone thinks that is too late, a suitable reply would be: yes, as things are. But if on the other hand he thought about the way things were done in the old days, *if he bore in mind how acceptable it was for a woman as well as a man to work*, he would no longer hold the opinion that 18 years is late for a girl to marry. (18.4–5)

Another relevant factor is the distinct physiological needs of women (and men). Here ancient thought went down a blind alley. Health, it was believed, was a product of the harmony of four bodily fluids or humours, which in turn had to be understood in connection with the four elements and the four primary qualities. Food and drink were one of several factors that influenced the humours and preserved or undermined health. The task of the physician was to regulate the daily life of the patient, including his or her consumption of food and drink, in such a way as to maintain the normal balance of the humours. So we routinely find in the medical writings such statements as this, cited by Oribasius from Athenaeus of Attaleia:

The cold and wet constitution of the body of the woman has to be corrected by a regime which is weighted towards the hot and the dry. Women should therefore avoid the cold and the wet, air or places, and choose foods that are drying rather than moistening, as in any case nature itself teaches us, since women show very little need of liquid. Women should take little wine because of the weakness of their nature. (21.1–3)

Or, in more detail, from Rufus:

Everyone agrees that the body of a woman is wetter and colder than that of a man. So she must follow a regimen which is hotter in order to re-establish the equilibrium which is disturbed by the excess of their temperament. So they have to exercise themselves just as much as men must . . . Baths are less suitable for women, because they are wet. On the other hand, drying baths, that is to say, those of mineral water, are better for women than for men . . . As for suitable foods, they are those which heat and dry, while those which act in the opposite way are very harmful to them. So it is necessary to avoid foods that will make them colder and wetter: they include, among fish, eels, sheat-fish, sturgeons, turbots, and, in general, river fishes; among meats, they include those that are fat and come from new-born animals. (20.1–2, 13, 17)

Whether the 'science' is ultimately independent of the ideology is a moot point, but it does have a life of its own. The list of foods judged suitable for women reflects bizarre physiological theory rather than male prejudice and the social subordination of women. The two of course coexist and are intertwined, as the last two sentences of the first quotation show.

If the theory of the humours was a false trail, a statement of Aristotle has to be judged differently. He says in the *History of Animals* that women need less nourishment than men (608b14–15). Perhaps this idea or perception rather than straightforward anti-female bias lay behind the non-Spartan practice that Xenophon criticises, or indeed Aristotle's judgement? It happens that Aristotle is right. Women require 15–35% fewer calories than men. In general, the needs of the various family members are not identical. It follows that a precisely equal division of food would be a mistake. A fair distribution of food within the household is not an equal one.

This discussion raises a larger problem, which is related to the level of scientific knowledge existing in ancient societies. Supposing the principle *were* accepted in antiquity that women of child-bearing age (and young children) should receive rewards because of their crucial role in the reproduction of the society: were ancient societies aware of the needs of these crucially important and numerically very substantial groups? The answer seems to be, at most, only dimly, and in consequence, both women and small children were disadvantaged.

Take children first. There are two points to be made here and they go in different directions. There is no good reason for thinking that fathers and mothers in ancient societies placed a low valuation on their children, although this has been widely assumed and sometimes vigorously supported. Yet Greeks and Romans, by the way they fed their babies and infants, were preparing large numbers of them for early death, stunted development or selective malnutrition. They did this with the best will in the world. So, incidentally, did countless parents in later ages. This was not a specifically Graeco-Roman problem.[5]

Let us consider infant feeding practices.[6] Nobody understood colostrum, nobody before the nineteenth century, in fact. Colostrum is three times as protein-rich as mature human milk and its antibodies protect the neonate from bacterial infections. Here is what Soranus has to say on the subject:

---

[5] On attitudes to children, see Garnsey (1991b).
[6] See Fildes (1986), 81, 199–204 (colostrum); Fildes (1986) (weaning); Fildes (1988); Masciadri and Montevecchi (1982); Bradley (1980); (1986) (wet-nursing); Goodman and Armelagos (1989); Makler (1980); Whitehead (1989) (infant nutrition and disease).

Now, one must in most cases abstain from all food up to as long as two days . . .
After the interval one must give as food to lick . . . honey moderately boiled . . .
One must gently anoint the mouth of the newborn with the finger, and must
then drop lukewarm hydromel into it . . . From the second day on after the treatment one should feed with milk from somebody well able to serve as a wet-
nurse, as for twenty days the maternal milk is in most cases unwholesome, being
thick, too caseous, and therefore hard to digest, raw and not prepared to perfection. (*Gynaecology* 2.17–18)

It is hard to know if the attitude here expressed was exclusive to the
upper classes. Lower-class mothers would not have been able to give way
to a wet-nurse. It does not follow that they continued feeding their babies
longer than they wanted to. Soranus is probably criticising upper-class
women when he refers to 'those women' as 'too hasty' 'who after only 40
days try to give cereal food'. But early weaning was not necessarily an
upper-class preserve.

The well-off family had an advantage at the weaning stage because it
had access to a wider range of foodstuffs, including some that were good
protein sources. Soranus talks initially of 'crumbs of bread softened with
hydromel or milk, sweet wine, or honey wine', but later of 'soup made
from spelt, a very moist porridge, and an egg that can be sipped' (*Gyn.*
2.46). Galen prescribes first bread, then 'vegetables and meat and other
such things' (*Hygiene* 10.31). With both authors, the diet is for a time exclusively cereal, and one wonders how long this was persisted with. Cereal
was clearly the basic weaning food.

Absence of colostrum, early weaning, weaning foods low in nutrients,
late weaning: all of these undermined the nutritional status and life
chances of the small child. Yet, and this is a crucial point, parents were
unaware of the consequences of their actions. It was not that they placed
a low valuation on their children. Some individuals no doubt did, just as
some do now, but not fathers and mothers in general, then or in later
ages. Parents through the ages *have* shown ignorance of the needs of a
child.

When we turn to the situation of women, we find something rather
similar. There is, however, one important difference. Whereas writers in
antiquity had no deep-seated prejudice against children, they did as a
group have views of women which we would regard as unambiguously
prejudiced. Medical writers, as we saw, knew that pregnant women had
to feed the foetus and therefore needed to increase their food intake. This
did not prevent them issuing warnings against laziness, overeating and
the effects of wine. But sheer ignorance is also part of the picture. No
one in these societies could possibly have known, for example, that the

iron needs of women are three times those of men, let alone by what means those needs might be satisfied. So their failure to give women what they needed to ward off anaemia was a function in the first instance of ignorance, not discrimination.

To sum up the discussion so far. It would be absurd to suggest that ancient societies were systematically unwilling to recognise the food needs of women and children. It would have been suicidal to have taken such a stand. In practice, however, it was difficult if not impossible to meet the real needs of the various family members in a pre-scientific society. Ignorance in the matter of nutrition stood in the way. In any case, unequal division of food did not automatically produce a nutritionally unfortunate result, because the food needs of the various members of the family are not in fact equal. Finally, cultural factors, notably, the values of a patriarchal society, probably were a factor in unequal distribution. We can turn to this aspect now.

STATUS AND POWER

The guiding principle of the cultural explanation of food allocation is that food behaviour reflects the social hierarchy and social relationships. So the status of an individual in the household and in the society at large will be crucial in food allocation. The implications of this are straightforward. In a patriarchal society, men, teenage boys and, to some extent, older adults will be favoured over children and women, especially young women.

The inferior status of women may be expected to have played a role in the division of food within the family. The withholding of wine from women, as recommended by physicians, is a product of the way women were perceived, in a male-dominated society, as weak and fickle, a prey to their emotions, and easily tempted and led astray by the sins of the flesh. The denial of meat and other 'nourishing' foods, and the general instruction to restrict food consumption, were represented as a necessary response to the natural concupiscence of young women.

To isolate one variable is, inevitably, to oversimplify. We saw that the failure to feed vulnerable groups adequately was to some extent an intellectual failing, traceable to inadequate perceptions of need. Furthermore, when we looked at the prescriptions by doctors of the foods that should and should not be fed to women, we found pseudo-scientific principles at work as well as, and often side-by-side with, value-judgements which are rooted in social inequalities.

Power, another aspect of the social hierarchy, might be assumed to work closely in parallel to status in depressing the situation of women and children. But there is more in this than meets the eye. A crucial question is whether women work and control the product of their work. Again, one would expect adult males to dominate the scene. But older men, and perhaps women, might also be expected to do well if allocation proceeds in accordance with this rationale. Since the elderly hardly represent the active work-force, in their case the control of food once produced would be the crucial factor. Power, here, means resource-control.

This sends me to the hostile representation of women in the archaic Greek writers Semonides and Hesiod and the somewhat milder prejudices of the classical writer Xenophon, and to the idea that food acts as a 'feminine signifier' partly because historically food is a resource, perhaps the only one, over which women have exercised some control, in the spheres of both preparation and storage. One can perhaps detect in the paranoia of Greek writers a feeling that women were manipulating their power for their own benefit.[7] Hesiod employs an image of bees, presenting men as the hardworking producers, and women as the all-consuming drones: 'Throughout the whole day until the sun goes down, the bees toil to lay down the white combs, while the drones remain inside beneath their shelters and take the labour of others into their bellies' (*Theog.* 594–602). Xenophon's model landowner Ischomachus, who is his spokesman in *Oikonomikos*, is more patronising than misogynistic, as he lectures his young bride of all of 14 years about her tasks in the home. The wife is not named but simply addressed as 'woman'. Xenophon also uses the bee metaphor, but the woman in his house is queen bee rather than drone.[8] There is, however, an undercurrent of suspicion in Xenophon, not so much of the character of the girl herself, as of her sex. Right at the beginning of the passage he hints at the trouble that might arise when a woman comes into a house. Socrates asks Ischomachus if he had to train his wife in her duties or whether her parents had already done so. He replies:

Why, what knowledge could she have had, Socrates, when I took her for my wife? She was not yet 15 years old when she came to me, and up to that time she had lived under close control, seeing, hearing and saying as little as possible. If when she came she knew no more than how, when given wool, to turn out a cloak, and had seen only how the spinning is given out to the maids, is not

---

[7] Currie (1989), citing Walker Bynum (1987).
[8] Xen. *Oik.* 7.33–4; Pomeroy (1984). On Hesiod, see Sussman (1978).

that as much as could be expected? For she had been excellently trained, in my opinion, in the matter of her appetite, and this sort of training seems to me the most important to man and woman alike. (*Oik.* 7.5–6)

This may sound evenhanded – 'man and woman alike' – but a woman's self-control is primary, crucial, because she controls the storage and preparation of food, as Ischomachus reminds her in some detail. The weakness of women for food and drink is a standard theme in Greek and Roman literature.[9] Ischomachus knows the score; and so does the young woman. Her first words are: 'How can I possibly help you? What power have I? Everything depends on you. My duty, as my mother told me, is *sophronein.*' The virtue of *sophrosynē* is immediately defined by Ischomachus as adding to one's possessions and safeguarding them (by implication), rather than depleting them, consuming them, running them down.

The dilemma facing the male head of the house is clear. If women were confined to the home, as they more or less were in upper-class society, then they were handed the power to indulge their alleged weakness in the matter of food and drink. In practice, the presence of household servants must have made a difference, in limiting the woman's access to food resources. Ischomachus' wife supervises others rather than doing the work herself. And no doubt the cook was male (as is suggested for this period by many comic fragments in Athenaeus).[10]

It is time we asked how the other 90–95% lived, more particularly in a rural context. Whether women took part in agricultural work is an important consideration. Active workers receive more food. This was a rule of thumb even to mean old Cato. The rations he served his slaves reflected the labour demands he was making on them.

In antiquity, it is commonly assumed, women did not work in the fields. 'Barbarian' women certainly did. Plato in the *Laws* (805d–806a) talks of three alternative systems in vogue in his time. One is that of 'the Thracians, and many other tribes', 'who employ their women in tilling the ground and minding oxen and sheep and toiling just like slaves'. Plato's interlocutor contrasts this with the Laconian system, which he doesn't like because it falls between two stools, and the Athenian system, which is recognisably Xenophontic, and is described as 'ours and of all the people of our district': 'We huddle all our goods together, as the saying goes, within four walls, and then hand over the dispensing of

---

[9] Women and wine: see Richlin (1984), 68–9, with refs.; also Durry (1955); Gras (1983); Pucci (1989).
[10] Goody (1982), 193: in past societies the difference between high cooking and low cooking tends to be one between male and female.

them to the women, together with the control of the shuttles and all kinds of wool-work.' Other tribeswomen who are said to work, and bear and feed children while at work, are the Ligurians in Strabo (amongst other sources) and the Illyrians in Varro,[11] concerning whom Varro's interlocutor addresses another man thus:

As I have heard you say that you, when you were in Liburnia, saw mothers carrying logs and children at the breast at the same time, sometimes one, sometimes two; showing that our newly-delivered women, who lie for days under their mosquito-nets, are worthless and contemptible.

This is the noble savage motif, prominent in ethnographic writing like that of Strabo or Tacitus. What I want to suggest is that women worked in the fields as a matter of course in peasant communities within the Graeco-Roman orbit.[12] There is substantial comparative evidence for the active participation of women in agricultural work, and not just in livestock raising, but also in such vital areas as harvesting, when all hands had to be mobilised. My hypothesis is that participation in farmwork on this level had its rewards in the distribution of food, and this in the context of a patriarchal society.

CONCLUSION

Allocation of food within the household is a complex matter, because a diversity of considerations and values interact and clash. People in ancient societies had some conception of the food needs of individuals – guided no doubt by pragmatic rather than humanitarian considerations. The base line is that it was counter-productive and counter-reproductive to exploit women and deny them food too much, just as it was imprudent to overexploit or starve slaves. In addition, if women and children were disadvantaged nutritionally, as I have suggested they were, then this was in part a result of ignorance rather than prejudice. Still under the heading of need, and along the same line of argument, food needs are not in fact equal, and in so far as this was recognised in ancient society, this should not be put down to (just) prejudice.

Cultural values were a vital, controlling force. We are dealing with patriarchal societies. So adult males can be assumed to have scored well in the division of food resources. Still, there may not have been gross

---

[11] *Ligurians*: ps.-Arist. *Mirab.* 91 cf. Diod. 4.20.1ff.; also Posidonius in Strabo 3.4.17, told the story by his host, a man of Marseilles. *Illyrians*: Varro 2.10.8.

[12] Here I am taking a lead from Scheidel (1995); (1996).

inequality, especially if there was plenty of food to go round. The test
would come if food was short, choices had to be made and restrictions
imposed. Male power was mitigated to a degree by the control exercised
by women, within limits, over food storage, preparation and serving. On
the other hand, women have not always used this power to their own
advantage. It was the mother of the wife of Ischomachus who taught her
to control her appetites. Jack Goody states the general principle thus:
'While women feed young children irrespective of sex, they may not necessarily feed them equally, at least after they are weaned. In societies
where preference is given to sons rather than daughters, women may
themselves be the instruments of their own subordination.'[13]

The necessity of extracting labour out of women in households other
than those of the minority, who belonged to the leisured classes, might
be expected to have done something to redress the balance. That is to
say, where women participated in work outside the household, the gap
between the sexes in the division of food would have been narrower than
where women were confined to the home.

My expectation is that ancient evidence, had we more of it, would also
be equivocal and not produce a uniform picture. Although the subordination of women was universal, their treatment is not likely to have
been identical in all societies. By the same token, their nutritional and
health situation is unlikely to have been homogeneous throughout the
Mediterranean world.[14]

---

[13] Goody (1982), 68.
[14] Barbara Harriss-White, on the basis of research carried out in the Indian subcontinent in the
1980s, found that a gender bias in favour of males was more evident in access to medical and
health care than in distribution of food within the family, which in some surveys turned out to
be reasonably equitable. The factors at play are complex, but are apparently cultural as well as
economic. She now writes pessimistically about 'growing gender imbalances' in Tamil Nadu,
South India, on the basis of new evidence for female neglect in feeding and a 'culling of girls'.
See Harriss (1990); (1993); Harriss-White (1997); Harriss-White, Janakarajan and Arya (1996). I
am very grateful to her for sending me both published and unpublished work. The earlier
research may be dated, but it still stands as an indication that discrimination against women can
be muted in a patriarchal society.

CHAPTER 8

Haves and havenots

PRELIMINARIES

Flamingo. Pluck the flamingo, wash, truss, and put it in a saucepan; add water, dill and a little vinegar. Half-way through the cooking make a bouquet of leek and coriander and let it cook with the bird. When it is nearly done, add defrutum to give it colour. Put in a mortar pepper, caraway, coriander, asafoetida root, mint, rue; pound; moisten with vinegar, add Jericho dates, pour over some of the cooking-liquor. Put in the same saucepan, thicken with cornflour, pour the sauce over the bird, and serve. The same recipe can also be used for parrot. (Apicius 6.1)

My man is a pauper and I am an old woman with a daughter and a son, this boy, and this nice girl besides, five in all. If three of us get a dinner, the other two must share with them only a tiny barley-cake. We wail miserably when we have nothing, and our complexions grow pale with lack of food. The elements and sum of our livelihood are these: bean, lupine, greens, turnip, pulse, vetch, beechnut, iris bulb, cicada, chickpea, wild pears, and that god-given inheritance of our mother-country, darling of my heart, a dried fig. (Athen. 54e, Alexis)

In Graeco-Roman society, there was a large gulf between the *haute cuisine* of the few and the frugal menus of the mass of the population, rural and urban. *Haute cuisine* Greek- and Roman-style was marked by variety of foods (home-produced and imported), elaboration, novelty, professionalism and luxury. The diet of the poor and lowly was basic and repetitive, built around the staples of cereals and dry legumes, with simple and cheap additions (in the Greek, *opson*).[1]

In strongly hierarchical and status-conscious societies, rich men use food as one of a number of ways of signalling their wealth and winning or maintaining prestige in the sight of the world. Food in pre-industrial society was the more effective as a marker of economic and social distinction for the fact that it consumed the greater proportion (perhaps 66–75%) of family income.[2]

---

[1] See Davidson (1995).   [2] Jongman and Decker (1989), 115.

113

Wealth and status are not hard and fast categories. There is no clear cut-off point between wealth and poverty, or high and low status, and what ranks as great riches and lofty prestige in one society may appear rather more modest in another. Again, wealth and status are not the same thing. For example, a rich freedman in the context of Roman society, however enormous his wealth, was of low status by comparison with aristocrats of senatorial and equestrian rank or local councillors and magistrates. Still, his wealth gave him an elevated position and importance in comparison with the majority of the population. This was not just because he was potentially the founder of a family which, in a highly mobile society, might rise fast in the social order on the basis of inherited wealth. Trimalchio in Petronius' classic portrait (or rather, caricature) illustrates both the possibilities and the limitations of crude wealth. Trimalchio can act the grand patron of people of his own social background and below, but has no access to upper-class society. His best efforts in aping his social superiors fall short in another way, in that the fare he produces for his guests is not in fact of the highest quality and cost.[3] Culture and good taste cannot be acquired overnight.

I explore below the presentation of social and economic differentiation in the sources in the context of food and foodways, and ask whether the relativity of social class and status is reflected in the foods that were consumed and the manner of their consumption. Were there clearly identifiable foods for the rich and foods for the poor?[4]

THE EVIDENCE

The writers of literature were, like their audience, upper-class. Hence we are told a great deal about the diet of the rich and very little about the diet of the poor. Not surprisingly, in the world of the rich food supplies were ample and overindulgence normal. There are exceptions. Hesiod evokes in *Works and Days* the hard life of the countryman and his vulnerability to shortage and hunger. In a Latin poem called *Moretum* of authorship unknown from the early first century AD, a farmer is shown making ready his lunch, going to market, and starting to plough his field. This is not a slice-of-life portrait of a standard Italian peasant. Our poet had not done a day's work in his life, and he had his own literary and moralistic purposes in view in creating this vignette.[5] Despite this, he does manage to convey something of the flavour of rural life and, more

---

[3] Schmeling (1970).   [4] Corbier (1996).   [5] Kenney (1984); Gowers (1993), 46–7.

particularly, of the attitudes of a morally sensitive member of the elite on such matters as poverty, frugality and rural simplicity.

Galen, the doctor and philosopher from Pergamum in the second century AD, like his near-contemporary Soranus of Ephesus, drew his clientele from upper-class circles in Rome and Asia Minor. This no doubt helps to explain why he wrote a treatise *On Slimming Diets* but not one on malnutrition. His major study of food, *On the Properties of Foodstuffs*, was aimed at men of means. It was a work of great erudition, surveying the medical properties of the whole range of foodstuffs available in the Roman empire, and arguing that good health could only be attained through correct dietary practice. Unusually, Galen shows a serious interest in the diets of ordinary people in the Roman empire, and documents them in detail.[6] At the other extreme, the Roman cookery book of Apicius, of date disputed, could only have been composed for the rich and tells us nothing of the diet of the poor.

Athenaeus' vast culinary treatise does give glimpses of frugal or poor diets – which have to be treated with caution by the historian, as everything in this scissors-and-paste author – but is essentially interested in the extravagant eating of the rich. Drawing largely on Greek sources, he shows that gastronomy was not a Roman invention, even if it was a Roman speciality. One of his favourite sources, Archestratus, a Sicilian Greek of the fourth century BC, wrote *The Life of Luxury*, a kind of cookbook in verse. Archestratus is revealed in his fragments as cosmopolitan in his interests, professional in his attitudes, discriminating in his tastes and full of the pleasures of food. He is a representative consumer of the Greek *haute cuisine*, to which the ordinary Greek had no access.

Archaeology is a useful supplement to literature. Plant remains, animal bones and human faeces can tell us something about diets of people and places about which the literary sources are silent. Pompeii supplies a rich store of data of this kind, largely unspecific in terms of class. Similar finds, complemented by written materials (papyri in Egypt, wooden tablets in Vindolanda near Hadrian's Wall), enable us to reconstruct the diet of Roman soldiers in various frontier zones of the Roman empire. This evidence relates to a specific social group, the army, which formed a sub-elite class, distinct from both the elite and the mass of the people. Then, human skeletal data are informative as to nutritional status and health – again, this evidence is often undifferentiated in terms of social class, although it sometimes reveals the existence of social hierarchies.

[6] Nutton (1995).

It remains the case that the weight of evidence for food comes from literature and concerns the rich, and it is their view of the poor that we have, in so far as the poor are mentioned at all.[7]

HUMBLE DIETS IN ATHENAEUS

There is a sprinkling of diets of the poor among the comic fragments preserved by Athenaeus.[8] Those which mention fish are particularly interesting to us, for fish appears to have divided rich and poor in Athens. In one fragment, a stingy cook is accused of giving the general public miserable fare at the festival of Aphrodite Pandemos, the goddess with responsibility for lower sexual life and prostitution[9] – pease-porridge, or porridge made of pulses (*lekithos*), pressed olive skins (*stemphula*) and sprats (*membrades* or *bembrades*). The last item stands for sundry tiny fish, small fry, often linked in Athenaeus with consumers of humble station. Chrysippus, no comic poet but a Stoic philosopher, wrote: 'In Athens they despise anchovy (*aphuē*) on account of their abundance, and declare that they are a food for beggars; but in other cities people like anchovy extravagantly, though it is much inferior to the Athenian' (Athen. 285d). Chrysippus flourished in the mid-third century, therefore after the collapse of democracy. Were the attitudes he depicts exclusively post-democratic?

Apparently not. Around a century earlier, a character in a comedy of Antiphanes is made to refer contemptuously to sprats as Hecate's food, 'because of their small size', and elsewhere to the same fish as Helen's food. They are meagre fare (as we saw) in Antiphanes' mid-fourth century contemporary, Alexis, and mere bait along with a small shrimp in Numenius' *Art of Angling*, a technical work. In other comic fragments they (plural) are priced at one obol, and said to be the last thing anyone would want to buy. If none of them were for sale, then the market really was completely bare.[10]

In another group of texts salt fish is regarded as *infra dig*. There is an early comic fragment along these lines: 'My God, would you even eat salt fish?' This comes from the (significantly titled) play *Beggars* by one Chionides, who with Magnes is the earliest comedian known to us,

---

[7] Diets of ordinary people are also represented in various literary genres, especially Roman satire and epigram. See Bramble (1974), esp. 45–56; Morford (1977); Classen (1978); Hudson (1989); Gowers (1993).   [8] See Athen. 54e (cited above); 60b–d.
[9] See Burkert (1985), 155, referring e.g. to Plato, *Symp.* 180d; Xen, *Symp.* 8.9.
[10] Athen. 313b; 358d; 287. For Alexis, see Arnott (1996). Salt-fish were a talking-point in Alexis' period too. See Athen. 119f–20a.

dating from the first decades of the fifth century, before the introduction of radical democracy in 462/1. Next, chronologically, comes Pherecrates, an Old Comedian of the age of Pericles and after. His play *Deserters* provides the following snippet: 'Meanwhile our wives are waiting for us, boiling for each some pease-porridge or lentils and broiling a tiny orphan salt-fish.' Here salt-fish plays a similar role to sprats in the Alexis fragment.[11] One could in principle buy salt-fish as small fry, or as a piece of a larger fish. The price paid depended on the variety, place of origin (the Pontus produced the best) and size of the piece.[12]

If ordinary Athenians could sometimes afford fresh small fry and salt-fish, a tiddler or a piece of a larger fish if the price was right, the larger and more desirable fish, fresh or preserved – sea bream, tuna, grey-fish, eel, conger eel, and so on – were monopolised by the rich. These were, it seems, the great delicacies of the Athenian table. James Davidson argues that an acrimonious political rhetoric grew up around fish in Athens. Political opponents were charged with being hooked on costly fish, wasting their patrimony on fish.[13]

One can of course argue about the reality (if any) behind the fish fragments, starting with the issue of prices. The prices are incidental to the purposes of the dramatists. They set no great store by them, and neither should we.[14] Rather more seriously, the texts suggest that inequality persisted in democratic Athens, and that fish was a conspicuous social divider. There were fish, and fish, small fry for the poor, conger eels for the rich. The fact that it is fish that is employed to expose the reality of inequality is not a problem. The dramatists, had they been social historians or moral philosophers, might have tackled more central aspects of inequality in Athens. They chose fish because they were comedians, perhaps too because Athenians liked their fish. At a deeper level, the comedians are interested in depicting attitudes – not forgetting that comedy was first and foremost aimed at raising a laugh. It seems that the persistence of social and economic inequality was a highly sensitive issue in democratic Athens. The conspicuously consuming rich were thought to be showing disloyalty to the democracy. It does not follow that the comic poets were single-minded champions of the poor, or engaged in promulgating any political programme whatsoever.

There is more to the rich/poor divide than the individual food items: for example, the manner of preparation. Alexis has a cook who gives the

---

[11] Athen. 119d–e; 287b.   [12] Athen. 117d–e.   [13] Davidson (1993); (1997).
[14] Schaps (1985–88) argues that 'one may make some use' of the prices in Athenaeus.

following salt-fish recipe, which includes silphium, an exotic spice from
Cyrenaica: 'I must wash it well. Then I will sprinkle seasoning in a casse-
role, place the slice in it, pour over it some white wine, stir it in oil and
stew it until it is as soft as marrow, covering it generously with a garnish
of silphium' (Athen. 117d). In the case of cereals and other staples too,
preparation could raise the social status of the dish.

STAPLE FOODS

By staples I mean, loosely, items in the diet that were regarded as basic
and essential, that more or less everyone would want and expect to have.
They include cereals and other seed crops (dry legumes), and in the
Mediterranean context oil and wine. The quality and quantity of what
was consumed varied and in such a way as to reflect the rich/poor,
high/low divides.

(i) Drink

Cheap wine was for the poor, expensive wine for the rich. In Egypt,
where beer made of barley was the most popular drink and according
to Athenaeus 'was invented to help those who could not afford wine'
(Athen. 134b), the poorer *vin ordinaire* was none the less accessible to ordinary Egyptians (Strabo 17.1.14). The high-class home-grown vintages,
like the Mareotic wine favoured by Cleopatra according to Horace, and
imported wine in general, were another matter.[15] Conversely, the upper
classes in Egypt were not averse to beer. Unlike the fellahin, they could
pick and choose.

Gaul provides something of a parallel to Egypt, at least when it was
coming under Greek and then Roman influence. Wine both imported
and local increasingly made an impact on a mainly beer-drinking zone,
through the agency of the elite, who in the process acquired another
marker of their high status. As Posidonius wrote: 'The liquor drunk in
the houses of the rich is wine brought from Italy and the country around
Massalia, and is unmixed, though sometimes a little water is added. But
among the needier inhabitants a beer is drunk made from wheat, with
honey added; the masses drink it plain. It is called *corma*' (Athen. 152c).

Wine was a social divider even where an alternative stimulating drink
such as beer (or mead) was lacking. Prices at shops in Pompeii and

---

[15] Rathbone (1983).

Herculaneum tell the obvious story that customers paid in accordance with the quality and rarity of the wine. Still, the best wine was not likely to have been for sale at all at the ordinary street-shop in these towns. Conversely, the worst, which was not much better than vinegar, would have been on tap at the lower dives. The region (Campania) produced not only famous vintage wines like Falernian for the epicure, but also a lot of cheap plonk for the mass Roman market. Also at the top end of the market, various Greek wines were imported at some expense into the Naples region and Rome. Again, these wines would not have been for the poor to buy.[16]

(ii) Food

Even in the case of *the* staple food, cereals, different consumption patterns reflected the social and economic hierarchy. There are several oppositions or choices that are worth considering, between wheat and barley, naked and hulled wheat, bread and other cereal products, and different classes or grades of bread.

(a) *barley/wheat* The barley/wheat division is in part a split between Greece and Rome. Barley was more valued in Greece than it was in Rome and Italy. It is the more drought-resistant crop, and does well in semi-arid parts such as Attica and the islands to the south and south-east. Barley did lose ground to wheat, but only gradually. A number of texts from the Roman period point to both the low status of barley and its continued consumption in the countryside in the late second and early third centuries AD.[17] The idea that already in classical Greece, around half a millennium before this period, barley was essentially food for slaves and the very poor, and fodder for animals, has been shown to be erroneous.[18] At this time wheat is more accurately described as a prestige food than as a staple food, and barley was the staple food for most Greeks. This is reflected in religious ceremonial, which features barley rather than wheat.[19] The rarity of wheat in the south of Greece, and the

---

[16] Tchernia (1986).
[17] See e.g. Galen vi 507; Origen, *Hom. Gen.* 12.5: 'Barley is the food especially of beasts or of peasants . . . Isaac is the word of God. This word sows barley in the Law, but wheat in the Gospels.' Origen goes on to say that Jesus regarded barley as food for beginners (the 'inexperienced and natural'), and wheat as food for those who had made progress through instruction (the 'perfect and spiritual'). For further discussion of cereals, see above, pp. 17–21.
[18] Gallo (1983); Sallares (1991), 313–61, for shifts in cereals in antiquity.
[19] Dion. Hal. 2.25; Plut. *Mor.* 292b–c.

growing taste for bread, which was better when made from wheat, gave wheat extra appeal to those who could afford to buy it. The elite prefer-ence for wheat was bolstered by the (inaccurate) judgement of medical men that barley had lower nutritional value than wheat.

In Rome and Italy things were rather different. Barley began life in Italy as a crop of minor importance, and it declined to the status of fodder for animals. Galen writes that soldiers took barley-meal on cam-paign 'in the old days', whatever that means – and how did he know? In the historical period, barley bread was a punishment for a Roman legion in disgrace, if it escaped decimation.[20]

(b) *Naked wheat and other cereals*   In antiquity hulled grains gradually gave way to naked grains, principally wheats, that is, grains whose hulls were easily removed in processing. Such grains lend themselves better to breadmaking. This mini-revolution in agriculture is reflected in chang-ing linguistic usage. The meanings of *sitos* and *frumentum* were trans-formed from 'grain' to 'naked wheat'. Meanwhile, *puros* and *triticum*, the specific words for wheat, dropped out of use. For the Romans, the most ancient wheat was *far*, emmer wheat (*Triticum dicoccum*). This was a husked grain best turned into pottage or porridge (*puls*). The continuing role of *far* in sacrifice and cult and its contribution to the Latin language are evidence of its importance in early Rome. Pliny cites Verrius, a younger contemporary of his, as saying that *far* was the only wheat used by the Roman people over a period of 300 years (*Nat. Hist.* 18.62). Eventually, around the first half of the second century BC, porridge lost ground to bread (*puls* to *panis*). The rich presided over this transition, which would also have involved the introduction of bakers into private households.[21]

(c) *Naked wheats*   Among the naked wheats there is soft or bread wheat (*siligo*, *Triticum aestivum*), and hard wheat (*Triticum durum*), the ancestor of today's pasta wheat, probably then eaten mainly in the form of flat unleavened cakes cooked on a griddle. Soft wheat made the best bread, but preferred a wetter climate than the Mediterranean could offer, and was mainly grown in the transitional climates of South Russia, the Northern Balkans, North Italy, Gaul and Britain. Being not readily avail-able, it had to be imported or specially purchased, and so was sought after by the rich from the classical period in Greek history on. I suspect

[20] Polyb. 6.38.3; Frontinus, *Strat.* 4.1.25, 37.   [21] Pucci (1989); Ampolo (1995); Braun (1995).

that ordinary Athenians had no access to this higher-status wheat except in so far as it was distributed by the state authorities.

(d) *Bread and other cereal products* Athenaeus cites Greek writers of the late fifth to the third centuries BC who claim to recall a time in the past when the barley cake, *maza*, was in active competitition with wheat bread (Athen. 268b). And in Archestratus' *Life of Luxury*, the white barley of Lesbian Eresos, Thebes and Thasos is praised before Thessalian buns, also made from barley, and wheat bread from Tegea, Athens and Erythrae. All this is soundly squashed by Arrian, one of Athenaeus' diners, who cites an unidentified comic verse which runs: 'We have no interest in barley meal, since the city is full of loaves of wheat bread' (Athen. 111–113a). In the Roman context, as already indicated, the popularity of *far*, a product of the husked wheat emmer, declined as bread from naked wheats became available. The fact that bread and wine were given a central place in Christian ritual practice and symbolism presumably reflects consumer preference for bread, and the predominantly urban environment of early Christianity. In the countryside bread was often not eaten at all. If wheat suitable for bread-making was grown, it was marketed in the city, while the peasants were left with 'inferior cereals', for which incidentally their land was quite likely to have been better suited, to be consumed in one form or another. To 'inferior cereals' we may add the main dry legumes.[22] In both Greek and Roman contexts, the rich did not exclude themselves from lentils, beans and chickpeas. Everyone ate them in some shape or form. Beans even feature in the recipes of Apicius. But whereas ordinary people had recourse to legumes as virtual staples, the rich had no need to. That is the difference.

(e) *Bread – and bread* Athenaeus' long list of breads reflects a sophisticated urban environment. The number of varieties – no fewer than 72 are named – is in itself a sign of luxury. Add the culinary elaboration (in, especially, the shaping of the bread), the regional specialities, the employment of exotic foreign cooks (Cappadocian were best), the use of bread in banquets (e.g. brazier bread), the technical literature on bread and its preparation, and it becomes clear that bread could be a high-status food. The other side to this is that bread reflects social divisions: it could be consumed conspicuously or in the most humble way and form. As we saw earlier, the comedians spoke of the poor man's bread as black,

---

[22] See Garnsey (1998), ch. 12, on the cereal-and-legume hierarchy employed by Theophrastus, our main source for seed-crops in Greece.

barley bread with chaff mixed in the kneading, eaten twice a day
(Athen. 60b–c; cf. 246). The expenditure of extra labour-time and
money on milling and sieving will turn out a product judged to be superior, a whiter bread. In late classical Greece, barley products too, meal
and flat-cakes, won praise if they were white (Athen. 111–12). Food
preparation was already a laborious process, and if anything more
special than gruel or porridge was required, the list of tasks was much
lengthened. The result of all the effort was no 'Wonderloaf'. The light-
est bread known to Galen still sank in water.

PRESTIGE FOODS

Meat stands head, shoulders, and rump above other foods – in the orthodox
Western hierarchy, at least. It is the pivot around which we plan meals, the focus
of festivities. A steak to celebrate; turkey at Christmas; bacon for breakfast; a
burger when we're peckish; a joint on Sundays; or maybe mince, since times are
hard. The roast gets the family's oohs and aahs, seldom the spuds . . . The reason
we eat so much meat is that we love the feeling of supreme power we get from
devouring portions of once living, breathing creatures. Our apparent obsession
derives from a desire to dominate the beasts whose carcases we consume. We
adore meat not in spite of the implications for the creatures whose breeding,
growth, and slaughter we ordain, but rather because of that . . . Understanding
our valuation of meat primarily as an increasingly unfashionable statement of
(mainly masculine) power in the world explains much that is otherwise opaque:
why we date human evolution to the advent of hunting (or to our Fall from a
vegetarian Eden); why Real Men don't eat quiche; why most foodscares involve
animal produce; why the rich enjoy slaying big game; why Monty Python's rat
recipes never caught on; and why red meat is in decline amid rising affluence.[23]

The fragments of the writings of Archestratus the fourth-century
Sicilian gastronome are full of 'foreign' products, reflecting his travels
throughout the Greek world. He was disparaging about those who 'like
to praise products from their own locality' (Athen. 29b). Prestige foods,
that is, those foods likely to be relatively scarce and expensive, and therefore reserved for men of means and rank or for important occasions, are
to be sought in the first place among imported foods. Some imports were
rare, exotic, and invariably expensive. Spices, especially pepper, are
sprinkled liberally through the recipes of Apicius. Exchanged for pre-
cious metals, they flowed into (especially) Rome from China, India,
Arabia and Africa. Rome and other large cities also received oil, wine,

---

[23] Nick Fiddes, *Weekend Guardian*, 14–15 Sept., 1991, p. 16; cf. Fiddes (1991); Corbier (1989); (1996).
For further discussion of meat, see above, pp. 16–17.

fish-sauce and other more familiar items of consumption, and in bulk. Unlike spices, they were relatively cheap and intended for mass consumption. Archestratus was interested only in the best varieties of familiar products of this sort, and the premium placed on these would have put them out of the reach of ordinary people.

How 'familiar' a product was meat? Is it to be classed together with oil and wine as something consumed in quantity but in a wide variety of forms over a wide range of values? Or was it scarce and invariably expensive? There is a middle road. Meat was highly valued and relatively scarce, but also accessible to some degree and in some forms for popular as well as elite consumption. There were, however, aspects of its consumption which were problematic in the eyes of the elite.

Meat, then as now, cannot be produced in quantity in the heart of the Mediterranean region. The growing season for plant life is short. Grass and fodder are in meagre supply. So there could be no mass production of meat. When it is added that trade was backward and the technology underdeveloped for preserving perishable foodstuffs, it is clear that there could be no mass consumption of meat either. Meat and other foods of animal origin must have been of minor importance in the diets of the mass of the Mediterranean population. In particular, there was little red meat available. Carnivorous central and northern Europeans could be 'macho males' on a regular basis, but not the people of the Mediterranean region. Was it partly out of envy that their diet was stigmatised by Greeks and Romans as brutish and uncivilised?

High-grade red meat was available to some degree and in some contexts. Not among classical and Hellenistic Greeks perhaps, as distinct from Thracians and Macedonians, whose meat consumption at banquets roused the jealous interest of their southern neighbours. Rich Athenians appear to have eaten expensive fish rather than (expensive) meat. In the context of Rome, Italy and the Roman Empire, meat-eating must have been standard among the rich, who as large landowners could afford to turn arable, of relatively short supply, into meadowland for livestock raising, and could pay for meat to be brought from elsewhere, preferably on the hoof.

Secondly, meat was the food of sacrifice *par excellence*, and was offered to participants in religious ceremonies. By the same token, it was *only* available on such occasions, and did not make a significant contribution to the regular diet.[24] In the religious context, meat was apparently more

---

[24] Jameson (1988); Loraux (1981); Durand (1986).

widely available among ordinary Greeks than among ordinary Romans. At Rome the ceremonial eating of sacrificial meat was reserved for the upper classes, and any residue was sold in the market.[25] This looks to have been a deliberate strategy to prevent meat of good quality reaching the common man. It is a clear sign that meat, especially red meat, was a prestige food, and that meat-consumption was a sensitive matter. Who ate it, and the way it was obtained, mattered to the elite, especially to aristocratic Romans.[26]

There were at least five problematic areas. First, barbarians ate meat in quantity, and so did they, the Graeco-Roman elite. Secondly, there was moralistic rhetoric against overindulgence, excess, ostentation and waste, and at the centre of it was meat-consumption by the rich. Thirdly, there was the issue of how widely sacrificial meat should be distributed, given that it was usually limited in quantity and could not possibly be offered to all those who took part in religious ceremonies. Fourthly, ordinary people in Rome sometimes received meat from the wealthy and ambitious as individual clients, or *en masse* in public displays of philanthropy or euergetism. The state authorities were, or became, increasingly uneasy about private munificence. Fifthly, low-grade meat as an ingredient in cooked food could be bought cheap on the streets or in cookhouses.

On the first two points, there was a recognisable middle ground which leading Romans of common sense and good judgement could occupy. The Romans were on the whole practical people and did not let ideology or morality force them into a corner. Meat-eating was not wrong in itself. There was no taboo against it. Vegetarianism was an ascetic choice, for the very few. What *was* unacceptable was:

(i)   Eating meat raw, as the Huns did, according to Ammianus Marcellinus. It is through cooking that the transition from nature to culture is achieved.

(ii) Eating meat without any display of table manners, as animals did – and the Celts, according to Posidonius (in Strabo).

(iii) Eating meat by itself, or as a staple, as the stereotypical pastoral nomad did. The third-century emperor Maximinus, uncivilised in the eyes of aristocratic sources, was said to have eaten only meat, never vegetables (*SHA, The Two Maximini* 4.1–2).

(iv) Eating meat in huge quantities. The same Maximinus was alleged to eat 40 or even 60 lb. of meat per day. This was the behaviour of a wild beast.

---

[25] Scheid (1988); (1990).   [26] For the 'ambiguity' of meat, see Corbier (1989).

As for the rhetoric of frugality and excess: from time to time moralists gained the upper hand and sponsored sumptuary laws. We know only a little about such laws, which in Rome begin in the first half of the second century BC.[27] The laws were designed at one level (for they also had political implications) to prevent extravagance and the importation and consumption of new, exotic foods. The *lex Fannia* of 161 BC ruled out the eating of all birds apart from chickens, which also had to be non-fattened (Pliny, *Nat. Hist.* 10.140). Such laws were unenforceable and the boundaries were constantly shifting. Who could say where moderation ended and excess began?

The next three areas of sensitivity concern *popular* meat consumption. In all cases the Roman state took an active interest. As we saw, the state reserved sacrificial meat for its leaders and key participants in religious ritual. This may not always have been the practice, but attitudes changed as the political and demographic climate of Rome was transformed. Similarly, the sporadic distribution of meat to sub-elite Romans by the rich acting in a private capacity was bound to come under scrutiny, as Roman politics became ever more competitive and faction-ridden, and the 'generosity' of the ambitious developed new forms. They no longer confined themselves to patronal distributions at their houses or on public occasions such as family funerals, both traditional practices, but threw banquets for all the members of their tribes or to all comers. Even the distribution of cut-price, later free, grain under the aegis of the state was regarded by conservative Romans as a form of bribery subversive of the rule of the collective oligarchy, and its continued existence was seen by Augustus as an invitation to demagogues and a threat to his regime. His solution was to take over and reorganise the grain distribution, and monopolise the role of public benefactor. Still, it was not until the 270s that an emperor, Aurelian, took the step of handing out free pork for those Roman citizens already receiving free grain, wine and oil. In effect, the urban plebs, or, more accurately, a substantial minority of the inhabitants of Rome, received meat as the emperor's own special constituency, a privileged class.

The army, another prop of the imperial regime, provides something of a parallel.[28] The basic diet of Roman soldiers was bread made from wheat, bacon, cheese, vegetables, sour wine, salt and olive oil. A modest amount of meat therefore was common. Soldiers in Britain, the

[27] For the laws, see above, p. 172.
[28] Davies (1971); Knights et al. (1983); King (1984); Groenman-van Waateringe (1989); Bowman et al. (1990); Bowman and Thomas (1994).

Rhineland and the Danubian provinces did better than those stationed elsewhere. In Britain they ate meat from ox, sheep, goat and pig, also deer and wild boar. Such a variety of meats was available locally at no great cost – and the men in question came largely from Britain and Gaul, that is from the locality or not far away, and the diet was not foreign to them. Soldiers in any case were a privileged group.

The normal way in which ordinary Romans got meat was through buying cheaply low-grade cooked food from street vendors or in cook-houses and inns: items like blood pudding, forcemeat, sausages. It appears that the emperors did not like this fast-food industry. They put the inns under surveillance and sometimes persecuted them. They pro-duced measures regulating the sale of cooked meat, pastries and even, on one occasion, hot water in a period of public mourning. What were they worried about? The puritanical streak, which surfaced from time to time in the Republican period, died hard. Cookhouses were associated with gambling, some kinds of which were prohibited, and sexual licence, which emperors also legislated against. Class bias might also have been a factor. We note too that inns were a haunt of the occasional renegade aristocrat. It is not necessary to believe that emperors were concerned about the health risk provided by contaminated meat.[29]

I conclude with a glance at one *un*problematic area of sub-elite meat consumption, to be added to the army and a select group of the *plebs urbana* in Rome (to be joined, from AD 330, by a similar privileged group in the late imperial capital of Constantinople). In Mediterranean rural contexts, peasants who had any livestock at all would have eaten some meat, as a corollary of the normal business of raising animals. Pigs were the only animal raised solely for meat (apart from for sacrifice), and were also the animal most easily raised. Varro wrote: 'Who of our people cul-tivate a farm without keeping swine?' (2.4.3). He was speaking of Italians, though of what social level is not specified. If he had in mind, among others, peasant proprietors, then there was no special problem for the elite. This meat was home-grown, involved no outlay of cash, and amounted to the odd flitch of bacon. It was part of the balance of a recognisably Mediterranean diet, and did not upset that balance.

So much for the usages and the ambiguities of meat. The basic ambiguity is that meat was a prestige food but that others besides the elite had access to it *in some shape or form*. What counted, as with other foods that had a more central place in diets, was the amount eaten, its

[29] Corbier (1989); Toner (1995). For cooked-meat shops in Alexandria, see Athen. 94a.

kind and quality, the way it was prepared – and consumed. One could eat it 'like a lion' in Celtic style, or in a civilised way like a sophisticated urbanite.

CONCLUSION

The cuisines of the Greeks and Romans were markedly differentiated and hierarchical. Jack Goody has argued that a strongly hierarchical cuisine reflects a pronounced social hierarchy, characterised by sharply contrasting styles of life and based on a relatively advanced agricultural system, involving, among other things, the use of plough rather than hoe and the exploitation of a class of slaves.[30] If the connections and associations that he posits are accepted, then we are given a clear reminder of the fact that a century and a half of radical democracy did not eradicate class divisions in Athens. Romans were always under an oligarchic or monarchic form of government, and never shared the social and political aspirations of the radical democrats of Greece.

Few foods were completely monopolised by the rich. They, however, had access to every kind of food, whether standard or prestige, in greater quantity, with greater frequency, at higher cost, and in better quality. Moreover, in their households the food was prepared and presented with greater labour, elaboration and culinary expertise. Innovation was also in the hands of the rich, and those of their cooks. As in other periods of history, the elite were the first to introduce new foods, and monopolised them while they were new, rare and showy. This applies equally to the introduction from outside of new strains of wheat or of exotic fruits, or to Nero's own invention, snow-cooled water.[31] Their display of luxury and indulgence was a mark of status and of wealth. Those below them in the social scale envied them their patterns of consumption and would have liked to do the same.

[30] Goody (1982).   [31] Pliny, *Nat. Hist.* 31.40; taken up by Trimalchio in the *Satyricon*.

CHAPTER 9

You are with whom you eat

PRELIMINARIES

Ceremonial eating and drinking are a conspicuous feature of ancient society. They brought together families and their guests, patrons and their dependants, politicians and their friends, aristocratic youth, members of occupational groups, social clubs, religious brotherhoods, the soldiery, the citizenry, the population of a town. Large or small, these displays of commensality or collective consumption carried significance well beyond the nutritional function of the meal that was consumed. In the domestic setting, they might demonstrate, as in the act of hospitality shown by Baucis and Philemon to two strangers (who happened to be gods) the moral integrity of the simple peasant household; or they might celebrate *rites de passage*, a funeral, or the acceptance of a neonate into the family, in classical Athens, the Amphidromia:

Ephippus says in *Geryones*: 'If that is so, then how is it that there is no wreath before the doors, no savour of cooking strikes the tip end of the projecting nose, though the feast of the Amphidromia is on? For then it is the custom to toast slices of cheese from the Chersonese, to boil a cabbage glistening in oil, to broil some fat lamb chops, to pluck the feathers from ringdoves, thrushes and finches withal, at the same time to devour cuttle-fish and squids, to pound with care many wriggling polyps, and drink many a cup not too diluted.' (Athen. 370c–d)[1]

Outside the home, commensality demonstrated and confirmed the membership and solidarity of the group, paraded the status of the group *vis-à-vis* outsiders, and set out the hierarchies that existed both in the society at large and within the group itself. The settings were diverse – from a grandiloquent display of opulence by an emperor posing as a god to a showy feast staged by a freedman *arriviste* (as caricatured in the

---

[1] Ovid, *Met.* 8. 646ff. (Baucis and Philemon). For the Amphidromia, see Hamilton (1984); Garland (1990), 93–6. The subject of this chapter is well covered in recent literature, especially in the work of Oswyn Murray and Pauline Schmitt, to both of whom I readily acknowledge my debt.

9. Symposium scenes. Tomba del Tuffatore, Paestum. Greek, late sixth century BC.

Satyricon of Petronius) to the common meal of a religious group (Jesus and his disciples, Basil of Caesarea and his monks) or a Celtic version of potlatch in the account of Posidonius.[2]

SYMPOSIUM AND *DEIPNON*

The symposium is, properly, the post-eating stage of a banquet during which drinking for pleasure took place, accompanied by entertainment, in the form of recitation, music, dancing, conversation, sex (Fig. 9). In its heyday in early Greece, the symposium had social and political as well as cultural significance, so that it can be called by its historian, Oswyn Murray, 'the organizing principle of Greek life'. The symposium of the archaic period was a private club, in that its membership was restricted and met in private premises, in the household. It belonged to the public, or better, political, sphere, in the sense that the people who came

---

[2] For the banquet of the emperor Domitian, see Suet. *Dom.* 8.5: 'In the course of one of his shows in celebration of the feast of the Seven Hills, he gave a plentiful banquet, distributed large baskets of victuals to the senators and equestrians and smaller ones to the commons; and he himself was the first to begin to eat.' For Celtic 'potlatch', see Athen. 152d–e, with Feuvrier-Prévotat (1978). In potlatch, as practised among the Indian tribes of the north-west coast of America, a tribal leader gave a great feast or succession of feasts, lasting one full phase of the moon, at which guests, who included members of other tribes, were stuffed with food and drink and showered with gifts. This was not the end of the story, because chieftains of rival tribes were shamed into replying in kind. Potlatch was competitive feasting which served to exchange and redistribute resources within tribal society. See Clutesi (1969); briefly, Fieldhouse (1986), 86–9.

together in this way were precisely the citizens of the early *polis* and the men who formed its political and, in the Homeric period at least, its military leadership.[3]

As the aristocracy lost its grip on the *polis*, the symposium also declined in significance. In Athens the democratic reformer Cleisthenes relegated to the political wilderness the symposium and the aristocratic friendship group (*hetaireia*) that was rooted in the symposium. Under the Athenian democracy these 'clubs' had mainly nuisance value. In 415 a particularly lively symposium spilled over into the street late at night. In the aftermath it was discovered that religious statues, the Hermai, had been systematically mutilated.[4] When naval disasters befell the democracy, in 413 in Sicily, and in 405 at Aegospotami, oligarchs based on the clubs crawled out of the woodwork and staged *coups d'état* (in 411 and 404). Democracy in due course came back and things returned to normal, which meant that the clubs were again marginalised and indeed made illegal. It is in this period of the restored democracy that the banquet was born as a literary genre, in the *Symposium* of Plato. In Plato's hands the symposium became a form of sociability in which a company of friends discuss a theme, in this case the nature of love, in the form of a dialogue.[5] Xenophon's *Symposium*, Plutarch's *Dinner-Table Conversations*, Athenaeus' *Deipnosophists* and Methodius' *Banquet of the Ten Virgins* are among the ancient works that follow his model, and the genre has a long history in later literature.

In Sparta, though it was an oligarchy, there was no room at all for the symposium. Instead of a drinking club of the *jeunesse dorée*, optional and private, where conversation was free, open and often antipathetic to the prevailing values of the state, the Spartans established dining groups or messes (*syssitia*) which were compulsory, an arm of the state and designed to inculcate and perpetuate its ideology. Furthermore, whereas the traditional symposium had promoted equality among members of a single age and social group, at Sparta the equality of the Equals (Homoioi) was tempered by hierarchy, both in terms of age and social/economic status. Elders dominated a group in which no single age-group was exclusively represented, and the wealthier members used the occasion to show their superiority in acts of food redistribution – for this is the function of the desserts (*epaikla*).[6]

In fourth-century Greece as a whole, the symposium was finished as

---

[3] Schmitt-Pantel (1990), 25–6.   [4] Murray (1990a).

[5] For Plato's attitude to the symposium as an institution, see Teçusan (1990).

[6] For the Spartan mess, see Fisher (1989); Figueira (1984).

a civic or political institution. The collapse of Greek freedom at the hands of the Macedonians was simply the last nail in its coffin. The symposium survived or even thrived in the Hellenistic age at the courts of the Ptolemies and Antigonids as a cultural institution. As such, its golden days may have been far in the past, in the archaic age again, when the aristocracy of leisure patronised painters and poets of class, but the new setting was conducive to the production and performance of poetry, especially epigram.[7]

The case for decline in the second and first centuries BC and the early Roman period is stronger. Or, if we are chary of the word 'decline', then we can speak of cultural change. The role of symposium no longer provides a stimulus and context for the creation of performance of poetry. Instead, learned conversation, already an ingredient in the late classical and Hellenistic symposium, takes over and dominates the occasion. Moreover, one might gain the impression from Athenaeus that the symposium has been swallowed up by the dinner (*deipnon* or *cena*).[8] It is a *deipnon* that Athenaeus himself stages. True, there is a superficial division in the work between a *deipnon* and, right at the end, a *symposion*. But the conversation extends over the whole, it closely follows the order of the banquet, and it takes its cues from the food that is served at each stage. And the work is named *Deipnosophistae, Professors of the Dinner-Table*. Athenaeus' work (I suggest) bears witness to changes in the tradition of sympotic literature, but not necessarily to the demise of the symposium as a social and cultural event in which well-off friends came together for wine, song, conversation and, no doubt, 'aphrodisia'.

THE CIVIC BANQUET

If there is a characteristic Greek or Roman party, one that stands out above the rest – as potlatch does among the Native Americans of the north-west coast – it is the civic banquet arranged by the political authorities. This typically follows a public sacrifice, and uses the sacrificial food as the ingredients for the meal. However, as the historian of the civic banquet, Pauline Schmitt, has stressed, it is not the association with religion in itself that marks off this kind of banquet from

---

[7] Cameron (1995), 71–103 (who argues persuasively against decline in the Hellenistic period); Murray (1996).
[8] Athenaeus is a source of dubious worth for the symposium. In his usage, *symposion* is a synonym for or variant of *deipnon*, and his preoccupation is with feasting and luxury.

others.[9] All commensality in antiquity has a religious element. It varies in prominence and intensity, but it is always there. At one end of the spectrum there are the Arval Brothers, a high-status brotherhood in the city of Rome, who are shown in the epigraphic record making sacrificial offering to Dea Diva and subsequently feasting themselves and their retainers, to the accompaniment of a most elaborate religious ritual.[10] At the other end is a feast such as that depicted in the *Deipnosophists*, where libations are poured to the gods – and that is all the 'active' religion in the work. In between these extremes lie a great variety of public ceremonial occasions revolving around a dinner, where the meal follows a sacrifice and consists of sacrificial food in the first instance. The 'sacrificial banquet' is the quintessential 'civic banquet'. As a public event integrated into the life of the city, and involving more members of the community than any other, it has a special significance. For present purposes my main concern is to explore the implications of the banquet for the relationship between the participants as consumers.

The sacrificial banquet is the last act, or one of the last acts, of the ritual of blood sacrifice (animal sacrifice being the classic form of sacrifice). The meat is divided out equally. This is crucial. As Nicole Loraux wrote: 'To eat equal shares is to produce and reproduce civic equality.'[11] Equality among whom? Among the citizens, who might represent only a fragment of the population (of adult males), as in the archaic Greek *polis*. Equality survives as the principle of distribution in later periods of Greek history, but its implications for the size of the feast differ, according to the character of the regime.

The feasts put on by the Athenian *polis* for its citizens under the radical democracy were immense in scale, as befitted a democracy that was also a rich empire. As Michael Jameson puts it: 'In Athens the democracy through the mechanism of the state provided the many with the style of life of the few.'[12] In 410/9, when Athens was losing the war against Sparta, 5,114 drachmas, perhaps a day's wages for the same number of men, was spent on 100 cows for the Great Panathenaic Festival (only a four-yearly event, to be sure), and the meat was shared out among the participating demesmen. The number of cattle sacrificed in the year 334/3 was between 1,400 and 1,700. The Old Oligarch, a cranky reactionary who wrote a tract against the democracy in perhaps the 430s, complained:

[9] Schmitt-Pantel (1990), 24.   [10] Scheid (1990).   [11] Loraux (1981), 620.
[12] Jameson (1988), 96.

The Athenian populace realises that it is impossible for each of the poor to offer sacrifices, to give lavish feasts, to set up shrines, and to manage a city which will be beautiful and great, and yet the populace has discovered how to have sacrifices, shrines, banquets and temples. The city sacrifices at public expense many victims, but it is the people who enjoy the feasts and to whom the victims are allotted. (Ps.-Xen. *Ath. Pol.* 2.9)

What did the experience do for the Athenian citizenry, apart from fill their stomachs, and make a change from the usual, boring menu? It helped to bind together the community of citizen-consumers.[13] Of course, even under the Athenian democracy, citizens were a privileged class, and the adult males who assembled for a feast were highly conscious of their separateness and superiority. That said, the democracy did transform the public sacrificial banquet simply by greatly swelling the number of citizens. Democratic Athens took a predemocratic institution, controlled by the aristocracy and favouring the few, and made of it a democratic institution benefiting the many.

Meanwhile, the democracy devised its own, characteristically democratic, system of eating, and put up its own building for it as well (*c.* 480–460), the Tholos in the agora. Here on every day of the year could be found the prytaneis, the standing committee of the council, eating their dinners. This was not a fixed and stable group of people. Far from it – the democracy made it its business to ensure that its membership rotated. The eating party consisted of the 50 councillors who belonged to whichever tribe happened to be 'prytanising', that is, forming the standing committee of the council. This was the tribe which had been chosen by lot from the ten tribes to control the business of the *polis* for a prytany, that is, for 36 or 37 days. They ate what they bought with their pay, which amounted to 1 obol a day, and was intended to cover their food expenses. It was their choice how they were to spend it.

It is not the case that the Athenian democracy paid no consideration at all to status in the public allocation and distribution of food.[14] The democracy preserved, more or less untouched, a practice which was carried over from the aristocratic period. This was the offering of free dining rights, *sitesis*, in the town-hall, or prytaneum, not in the Tholos. There were two kinds of *sitesis*: the first was one-off, for foreign guests or citizen honorands; the other was for life, awarded to a few, such as the

---

[13] For this message, see Xen. *Hell.* 2.4.20, set in 404/3, a period of intense civil strife in Athens: '... Fellow citizens ... we have shared with you the most solemn rites and sacrifices and the most splendid festivals ...'

[14] For eating in the Tholos and the prytaneum, see Schmitt-Pantel (1992).

priests of Eleusis, the male descendants of the tyrannicides, a soothsayer chosen by Apollo, and winners at major games. This sounds like a fairly innocent list, but its existence grated with the democrats, because it involved *ad hominem* privileges. Socrates annoyed the jury at his trial by suggesting that they should be rewarding him with dinners for life in the prytaneum instead of offering him hemlock (Plato, *Ap.* 36d–e). Still, despite their disapproval, the democrats kept the custom going without any change. A sign that democracy was a spent force from the end of the fourth century is the swelling of the *sitesis* list through the addition of foreign benefactors.

When we proceed out of the classical into the Hellenistic era we find that public banquets were popular and thrown for large numbers; they were preceded, as ever, by sacrifice; and they were financed by the elite, the euergetists or public benefactors, whether by 'private' munificence or formal liturgies. The number of feasts appear to be on the increase. The celebration of the standard religious festivals proceeds, as usual, but in addition, euergetists are going outside the religious calendar, creating feasts out of nothing. Quite often a feast is provided for the people by an incoming official. Moschion of Priene offered the whole population a collation, on the first day of his tenure of the office of *stephanephoros*. Why did Moschion and the other euergetists do it? For the same reason as they performed other benefactions: for their self-esteem, for their survival as a social group, to reaffirm their legitimacy. The crowds who joined in, by their very presence, sanctioned the domination of the elite over society and politics.[15]

Already in the Hellenistic era, the social hierarchy was beginning to be reflected in the form of restricted access to sacrificial meals. This tendency is confirmed and extended under the Romans, that is, the Romans of Rome. Division of the meat after the sacrifice continues, but participation is limited to those at the top of the social hierarchy. 'Dining rights' (the *ius epulandi publice*) is a privilege for priests, magistrates and senators in general, perhaps equestrians (lesser aristocrats). Other citizens benefited from sacrifices only in so far as they could purchase the portion of the sacrificial meat released on the market; or, if they were admitted to the banquet, they sat apart from their social and political superiors, and ate less.[16] Where large numbers of citizens *did* sit down to dinner in Rome, conservative senators did not approve. I have alluded

---

[15] For euergetism, see above, p. 33. For Moschion, see *Inscr. Priene* 108, lines 253–5.
[16] Scheid (1988).

already to their hostility to gratuitous acts of euergetism. A magistrate acting *ex officio* could just about get away with it. Games organised by the aedile (a junior magistrate), were regularly accompanied by banquets. When Murena, a friend of Cicero, in his canvass for the consulship in 63 BC threw a meal for the people, he was courting prosecution.[17]

So hierarchy ruled in the division of food after the sacrifice. Another example from Rome concerns the Arval Brothers (referred to above). Exclusive priesthoods and brotherhoods held their own sacrifices for public causes, and feasted on the sacrificial meat. This is another form of discrimination in favour of the elite, because only the highest aristocracy could be members of these organisations. Within the Arval Brothers, the president ate first after the god and the ordinary members followed. At a certain point on the second day of the three-day feast of Dea Diva, the slaves and freedmen of the brotherhood participated in the banquet, but were given white bread decorated by laurel rather than meat.

A similar principle operated in the municipalities. In sizeable numbers of Italian and provincial towns, public meals were laid on by benefactors, occasionally for the plebs, but more often for the city councillors, or decurions, or for the decurions and the College of (six) Augustales, a select group of wealthy freedmen responsible for the cult of the emperors; or for all three orders, in which case they were not fed equally. The decurions received a proper meal, the plebs a snack.[18]

In the plebeian dining and funeral clubs of Italian towns, too, differentials were observed. The dining customs of the college of Diana and Antinous at Lanuvium, a town in Latium not far from Rome, are known from a long inscription. The presiding officers (*magistri cenarum*) had to ensure that each man got a loaf of bread worth 2 asses, 4 sardines, and an amphora of wine (a substantial quantity, and later on we read that there were fines for unruly behaviour). An internal hierarchy existed, so that the Board of Five (*quinquennales*) received a double portion in all distributions (and were protected from insults by the threat of a fine of 20 sesterces), while the scribe and the messenger got one and a half times the ordinary share. A more complex vertical ordering is reflected in seating arrangements. Members were threatened with a fine

---

[17] Cic. *Pro Mur.* 72–7; 67; cf. *De Off.* 2.56–7; Sall. *Iug.* 4.3.

[18] There are numerous variations, but the principle is the same. Status differences are reflected in the quantity and quality of the food served, just as in money hand-outs (*sportulae*) which often accompany the feasts, and are in general attested more often than meals in the municipal inscriptions. See Duncan-Jones (1982); Mrozec (1987).

of four sesterces if they tried to change their seat. The quantity (at least) of the food they received does not seem to have been affected by their place at the table.

CONVIVIUM

Cicero, Seneca, Tacitus and Pliny the younger, among others, show that daily dining with friends was an established social and cultural institution at Rome, part of the normal routine of life. This was a formal meal at a set time, dividing the Roman day between 'business' and 'leisure' (*negotium/otium*). In a letter to Paetus, Cicero talks of the convivium as the ideal setting in which Romans can *live together* (*con-vivere*; Cic. *Ad Familiares* 9.24.3). It was the obvious place for interaction, conversation and relaxation, the place and the occasion where friendship was strengthened and cultural attainment displayed. This picture is confirmed by the importance of the dining-room (or dining-rooms), *triclinium*, in the aristocratic house.

Cicero represents the convivium as the same institution as the symposium – just a change of name was involved. The Roman name, he claims, is simply better. Murray says the Roman *convivium* was different in three ways: it was sexually mixed, it covered a wide social range and equality was not always the order of the day.[19] He identifies the inclusion of women as diners (not performers or waitresses) as the main element taken over from the Etruscans. There is unfortunately no account of Etruscan dining practice that even approaches objectivity. So Theopompus, the fourth-century BC historian from Chios, contributed a scurrilous passage about these 'barbarians of the West'. It was the liberty that they allegedly allowed their women that particularly grated with him (Athen. 517–8a). Livy was dealing in stereotypes when he contrasted an Etruscan banquet at which wives of princes made merry, with a male-only dinner of Roman princes where they discussed the virtues of their wives while the exemplary virtuous wife, Lucretia, sat at home and spun (Livy 1.57ff.). Cornelius Nepos, addressing Atticus in the preface of his *Lives of Famous Men*, suggests that the appearance of wives of Romans at banquets was not considered at all scandalous, whereas in the Greek world they came only if the diners were related to them (pref. 6–7). However, there is little supporting evidence for this assertion in other sources, Cicero included. The exclusion of women from banquets

---

[19] Murray (1983a), 51.

may be a case of a rule or custom inherited from earlier tradition (Greek, Roman, Etruscan) which, though not formally abandoned, was applied only in a patchy way in Roman households.

Similarly, the banquet as a gathering of friends treated as equals survived as an ideal, but often did not correspond to practice. In this respect, there were banquets – and banquets. I distinguish three kinds, on which there were many variations.

First, the client dinner. Here social inferiors are entertained. On the surface, social barriers are ostentatiously lowered and normal social conventions relaxed. But there is tension. Can the patron keep up the pretence of social equality? We can be sure that he did not always succeed in doing so, supposing he had made an attempt in the first place. Many did not, placing and feeding their guests according to status. The client in question would never rise in the social scale, or at least his prospects of doing so were very limited. Horace tells a story of a distinguished senator who was once impressed by a simple artisan. He invited him to dinner and eventually settled him on a peasant plot in the countryside. That was it. The more familiar lower-class client, familiar for example from the epigrams of Martial, is the importunate client, desperate to gain access to his patron's table.

Second, the protégé dinner. A prospective recruit into the governing class is brought as a dinner-guest, perhaps by a fellow townsman who has made good, in order to meet important people, as a way of aiding his chances of being co-opted into the aristocracy, and acclimatising him to its *mode de vie* (e.g. Pliny, *Ep.* 9.24.4). This was a regular practice in a socially mobile society such as Rome was. The Rome-based aristocracy, in order to survive, had to be, and constantly was, engaged in promoting new members. It did so by exploiting existing links of friendship (*amicitia*) between established aristocrats.

Third, the peer-group dinner. This dinner brought together social equals. It is the kind of dinner that Cicero was urging his friend Paetus, who had dropped out, to rejoin. This could be or seem to be purely social, but in the heady world of late Republican Rome was likely to be a highly political occasion. Here political plans were laid, alliances confirmed, allegiances sought.

The wheel has come full circle. The peer-group dinner, paradoxical though it may sound, bears comparison with the archaic Greek symposium in one important respect. Neither was a private event, both were political, in the sense that we are dealing in each case with the assembling of a slice of the aristocracy that was already dominant in the *polis*/state. For that matter, almost everything a prominent politician in Rome did – and certainly all the social relationships in which he engaged – had public or political significance, not excluding his entertainment to dinner of protégés and clients. It was by such means that the governing class of Rome perpetuated itself and maintained its hold on society.

Conclusion: choice and necessity

Why do people eat what they eat?[1] There are four main factors. The first is physiological. People eat to live and be healthy. This explains why they need food, but not why they choose to eat a particular food or combination of foods. On the whole people have chosen well, and the human race has survived. Errors have been made in ignorance: in antiquity a poison, lead, was ingested through the making of *sapa* (must), and colostrum in certain social circles was routinely withheld from babies. (These days, nutritionally undesirable choices are sometimes made knowingly, or out of avoidable ignorance.) In general, humans like other animals have selected food that is good for them, and this without any knowledge of nutritional science. Galen, following the Hippocratic tradition, thought that good health depended on the proper blending of the four qualities, hot, cold, dry, wet, corresponding to the four essential humours of the body, blood, black bile, yellow bile, phlegm. Thus precise knowledge of the qualities of the various foods was essential. These are primitive ideas, but the surprising thing is how often Galen was on the right lines. Just as the ancient farmer was not rendered helpless by his ignorance of plant biology, so the crude limitations of Galen's dietetics did not often lead him into absurdity, let alone into giving health-undermining advice.

The second factor is taste. Some foods simply appeal more than others. Humans can survive or flourish on a wide variety of foods. They have more choice than animals have. Some animals are mainly or entirely carnivores or herbivores. Others are not only limited in this way, but are also extremely selective. Koalas will eat only eucalyptus leaves from a few of the many varieties of eucalyptus tree, and the new leaves at that. The beetle *Caryedes brasiliensis* eats only the seeds of the liane (*Dioclea megacarpa*), and the moth *Seirarctica echo* only the leaves of the

---

[1] Yudkin (1978a) asked himself a similar question, and I have been influenced by his answer.

cycad (*Cycas circinnalis*). Man is successful as an animal because he can
eat more or less everything. The line will be drawn only at cannibalism,
which offends against standard sacrificial principles: cannibalism-taboo
has its roots in the central religious act. Galen's story of covert cannibalism at inns and his (non-) reaction to it suggest that this was a weak
barrier, that standards were relaxed at the verges of civilised society.
Galen was probably insouciant on this point because he felt he was
describing a world that was not his. It was the rustic poor who approached closest to omnivorousness, but under constraint rather than
through deliberate choice. Here we can set the peasants of ancient Asia
Minor alongside those of modern Provence, as portrayed by Galen and
Marcel Pagnol, respectively. Pagnol's rustic, François, smacks his lips at
the thought of lizard, badger, and especially hedgehog, preferring them
to snake, fox and squirrel, respectively, and has a ready answer for the
stunned city-dweller:

I could hardly believe that he followed such a peculiar diet, and asked: 'Have
you really eaten all those animals?' 'Certainly.' He turned towards Lili. 'City
people are shocked that we eat hedgehogs. But they happily gobble up sea-
urchins.' After this triumphant riposte, he seemed to think a moment, and sud-
denly added: 'And there are even apparently sons of bitches who eat frogs'.[2]

Galen's catalogue of edible and eaten land-animals (see above, p. 83), I
suspect, owes much to his observations of country people *à table*, topped
up by practices of the urban poor. In contrast, the urban elite employed
a high level of refinement in the choice of foods and their preparation.
Their *haute cuisine* provided another sphere in which they could express
their superiority as a group over 'others', whether barbarians, nomads,
mountain-dwellers, countrymen, or, for that matter, the urban poor.

   The third factor is availability. Choice may be limited for a number of
reasons. Members of simple or primitive societies have been, by and
large, dependent on food grown at home or near by. Their range of
choice is governed by the physical environment of the locality. Contact
with the outside world brings an increase in the range of foods that are
at hand. The growth of cities stimulated trade and other forms of
exchange. In antiquity there is the phenomenon of a huge metropolis,
Rome, at the hub of a command economy, able to draw to itself products from a wide range of climates and natural economies throughout
the Mediterranean basin and beyond. In an earlier era, classical Athens,

---

[2] M. Pagnol, *Le Temps des secrets: souvenirs d'enfance* (1988), 11–13. François's remark about frogs is a
   reminder that the French are expert at transforming marginal or famine foods into gourmet
   dishes through culinary genius. Snails are another example.

at the centre of a more modest empire, received products from far afield, partly because it had political and military power, and partly because its demographic size made it a profitable destination for merchants. But even the thousands of ordinary cities in the Graeco-Roman world had some capacity to draw products from outside.

In introducing cities, we have brought into play economic and political alongside environmental and ecological factors. In the economic model, the market pull of cities can overcome the limitations of their natural environment and increase the range of choice for the consumer. Political authority too is concentrated in the city, which can exploit its control of the legal and military apparatus to extract the surplus from the territory under its jurisdiction.

Access to the goods that flow into the city will not be equal. The haves can acquire what the havenots cannot. In addition, the haves, by misusing their coercive power and control of the movement and distribution of foodstuffs, may aggravate the position of the havenots, expose them to periodic food crises and, in combination with epidemic disease, increase their vulnerability to long-term malnutrition. The haves, typically, will rub salt into the wound by indulging in conspicuous consumption – typically but not invariably, and not always without restraint. We note first that opposition to extreme self-indulgence and extravagance was expressed, especially among the Romans, in politics and in literature – as attested, for example, by the various sumptuary laws, and by the idealised reconstruction of the life-style and system of values of the archaic community of Rome by comparison with the corrupt present. The effect of this critique cannot be accurately gauged and should certainly not be overestimated, but it can be believed that it acted as a restraining force in some quarters. A second qualification is that adduced by Pierre Bourdieu.[3] Economic power characteristically asserts itself in the destruction of riches, that is, in conspicuous consumption. However, those with greater buying power and greater potential choice of foods do not invariably squander their resources in luxurious living. Religious scruples, bourgeois principles, or taste may get in the way. The cultural component in food choice comes into the reckoning.

The fourth factor, then, is culture. Diet is profoundly influenced by the traditional practices and norms of the particular society – and not just diet, what we eat, but also how the food is obtained, who prepares it, where, when and with whom it is eaten. Some anthropologists, of whom

[3] Bourdieu (1979), 197–222.

an early representative was Audrey Richards in *Hunger and Work in a Savage Tribe* (1932), have argued that the cultural system is and always has been the main influence on food habits. The role of culture may be illustrated with reference to two Ethiopian tribes, as studied by the anthropologist William Shack. These are the Amhara and Tigrinya peoples of the northern highlands, and the Gurage of the midlands of south-west Ethiopia.[4]

The Amhara and Tigrinya inhabit a fertile land capable of producing cereals in abundance, and a variety of other foods. However, this is an Orthodox Christian people who have bound themselves to an elaborate regime of fasting: 165 fast days in the year for an ordinary Christian, 250 fast days for the truly devout. For the latter, the rich food resources of the region are enjoyed for less than one-third of the year. For the mass of the population, those economically disadvantaged, and especially for the more vulnerable groups, namely children and women, the consequence is severe nutritional hardship. The other tribe, the Gurage, are wedded to a plant, *Ensete ventricosum*, which happens to be very poor nutritionally, being low in protein and short of key vitamins. This plant, also called the 'false banana plant' (false because it bears no edible fruit), the main staple of their diet, is also 'the actual and symbolic core of Gurage social and cultural life', having a range of non-food uses. Moreover, the Gurage practise an ethic of frugality. They eat sparingly. Their hunger is rarely sated. While there is little on their plates, the pits in their gardens are filled with ensete pulp in the process of fermenting for later use in ceremonials and feasts.

In both these cases, social and cultural traditions are the primary factor governing food choice and consumption habits. These Ethiopian tribes do not make full use of the potentiality of their lands, and both of them adopt strategies that are injurious to their health. Harsh reality is against the dietary choices that they have made, but this counts for less with them than the weight of religious belief and inherited custom.

The general point, that cultural and social norms can govern dietary choice, might be made with reference to much more mundane examples from ancient and other societies. A few ascetic Christians apart, no one in antiquity fasted like the Ethiopians, and no ancient Mediterranean people, as far as I know, was unwise enough to fix on a staple as unnutritious as the false banana plant. There are some notable, if less extreme, instances from ancient societies of groups of consumers

[4] Shack (1978).

restricting their intake of food in quantity and in kind, in response to philosophical, religious and ethnic regulations: the Jewish nation, Pythagoreans, ascetics in a variety of traditions, Christians who abstained from sacrificial meat. They provide the most vivid illustrations of the function that food and eating can perform of defining the identity of a group with reference to excluded others. They are vivid but they are also few, and they create a partial and distorted picture of the way in which food divided people in antiquity. They turn the spotlight away from social, economic, political, legal and gender divisions, which are also flagged by divergent patterns of food consumption, and might be held to have a higher claim to be regarded as a defining feature of Graeco-Roman society than racial, religious or philosophical differences. In any case, for a fuller picture of diversity in ancient societies, it is necessary to admit the role of food not only in excluding others, but also in including one's own. Christians shunned the meat left over from pagan sacrifices (Pythagoreans happen to have done the same), but also made their central ritual the Eucharistic meal of bread and wine which represent the body and blood of their founder.

Bibliographical essay

ENTRÉE

There is no comprehensive bibliography of 'food and foodways' in antiquity, and in view of the size of the subject, that is not at all surprising. This essay is necessarily very selective, and is written primarily for those who are relatively new to the topic. My advice is to start with some of the recent, impressive, secondary literature. (All works mentioned below are cited fully in the bibliography.) A shortlist might include, in alphabetical order, Dalby, *Siren Feasts* (1996), Davidson, *Courtesans and Fishcakes* (1997), Gowers, *The Loaded Table* (1993), Grimm, *From Feasting to Fasting* (1996), Murray, *Sympotica* (1990), and Wilkins and others, *Food in Antiquity* (1995). It would be as well to consult at the same time some of the better-known anthropological and sociological writing on food, by such eminent practitioners as Lévi-Strauss, Barthes, Douglas and Goody. In addition, Farb and Armelagos, *Consuming Passions* (1980), and Fieldhouse, *Food and Nutrition* (1986) are to be recommended as fine works of synthesis, and Mennell, *All Manners of Food* (1985), as a model work of historical sociology. A useful survey of anthropological and sociological writing on food, without reference to antiquity, is Mennell and others, 'The sociology of food and eating' (1992). For the broader view and up-to-date discussion, a glance at *Food and Foodways*, an interdisciplinary periodical devoted to the subject of food and eating, can be rewarding.

GENERAL STUDIES AND COLLECTIONS

Brothwell and Brothwell, *Food in Antiquity* (1969) is still a useful introduction to the subject, as far as it goes. The authors' concern is with the historical development of ancient diets, in their diversity, from prehistoric times. They have a secondary interest in health, nutrition and disease. Two valuable books of essays on various aspects of food have recently appeared. Flandrin and Montanari, *Histoire de l'alimentation* (1996) is a large volume of commissioned papers (in French). Around 300 pages, or roughly one-third of the whole, is devoted to prehistory and classical antiquity. Wilkins and others, *Food in Antiquity* is a collection of conference papers on a wide variety of topics, many of them technical and specialised, but often of considerable historical interest. (For collections on the symposium and associated topics, see below.)

ANCIENT SOURCES

The ancient evidence for food and eating is copious. There is hardly a single ancient writer who does not touch on food, while archaeology, epigraphy, papyrology and numismatics all make a contribution – which I do not attempt even to summarise here (but see below, on skeletal remains). To return to literature, ancillary subjects such as agriculture and medicine are treated in a number of technical treatises. Thus, works on farming by Cato, Varro, Columella and Palladius span the period from the mid-second century BC to the late-fourth century AD; the botanical writings of Theophrastus from the late fourth century BC provide the closest parallel from extant Greek literature. One of the two most important single works of ancient literature on food is a medical treatise, Galen's *On the Properties of Foodstuffs*. Nutton, 'Galen and the traveller's fare' (1995), catches the flavour of the work (which remains untranslated). Other medical treatises contain relevant material. A few of the most accessible are the Hippocratic work *On Regimen* (Fr. tr. Budé), Celsus, *De Medicina* (tr. Loeb), Soranus, *Gynaecology* (tr. Temkin) and Anthimus, *On the Observance of Foods* (tr. Grant). Dalby, *Siren Feasts*, 168–79, is a useful introduction to Athenaeus, our other main source. Exeter University is a centre of research into Athenaeus, and we can expect much new work from that quarter, beginning with a volume of conference papers (in progress). Athenaeus preserves numerous fragments of the Sicilian gastronome Archestratus' *Life of Luxury* (fourth century, BC); these are collected, with translation and commentary, by Wilkins and Hill (1994). Gowers, *The Loaded Table* is an enlightening guide to imaginative literature on food (mainly Latin).

DIET

Dalby, *Siren Feasts*, is good and recent on Greek food and gastronomy. On Rome, André, *Alimentation* (1981) is a reference work for specific foods known to the Romans. White, 'Food requirements' (1976) is an extended essay of the same type, but it does touch on variations of diet according to social class. On particular diets, one can usefully consult, e.g., Darby and others (1977) on Egypt, Hamel (1990) on Palestine, Evans (1980) on peasant diets in Italy, and Davies (1971) on the Roman army, now supplemented by the important evidence from Britain, for which see Bowman and Thomas, *The Vindolanda Writing Tablets* (1994). On individual foods, Foxhall and Forbes, '*Sitometreia*' (1982) is a bold attempt to quantify cereal consumption, while Sallares, *The Ecology of the Ancient Greek World* (1991), contains a significant technical and historical discussion of changes in varieties of cereal. Amouretti (1986) on bread and oil, Tchernia (1986) on (Italian) wine (both in French), and Curtis (1991) on fish-sauce, can be recommended. Gallant, *A Fisherman's Tale* (1985) vigorously denies fish the status of a staple food; Purcell 'Eating fish' (1995) is a rejoinder.

HEALTH AND NUTRITION

Epidemic disease in antiquity, a traditional interest of palaeopathology, is well catered for in the literature (see e.g. Grmek, *Diseases* (1989), and Manchester and Roberts, *The Archaeology of Disease* (1995)), but with little attention paid to the impact on nutritional status. The 'synergism' of disease and nutrition, long familiar to third-world nutritionists, has attracted the attention of historians of early modern and modern nutrition such as Robert Fogel, but has had little impact on historians of antiquity. The scientific study of human skeletal remains for the information they convey on nutritional status has only recently begun, under the impetus of research conducted mainly in North America and for the most part focused on North American sites. Collections of essays of interest and importance include Gilbert and Mielke, *The Analysis of Prehistoric Diets* (1985), Cohen and Armelagos, *Paleopathology at the Origins of Agriculture* (1984), Isçan and Kennedy, *Reconstruction of Life* (1989), Price, *The Chemistry of Prehistoric Human Bone* (1989). Wing and Brown, *Paleonutrition* (1979) complements these studies. The pioneer of skeletal analysis in the Mediterranean world was Lawrence Angel, but the subject has moved on since his time. Examples of useful recent case-studies from the Graeco-Roman world are Bisel (1988) on Herculaneum and Molleson (1993) on Poundbury, Dorset. Much can be expected from the investigation of the cemetery of Isola Sacra at Portus (near Ostia), directed by Roberto Macchiarelli. Many other surveys contribute smaller samples of data, some of which are serviceable. Garnsey, 'Mass diet and nutrition' (1991a), introduces the topic from a historical point of view, and Morris, *Death-Ritual and Social Structure* (1992), ch. 3, offers a synthesis. There is as yet no general work on malnutrition in antiquity. For famine, see Garnsey, *Famine and Food Supply* (1988).

FOOD IN ITS SOCIAL CONTEXT

On 'wining and dining', the work of Oswyn Murray on the symposium stands out. This includes sundry articles and two volumes of conference papers, *Sympotica* (1990) and *In Vino Veritas* (1995; with Teçusan). See also the collection of Slater, *Dining* (1991). Schmitt-Pantel, *La cité au banquet* (1992) is the definitive work on civic feasting. Davidson, *Courtesans and Fishcakes* is a vivid treatment of the political implications of consumption in classical Athens, with special reference to fish. Veyne, *Le pain et le cirque* (1976), on food and political relationships, is monumental; the English translation (1990) is abridged. On constructions of cultural diversity especially involving 'barbarians' and food, Rosellini and Saïd, 'Usages de femmes et autres "nomoi" ' (1978), and Shaw, 'Eaters of flesh, drinkers of milk' (1982–83), are especially informative. Hartog, *Le Miroir d'Hérodote* (1980; Engl. tr. 1988), and Cartledge, *The Greeks* (1993; rev. edn 1997), among others works, are also instructive. Anthropological and sociological writing which pursues a 'contextual' approach on food includes Goody, *Cooking, Cuisine and Class* (1982), Harris, *Good to Eat* (1986) and 'Foodways' (1987), and Mennell,

All Manners of Food (1985). The debate over Goody's book, including a reply by the author, can be consulted in *Food and Foodways* 3 (1989). Attitudes to women and children are not new topics, but the implications of these attitudes for food distribution within the family have not been systematically drawn; medical texts furnish useful data, especially Soranus, *Gynaecology* (tr. Temkin) and Oribasius, *Libri Incerti* (Fr. tr. Daremberg). On the rich/poor divide, the evidence is abundant but discrete, and still awaits assembling and analysing. Corbier, 'La fève et la murène' (1996) is a pilot essay in this area.

FOOD AS SYMBOL

Classic anthropological work stressing the symbolism of food includes that of Lévi-Strauss (Eng. tr. 1970), Barthes (Eng. tr. 1979), Bourdieu (Eng. tr. 1984) and Douglas (1966) (1973), etc. Passiarello (1990) surveys the work of Douglas. Edmunds, 'Ancient Roman and modern American food' (1986), is a brief comparative study after Douglas. The structuralist approach of Lévi-Strauss is applied by Vernant, Detienne and Vidal-Naquet to Greece, with special reference to the role of food in mythology. One can sample their writings in English translation in Gordon, *Myth, Religion and Society* (1981). Critical assessments of structuralism include Sperber, *Rethinking Symbolism* (1975), Gordon, 'Reason and ritual' (1979) and Gellner, 'What is structuralisme?' (1985) The metaphorical dimension of food in Latin literature, with special emphasis on the poet as cook, is profitably explored in Gowers, *The Loaded Table*.

The food/sex association is discussed by, among others, Sussman, 'Workers and drones' (1978), Foucault, 'The battle for chastity' (1985) and *History of Sexuality* (1976–1984), Mason, 'Third person/second sex' (1987), Delaney, 'Seeds of honor' (1987), duBois, *Sowing the Body* (1988), Olender, 'Aspects of Baubo' (1990), Henry, 'The edible woman' (1992); and with special attention to ascetic Christianity, by Musurillo, 'The problem of ascetical fasting' (1956), Rousselle, *Porneia* (1988), Wilson, 'Alimentary and sexual encratism' (1985), and Grimm, *From Feasting to Fasting* (1996). For a later period, see Walker Bynum, *Holy Feast and Holy Fast* (1987), and Bell, *Holy anorexia* (1985). For food and morality more generally, in Rome, see Goddard, 'Moral attitudes' and 'The tyrant at table' (both 1994), and Toner, *Leisure* (1995). Edwards, *The Politics of Immorality* (1993) is enlightening in an adjacent area.

FOOD PROHIBITIONS

There is no synthetic treatment of food taboos in Graeco-Roman societies. For taboos in general the best discussion is still Simoons, *Eat Not this Flesh* (1961). Most of the literature relating to antiquity is specialised: it concerns the Jewish dietary laws, or ascetic groups, pagan – especially Pythagoreans – and Christian (see above under 'Food as symbol', end). Jewish prohibitions are discussed in Soler, 'The semiotics of food in the Bible' (1973) (from a structuralist perspective), Douglas, *Purity and Danger* (1966) (cultural idealist), and Harris, *Good to*

Eat (1986) and 'Foodways' (1987) (materialist). Recently both Soler, 'Les raisons de la Bible' (1996), and Douglas, 'The forbidden animals' (1993), and 'Atonement' (1993–94), have adopted a more contextual approach to the laws. On Pythagoras and his followers, the evidence is presented in full in Burkert, *Lore and Science* (1972). Commentators are divided between symbolist and materialist interpretations; see, on the one hand, Detienne, 'La cuisine de Pythagore' (1970) and 'Between beasts and gods' (1987), and, on the other, Katz, 'Fava Bean consumption' (1987) and Grmek, *Diseases*. *De Abstinentia*, by the third-century Neoplatonist philosopher Porphyry, is an impressive statement of the case against sacrifice and consumption of animals; translation with commentary by G. Clark is forthcoming. Sorabji, *Animal Minds* (1993) is a general treatment of attitudes to animals.

Bibliography

ALCOCK, S. E. (1993) *Graecia Capta: the Landscapes of Roman Greece*. Cambridge

ALLBAUGH, L. G. (1953) *Crete: a Case Study of an Underdeveloped Area*. Princeton

AMOURETTI, M.-C. (1986) *Le pain et l'huile dans la Grèce antique*. Besançon

AMPOLO, C. (1980) 'Le condizioni materiali della produzione: agricoltura e paesaggio agrario', *DArch* 2: 15–46

(1984) 'Note minime di storia dell'alimentazione', *Opus* 3: 115–20

(1986) 'Il pane quotidiano delle città antiche fra economia e antropologia', *Opus* 5: 143–51

(1995) 'Pane antico: mulini, panettieri e città: aspetti sociali della panificazione', in O. Longo and P. Scarpi, eds., *Homo Edens IV: Regimi, miti e pratiche dell'alimentazione nella civiltà del Mediterraneo, Atti del Convegno 'Nel nome del pane', Bolzano, June 1993*. Bolzano: 229–43

AMUNDSEN, D. W. and DIERS, C. J. (1969) 'The age of menarche in Classical Greece and Rome', *Human Biology* 41: 125–32

(1970) 'The age of menopause in Classical Greece and Rome', *Human Biology* 42: 79–86

ANDRÉ, J. (1981) *L'alimentation et la cuisine à Rome*. Paris

ANDREWS, A. C. (1949) 'The bean and Indo-European totemism', *Amer. Anthr.* 51: 274–92

ARIE, T. H. D. (1959) 'Pythagoras and beans', *Oxford Med. Sch. Gaz.* 2: 75–81

ARNOLD, D. (1988) *Famine: Social Crisis and Historical Change*. Oxford

ARNOTT, W. G. (1996) *Alexis: the Fragments. A Commentary*. Cambridge

AUERBACH, E. (1953) *Mimesis. The Representation of Reality in Western Literature*. Princeton (Ger. publ. *Mimesis. Dargestellte Wirklichkeit in der abendländischen Literatur* (Bern, 1946))

AUSTIN, M. M. (1981) *The Hellenistic World from Alexander to the Roman Conquest. A Selection of Ancient Sources in Translation*. Cambridge

BADIAN, E. (1958) *Foreign Clientelae*. Oxford

BARTHES, R. (1972) *Mythologies*. Tr. A. Lavers. London (Fr. publ. *Mythologies* (Paris, 1957))

(1979) 'Toward a psychosociology of contemporary food consumption', in R. Forster and O. Ranum, eds., *Food and Drink in History*. Baltimore and London 166–73 (Fr. publ. 'Pour une psycho-sociologie de l'alimentation contemporaine', *Annales ESC* 16 (1961), 977–86)

149

BELL, R. M. (1985) *Holy Anorexia.* Chicago and London

BILLIARD, R. (1913) *La vigne dans l'Antiquité.* Lyon

BISEL, S. (1988) 'Nutrition in first century Herculaneum', *Anthropologie* 26/1: 61–6

BLOEDOW, E. F. (1975) 'Corn supply and Athenian imperialism', *Ant. Class.* 44: 20–9

BODSON, L., ed. (1988a) *L'animal dans l'alimentation humaine: les critères de choix, Actes du coll. intern. de Liège 26–29 nov. 1986, Anthropozoologica,* second numéro spécial. Paris

(1988b) 'Quelques critères antiques du choix et de l'exclusion de l'animal dans l'alimentation humaine', in Bodson (1988a), 229–34

BORDES, J. (1982) *Politeia dans la pensée grecque jusqu' à Aristote.* Paris

BOSERUP, E. (1965) *The Conditions of Agricultural Growth: the Economics of Agrarian Change under Population Pressure.* Chicago and New York

(1983) 'The impact of scarcity and plenty on development', *Jl. Interd. Hist.* 14: 383–407 (repr. in Rotberg and Rabb (1985), 185–210)

BOURDIEU, P. (1979) *La distinction: critique sociale du jugement.* Paris (tr. as *Distinction: a Social Critique of the Judgement of Taste* (London, 1984))

BOWMAN, A. K., THOMAS, J. D. and ADAMS, J. N. (1990) 'Two letters from Vindolanda', *Britannia* 21: 33–52

BOWMAN, A. K. and THOMAS, J. D. (1994) *The Vindolanda Writing-Tablets (Tabulae Vindolandenses* II). London

BRADLEY, K. R. (1980) 'Sexual regulations in wet-nursing contracts from Roman Egypt', *Klio* 62: 321–5

(1986) 'Wet-nursing at Rome: a study in social relations', in B. M. Rawson, ed., *The Family in Ancient Rome: New Perspectives* 201–29

BRAIN, P. (1986) *Galen on Bloodletting.* Cambridge

BRAMBLE, J. C. (1974) *Persius and the Programmatic Satire. A Study in Form and Imagery.* Cambridge

BRAUDEL, F. (1973) *Capitalism and Material Life 1400–1800.* London (Fr. publ. *Civilisation matérielle et capitalisme* (Paris, 1967))

BRAUN, T. (1995) 'Barley cakes and emmer bread', in Wilkins et al. (1995), 25–37

BRIANT, P. (1982) *Etat et pasteurs au Moyen-Orient ancien.* Cambridge and Paris

BROSHI, M. (1986) 'The diet of Palestine in the Roman period – introductory notes', *The Israel Museum Journal* 5: 41–56

BROTHWELL, D. R. and BROTHWELL, P. (1969) *Food in Antiquity: a Survey of the Diet of Early Peoples.* London

BROWN, P. (1988) *The Body and Society: Men, Women, and Sexual Renunciation in Early Christianity.* New York

BURKERT, W. (1972) *Lore and Science in Ancient Pythagoreanism.* Cambridge, Mass. (Ger. publ. *Weisheit und Wissenschaft: Studien zu Pythagoras, Philolaos und Platon* (Nuremberg, 1962))

(1979) *Structure and History in Greek Mythology and Ritual.* Berkeley and London.

(1985) *Greek Religion Archaic and Classical.* Cambridge Mass. (Ger. publ.

Griechische Religion der archaischen und klassischen Epoche (Stuttgart, 1977))
BUXTON, R. (1994) *Imaginary Greece. The Contexts of Mythology.* Cambridge
CAMERON, A. (1995) *Callimachus and his Critics.* Princeton
CAMPORESI, P. (1989) *Bread of Dreams: Food and Fantasy in Early Modern Europe.* Oxford (It. publ. *Pane selvaggio* (Bologna, 1980))
CARRIÉ, J.-M. (1975) 'Les distributions alimentaires dans les cités de l'empire romain tardif', *MEFRA* 87: 995–1101
CARTLEDGE, P. (1979) *Sparta and Lakonia. A Regional History, 1300–362 BC.* London
    (1983), ' "Trade and politics" revisited': archaic Greece' in Garnsey, et al. (1983) 1–15
    (1987) *Agesilaos and the Crisis of Sparta.* London and Baltimore
    (1997) *The Greeks.* Rev. edn. Oxford
CASSON, L. (1954) 'The grain trade of the Hellenistic world', *TAPA* 85: 168–87
CHADWICK, H. (1959) *The Sentences of Sextus: a Contribution to the History of Early Christian Ethics.* Cambridge
CHAYANOV, A. V. (1986) *The Theory of Peasant Economy.* Manchester
CHIRASSI COLOMBO, I. (1968) *Elementi di culture precereali nei miti e riti greci.* Rome
CIPOLLA, C. M. (1981) *Before the Industrial Revolution: European Society and Economy, 1000–1700.* 2nd edn. London
CIPRIANI, M. and LONGO, F., ed. (1996) *I greci in Occidente: Poseidonia e I Lucani.* Napoli
CLASSEN, C. J. (1978) 'Horace – a cook?', *CQ* 28: 333–48
CLUTESI, G. (1969) *Potlatch.* 2nd edn. Sydney
COFFEY, M. (1976) *Roman Satire.* London
COHEN, M. N. (1977) *The Food Crisis in Prehistory: Overpopulation and the Origins of Agriculture.* New Haven and London
    (1989) *Health and the Rise of Civilisation.* New Haven and London
    (1990) 'Prehistoric patterns of hunger', in L. F. Newman, ed., *Hunger in History: Food Shortage, Poverty and Deprivation.* Oxford: 56–9
COHEN, M. N. and ARMELAGOS, G. J., eds. (1984) *Paleopathology at the Origins of Agriculture.* Orlando
COLEMAN, T. (1968) *The Railway Navvies: a History of the Men Who Made the Railways.* London
CORBIER, M. (1989) 'The ambiguous status of meat in ancient Rome', *Food and Foodways* 3: 223–64 (Fr. publ. 'Le statut ambigu de la viande à Rome', *DHA* 15 (1989), 107–58)
    (1996) 'La fève et la murène: hiérarchies sociales des nourritures à Rome', in Flandrin and Montanari (1996), 215–36
CORVISIER, J.-N. (1985) *Santé et société en Grèce ancienne.* Paris
COUILLOUD-LE DINAHET, M.-TH. (1988a), 'Les magistrats grecs et l'approvisionnement des cités', *Cahiers d'histoire* 33: 321–32
    (1988b) 'L'exploitation des domaines d'Apollon et le ravitaillement de Délos', *Mélanges P. Lévêque.* Paris: 115–40
CRAWFORD, D. J. (1979) 'Food: tradition and change in Hellenistic Egypt',

World Archaeology 11.2: 136–46

CUMONT, F. (1929) *Les religions orientales dans le paganisme*. 4th edn. Paris

CURRIE, S. (1989) 'The bellies of women and the minds of men: women and food in ancient society', in Garnsey (1989), 1–9

CURTIS, R. I. (1991) *Garum and Salsamenta: Production and Commerce in Materia Medica*. Leiden

DALBY, A. (1996) *Siren Feasts: a History of Food and Gastronomy in Greece*. London

DAR, SHIMON (1995) 'Food and archaeology in Romano-Byzantine Palestine', in Wilkins et al. (1995), 326–35

DARBY, W. J., GHALIOUNGUI, P. and GRIVETTI, L. (1977) *Food: the Gift of Osiris*. 2 vols. London and New York

D'ARMS, J. (1984) 'Control, companionship, and *clientela*: some social functions of the Roman communal meal', *Classical Views / Echos du monde classique* 28: 327–48

(1990) 'The Roman convivium and the idea of equality', in Murray (1990b), 308–20

DAVIDSON, J. (1993) 'Fish, sex and revolution at Athens', *CQ* 43: 53–66

(1995) 'Opsophagia: revolutionary eating at Athens', in Wilkins et al. (1995), 204–13

(1997) *Courtesans and Fishcakes: the Consuming Passions of Classical Athens*. London

DAVIES, J. K. (1971) *Athenian Propertied Families 600–300 BC*. Oxford

DAVIES, R. W. (1971) 'The Roman military diet', *Britannia* 12: 122–42

DEGANI, E. (1990) 'On Greek gastronomic poetry, I', *Alma Mater Studiorum* (Bologna): 51–63

(1991) 'On Greek gastronomic poetry, II', *Alma Mater Studiorum* (Bologna): 164–75

DELANEY, C. (1987) 'Seeds of honor, fields of shame', in D. Gilmore, ed., *Honor and Shame and the Unity of the Mediterranean*. Washington, DC: 35–48

DELATTE, A. (1930) 'Faba Pythagorae cognata', in *Serta Leodiensia* (Liège), 33–57

DE LIGT, L. (1993) *Fairs and Markets in the Roman Empire: Economic and Social Aspects of Periodic Markets in a Pre-Industrial Society*. Amsterdam

DETIENNE, M. (1970) 'La cuisine de Pythagore', *Arch. de sociol.* 29: 141–62

(1977) *Dionysos mis à mort*. Paris (tr. as *Dionysos Slain* (1979), 35–67 = 'Between beasts and gods', in Gordon (1981), 215–28)

DETIENNE, M. and VERNANT, J.-P., eds. (1979) *La cuisine du sacrifice en pays grec*. Paris (tr. as *The cuisine of sacrifice among the Greeks* (Chicago and London, 1989))

DIERAUER, U. (1977) *Tier und Mensch im Denken der Antike: Ideengeschichtliche Studien zur Tierpsychologie, Anthropologie and Ethik*. Amsterdam

DION, R. (1959) *Histoire de la vigne et du vin en France des origines au XIXe siècle*. Paris

DIXON, S. (1988) *The Roman Mother*. London and Sydney

DODDS, E. R. (1951) *The Greeks and the Irrational*. Berkeley

DONKIN, R. A. (1980) *Manna: an Historical Geography*. The Hague

(1981) 'Manna in the ancient world', *Anthropos* 76: 4–11

DOUGLAS, M. (1966) *Purity and Danger: an Analysis of Concepts of Pollution and Taboo.* New York
(1973) 'Critique and commentary', in Neusner (1973), 137–42
(1975) 'Deciphering a meal', in *Implicit Meanings* (repr. from *Daedalus* 101: 61–82). London and New York: 249–75
ed. (1987) *Constructive Drinking: Perspectives on Drink from Anthropology.* Cambridge
(1993) 'The forbidden animals in Leviticus', *JSOT* 59: 3–23
(1993–94) 'Atonement in Leviticus', *JSQ* 1: 109–30
DUBOIS, P. (1988) *Sowing the Body: Psychoanalysis and Ancient Representations of Women.* Chicago and London
DUBY, G. (1974) *The Early Growth of the European Economy: Warriors and Peasants from the Seventh to the Twelfth Century.* London (Fr. publ. *Guerriers et paysans, vii-xiie siècle: premier essor de l'économie européenne* (Paris, 1973))
DUMONT, J. (1988) 'Les critères culturels du choix des poissons dans l'alimentation grecque antique: le cas d'Athénée de Naucratis', in Bodson (1988a), 99–113
DUNCAN-JONES, R. P. (1976) 'The price of wheat in Roman Egypt under the Principate', *Chiron* 6: 241–62
(1982) *The Economy of the Roman Empire. Quantitative Studies.* 2nd edn. Cambridge
DURAND, J.-L. (1986) *Sacrifice et labour en Grèce ancienne: essai d'anthropologie religieuse.* Paris and Rome
DURRY, M. (1955) 'Les femmes et le vin', *REL* 33: 108–13
EDMUNDS, L. (1986) 'Ancient Roman and modern American food – a comparative sketch of two semiological systems', *Comp. Civiliz. Rev.* 5: 52–68
EDWARDS, C. (1993) *The Politics of Immorality in Ancient Rome.* Cambridge
ELLIS, H. (1969) *A History of Bladder Stone.* Oxford
EVANS, J. K. (1980) '*Plebs rustica*: the peasantry of classical Italy II. The peasant economy', *AJAH* 5: 134–73
FARB, P. and ARMELAGOS, G. (1980) *Consuming Passions: the Anthropology of Eating.* Boston
FEELEY-HARNIK, G. (1981) *The Lord's Table: Eucharist and Passover in Early Christianity.* Philadelphia
FERRARI, L. C. (1978) 'The "food of truth" in Augustine's Confessions', *Augustinian Studies* 9: 1–14
FERRARY, J.-L. (1997a) 'De l'évergetisme hellénistique à l'évergetisme romain', in *Actes du Xe congrès international d'épigraphie grecque et latine, Nîmes 1992.* Paris: 199–225
(1997b) 'The Hellenistic world and Roman political patronage', in P. Cartledge, P. Garnsey and E. Gruen, eds., *Hellenistic Constructs: Essays in Culture, History and Historiography.* Berkeley: 105–19
FERRO-LUZZI, A. and SETTE, S. (1989) 'The Mediterranean Diet: an attempt to define its present and past composition', *Eur. Jl Clin. Nutr.* 43, Suppl. 2: 13–29
FEUVRIER-PRÉVOTAT, C. (1978) 'Echanges et sociétés en Gaule indépendante: à propos d'un texte de Poseidonios d'Apamée', *Ktema* 3: 243–59

FIDDES, N. (1991) *Meat: a Natural Symbol.* London and New York
FIELDHOUSE, P. (1986) *Food and Nutrition: Customs and Culture.* London
FIGES, O. (1996) *A People's Tragedy: the Russian Revolution 1891–1924.* London
FIGUEIRA, T. (1984) 'Mess contributions and subsistence at Sparta', *TAPA* 114: 87–109
FILDES, V. A. (1986) *Breasts, Bottles and Babies: a History of Infant Feeding.* Edinburgh
  (1988) *Wet Nursing: a History from Antiquity to the Present.* Oxford
FINK, B. (1976) 'The banquet as phenomenon or structure in selected eighteenth-century French novels', in Th. Besterman, ed., *Studies on Voltaire and the Eighteenth Century: Trans. 4th Intern. Congr. on the Enlightenment.* Oxford: 729–40
FINLEY, M. I. (1985) *The Ancient Economy.* 2nd edn. London
FISHER, N. R. E. (1989) 'Drink, hybris and the promotion of harmony in Sparta', in A. Powell, ed., *Classical Sparta: Techniques behind her Success.* London: 26–50
FITTON BROWN, A. D. (1984) 'The contribution of women to ancient Greek agriculture', *Liv. Class. Mthly* 9: 71–4
FLANDRIN, J.-L. and MONTANARI, M., eds. (1996) *Histoire de l'alimentation.* Paris
FLOUD, R., WACHTER, K. and GREGORY, A. (1990) *Height, Health and History: Nutritional Status in the UK, 1750–1980.* Cambridge
FOGEL, R. W. (1991) 'The conquest of high mortality and hunger in Europe and America: timing and mechanisms', in P. Higonnet, D. S. Landes and H. Rosovsky, eds., *Favorites of Fortune: Technology, Growth, and Economic Development since the Industrial Revolution.* Cambridge, Mass.: 33–71
  (1992) 'Second thoughts on the European escape from hunger: famines, chronic malnutrition, and mortality rates', in S. R. Osmani, ed., *Nutrition and Poverty.* Oxford: 243–86
  (1993) 'New sources and new techniques for the study of secular trends in nutritional status, health, mortality and the process of aging', *Historical Methods* 26: 5–43
FOGEL, R. W., ENGERMAN, S. L., FLOUD, R. et al. (1985) 'Secular changes in American and British stature and nutrition', in Rotberg and Rabb (1985), 247–83
FORBES, H. A. (1976) '"We have a little of everything": the ecological basis of some agricultural practices in Methana', *Ann. NY Ac. Sc.* 268: 236–50
  (1982) 'Strategies and soils: technology, production and environment in the peninsula of Methana, Greece', unpublished PhD thesis, University of Pennsylvania
FORBES, H. and FOXHALL, L. (1978) 'The queen of all trees: preliminary notes on the archaeology of the olive', *Expedition:* 37–48
FORSTER, R. and RANUM, O., eds. (1979) *Food and Drink in History.* Baltimore and London
FOUCAULT, M. (1985) 'The battle for chastity', in P. Ariès and A. Bejin, eds.,

Western Sexuality: Practice and Precept in Past and Present Times. Oxford: 14–25 (1988) *The Care of the Self.* London (Fr. publ. *Le souci de soi* (Paris, 1984))

FOXHALL, L. and FORBES, H. A. (1982) '*Sitometreia:* the role of grain as a staple food in classical antiquity', *Chiron* 12: 41–90

FRAYN, J. M. (1975) 'Wild and cultivated plants: a note on the peasant economy of Roman Italy', *JRS* 65: 32–9

(1979) *Subsistence Farming in Roman Italy.* London

FRAZER, J. G. (1911–17) *The Golden Bough: a Study in Magic and Religion.* 3rd edn. 12 vols. London

FREUD, S. (1938) *Totem and Taboo.* Penguin, Harmondsworth (1st publ. 1919)

GALLANT, T. W. (1985) *A Fisherman's Tale: an Analysis of the Potential Productivity of Fishing in the Ancient World.* Ghent

(1991) *Risk and Survival in Ancient Greece: Reconstructing the Rural Domestic Economy.* Oxford

GALLO, L. (1983) 'Alimentazione e classi sociali: una nota su orzo e frumento in Grecia', *Opus* 2: 449–72

(1989) 'Alimentazione urbana e alimentazione contadina nell'Atene classica', in Longo and Scarpi (1989): 213–30

(1993) 'Le leggi suntuarie greche e l'alimentazione', *Ann. Arch. Stor. Ant.* 15: 173–203

GARLAND, R. (1990) *The Greek Way of Life from Conception to Old Age.* London

GARNSEY, P. (1988) *Famine and Food Supply in the Graeco-Roman World: Responses to Risk and Crisis.* Cambridge

ed. (1989) *Food, Health and Culture in Classical Antiquity.* Cambridge Faculty of Classics Working Papers no. 1. Cambridge

(1990) 'Responses to food crisis in the ancient Mediterranean world', in L. F. Newman, ed., *Hunger in History: Food Shortage, Poverty and Deprivation.* Oxford: 126–46

(1991a) 'Mass diet and nutrition in the city of Rome', in A. Giovannini, ed., *Nourrir la plèbe: Actes du Colloque tenu à Genève les 28 et 29.ix.1989 en hommage à Denis van Berchem.* Basel and Kassel: 67–101 (=Garnsey (1998), ch. 14)

(1991b) 'Child-rearing in ancient Italy: ideology and practice', in D. Kertzer and R. Saller, eds., *The Family in Italy.* New Haven and London: 48–65 (=Garnsey (1998), ch. 15)

(1992a) 'Famine in history', in J. Bourriau, ed., *Understanding Catastrophe.* Cambridge: 65–99 (=Garnsey (1998), ch. 16)

(1992b) 'La fève: substance et symbole', in M. Aurell, O. Dumoulin and F. Thélamon, eds., *La sociabilité à table: commensalité et convivialité à travers les âges.* Rouen: 317–23 (=Garnsey (1998), ch. 13)

(1992c) 'Yield of the land', in B. Wells, ed., *Agriculture in Greece.* Stockholm: 147–53 (=Garnsey (1998), ch. 12)

(1996a) 'Prolegomenon to a study of the land in the Later Roman Empire', in Strubbe et al. (1996), 135–53 (=Garnsey (1998), ch. 9)

(1996b) 'Les raisons de la politique', in Flandrin and Montanari (1996), ch. 13

(1998) *Cities, Peasants and Food in Classical Antiquity: Essays in Social and Economic*

History. Ed., with addenda, W. Scheidel. Cambridge

GARNSEY, P., HOPKINS, K. and WHITTAKER, C. R., eds. (1983) *Trade in the Ancient Economy.* London

GARNSEY, P. and RATHBONE, D. (1985) 'The background to the grain law of Gaius Gracchus', *JRS* 75: 20–5

GARNSEY, P. and SALLER, R. (1987) *The Roman Empire: Economy, Society and Culture.* London

GARNSEY, P. and VAN NIJF, O. (1998) 'Contrôle des prix du grain à Rome et dans les cités de l'empire', *La mémoire perdue: Recherches sur l'administration romaine.* Rome: 303–15

GARNSEY, P. and WHITTAKER, C. R., eds. (1983) *Trade and Famine in Classical Antiquity* (*PCPS* Suppl. vol. 8). Cambridge

GASPARRO, G. S. (1987) 'Critica del sacrificio cruento e antropologia in Grecia: da Pitagora a Porfirio', in F. Vattioni, ed., *Sangue e antropologia, riti e culto: Atti della V Settimana, Roma, 26 nov. – 1 dic. 1984.* Rome: 107–55

(1989) 'Critica del sacrificio cruento e antropologia in Grecia: da Pitagora a Porfirio. II. Il *de abstinentia* porfiriano', in F. Vattioni, ed., *Sangue e antropologia nella teologia: Atti della VI Settimana, Roma, 23–28 nov. 1987.* Rome: 465–505

GAUTHIER, PH. (1981) 'Le commerce du grain à Athènes et les fonctions des sitophylaques', *RHDFE* 59: 5–28

(1985) *Les cités grecques et leurs bienfaiteurs.* Bull. Corr. Hell. suppl. 12. Paris

(1986) 'Sur le don de grain numide à Délos', in D. Knoepfler, ed., *Comptes et inventaires dans la cité grecque. Actes du coll. int. d'épigr. tenu à Neuchâtel en l'honneur de J. Tréheux.* Neuchâtel/Geneva: 61–9

GELLNER, E. (1985) 'What is structuralisme?', in *Relativism and the Social Sciences.* Cambridge: 128–57

GERNET, L. (1909) *L'approvisionnement d'Athènes en blé au Ve et au IVe siècle.* Paris

GILBERT, R. I., JR and MIELKE, J. H., eds. (1985) *The Analysis of Prehistoric Diets.* Orlando

GODDARD, J. (1989) 'The distribution of money and food in the towns of Italy in the early Empire', in Garnsey (1989), 128–38

(1994a) 'Moral attitudes to eating and drinking in ancient Rome', unpublished PhD thesis, University of Cambridge

(1994b) 'The tyrant at table', in J. Elsner and J. Masters, eds., *Reflections of Nero: Culture, History and Representation.* London: 67–82

GOODMAN, A. H. and ARMELAGOS, G. J. (1989) 'Infants and childhood morbidity and mortality risks in archaeological populations', *World Archaeology XXI* 2: 225–43

GOODY, J. (1982) *Cooking, Cuisine and Class: a Study in Comparative Sociology.* Cambridge

GORDON, R. L. (1979) 'Reason and ritual in Greek tragedy', in E. Shaffer, ed., *Comparative Criticism. A Yearbook,* 1 Cambridge: 279–310

ed. (1981) *Myth, Religion and Society: Structuralist essays by M. Detienne, L. Gernet, J.-P. Vernant, P. Vidal-Naquet.* Cambridge

GOULD, J. P. (1980) 'Law, custom and myth: aspects of the social position of women in classical Athens', *JHS* 100: 38–59

GOUREVITCH, D. (1980) 'Le dossier philologique du nyctalope', in M. D. Grmek, ed., *Hippocratica. Actes du Colloque Hippocratique de Paris, 1978.* Paris: 167–88

GOWERS, E. J. (1993) *The Loaded Table: Representations of Food in Roman Literature.* Oxford

GRAILLOT, H. (1912) *Le culte de Cybèle, mère des dieux à Rome et dans l'empire romain.* Paris

GRANT, A. (1988) 'Food, status and religion in England in the Middle Ages: an archaeozoological perspective', in Bodson (1988a), 139–46

GRANT, M., ed. (1996) *Anthimus: On the Observance of Foods. Tr. and Comm.* Totnes, Devon

GRANT, R. M. (1980) 'Dietary laws among Pythagoreans, Jews and Christians', *Harv. Theol. Rev.* 73: 299–310

GRAS, M. (1983) 'Vin et société à Rome et dans le Latium à l'époque archaïque', in *Forme di contatto e processi di trasformazione nelle società antiche. Atti del Convegno di Cortona, Maggio 1981* Pisa and Rome: 1067–75

GREENE, K. (1986) *The Archaeology of the Roman Economy.* London

GRIFFITHS, J. G. (1970) *Plutarch's De Iside et Osiride.* Swansea

GRIMM, V. E. (1995) 'Fasting women in Judaism and Christianity in late Antiquity', in Wilkins et al. (1995), 225–41

(1996) *From Feasting to Fasting, the Evolution of a Sin: Attitudes to Food in Late Antiquity.* London and New York

GRMEK, M. D. (1983) *Les maladies à l'aube de la civilisation occidentale.* Paris (tr. as *Diseases in the Ancient Greek World* (Baltimore and London, 1989))

GROENMAN-VAN WAATERINGE, W. (1989) 'Food for soldiers, food for thought', in J. C. Barrett, A. P. Fitzpatrick and L. MacInnes, eds., *Barbarians and Romans in North-West Europe from the Later Republic to Late Antiquity, BAR IS* 471: 41–57

GUTHRIE, W. K. C. (1962) *A History of Greek Philosophy.* I. *The Earlier Presocratics and the Pythagoreans.* Cambridge

HALL, E. (1989) *Inventing the Barbarian: Greek Self-Definition through Tragedy.* Oxford

HALPERIN, D. M., WINKLER, J. J. and ZEITLIN, F. I., eds. (1990) *Before Sexuality: the Construction of Erotic Experience in the Ancient Greek World.* Princeton

HALSTEAD, P. (1981) 'Counting sheep in Neolithic and Bronze Age Greece', in I. Hodder, G. Isaac and N. Hammond, eds., *Pattern of the Past: Studies in Honour of David Clarke.* Cambridge: 307–39

(1987) 'Traditional and ancient rural economy in Mediterranean Europe: plus ça change?', *JHS* 107: 77–87

(1989) ' "The economy has a normal surplus . . ." Economic stability and social change among early farming communities of Thessaly, Greece', in P. Halstead and J. O'Shea, eds., *Bad Year Economics. Cultural Responses to Risk and Uncertainty.* Cambridge: 68–80

HAMEL, G. (1990) *Poverty and Charity in Roman Palestine, First Three Centuries CE.* Berkeley

HAMILTON, R. (1984) 'Sources for the Athenian Amphidromia', *GRBS* 25: 243–51

HARMANEH, S. K. (1973) *Al-Biruni's Book on Pharmacy and Materia Medica*. Karachi

HARRIS, M. (1986) *Good to Eat: Riddles of Food and Culture*. London

(1987) 'Foodways: historical overview and theoretical prolegomenon', in M. Harris and E. B. Ross, eds., *Food and Evolution: Toward a Theory of Human Food Habits*. Philadelphia: 57–90

HARRISON, G. A., ed. (1988) *Famine*. Oxford

HARRISS, B. (1989) 'Special report on differential female mortality and health care in south Asia', *The Journal of Social Studies* 44: 3–123

(1990) 'The intrafamily distribution of hunger in south Asia', in J. Dreze and A. Sen, eds., *The Political Economy of Hunger. I. Entitlement and Well-Being*. Oxford: 351–424

(1993) *Differential Female Mortality and Health Care in South Asia*. Famine and Society Series, Monograph 1. Centre for the Study of Administration of Relief. New Delhi

HARRISS-WHITE, B. (1997) 'Gender-cleansing: the paradox of development and deteriorating female life chances in Tamil Nadu'. Unpub. typescript

HARRISS-WHITE, B., JANAKARAJAN, S. and ARYA, A. (1996) 'Food, nutrition and the state in northern Tamil Nadu'. Paper to the Workshop on Adjustment and Development: Agrarian Change, Markets and Social Welfare in S. India 1973–93. Madras Institute of Development Studies

HARTOG, F. (1988) *The Mirror of Herodotus: the Representation of the Other in the Writing of History*. Berkeley and London (Fr. publ. *Le Miroir d'Hérodote: Essai sur la représentation de l'autre*, (Paris, 1980))

HAUSSLEITER, J. (1935) *Der Vegetarismus in der Antike*. Berlin

HEEN, E. and KREUZER, R., eds., (1962) *Fish in Nutrition*. London

HEICHELHEIM, F. M. (1954–55) 'On ancient price trends from the early first millennium BC to Heraclius', *Finanzarchiv* 15: 498–511

HENRY, M. M. (1992) 'The edible woman: Athenaeus' concept of the pornographic', in A. Richlin, ed., *Pornography and Representation in Greece and Rome*. New York and Oxford: 250–68

HERMAN, G. (1987) *Ritualised Friendship and the Greek City*. Cambridge

HERZ, P. (1988) *Studien zur römischen Wirtschaftsgesetzgebung: Die Lebensmittelversorgung*. Stuttgart

HOPKINS, K. (1980) 'Taxes and trade in the Roman empire (200 BC–AD 400)', *JRS* 70: 101–25

(1983a) 'Introduction', in Garnsey et al. (1983), ix–xxv

(1983b) 'Models, ships and staples', in Garnsey and Whittaker (1983), 84–109

HUDSON, N. A. (1989) 'Food in Roman satire', in S. H. Braund, ed., *Satire and Society in Ancient Rome*. Exeter: 69–87

HUGHES, D. D. (1991) *Human Sacrifice in Ancient Greece*. London.

HUNTER, R. L. (1983) *Eubulus. The Fragments. Edited with a Commentary*. Cambridge

(1985) *The New Comedy of Greece and Rome*. Cambridge

HUXLEY, G. (1971) 'Crete in Aristotle's *Politics*', *GRBS* 12: 505–15

INWOOD, B. (1992) *The Poem of Empedocles: a Text and Translation.* Toronto, Buffalo and London

ISAGER, S. and HANSEN, M. H. (1975) *Aspects of Athenian Society in the Fourth Century BC.* Odense

ISAGER, S. and SKYDSGAARD, J. E. (1992) *Ancient Greek Agriculture: an Introduction.* London and New York

IŞCAN, M. Y. and KENNEDY, K. A. R., eds. (1989) *Reconstruction of Life from the Skeleton.* New York

JAMESON, M. H. (1978) 'Agriculture and slavery in classical Athens', *CJ* 73: 122–45

(1983) 'Famine in the Greek world', in Garnsey and Whittaker (1983), 6–16

(1988) 'Sacrifice and animal husbandry in classical Greece' in C. R. Whittaker, ed., *Pastoral Economies in Classical Antiquity.* Cambridge: 87–119

JAMESON, M. H., RUNNELS, C. N. and VAN ANDEL, T. H. (1994) *A Greek Countryside: the Southern Argolid from Prehistory to the Present Day.* Stanford

JASNY, N. (1942) 'Competition among grains in classical antiquity', *AHR* 47: 747–64

(1944) *The Wheats of Classical Antiquity.* Baltimore

(1950) 'The daily bread of the ancient Greeks and Romans', *Osiris* 9: 228–53

JEANNERET, M. (1991) *A Feast of Words: Banquets and Table Talk in the Renaissance.* Oxford (Fr. publ. *Des mets et des mots: Banquets et propos de table à la Renaissance* (Paris, 1987))

JOHANSSON, S. RYAN (1994) 'Food for thought: rhetoric and reality in modern mortality history', *Historical Methods* 27.3: 101–26

JONES, A. H. M. (1940) *The Greek City from Alexander to Justinian.* Oxford

JONGMAN, W. and DEKKER, R. (1989) 'Public intervention in the food supply in pre-industrial Europe', in P. Halstead and J. O'Shea, eds., *Bad Year Economics: Cultural Responses to Risk and Uncertainty.* Cambridge: 114–22

KATZ, S. H. (1987) 'Fava Bean consumption: a case for the co-evolution of genes and culture', in M. Harris and E. B. Ross, eds., *Food and Evolution: Towards a Theory of Human Food Habits.* Philadelphia: 133–59

KENNEY, E. J., ed. (1984) *The Ploughman's Lunch. Moretum: a Poem Ascribed to Virgil,* ed. with transl., introd. and comm. Bristol.

KING, A. C. (1984) 'Animal bones and the dietary identity of military and civilian groups in Roman Britain, Germany and Gaul', in T. C. Blagg and A. C. King, eds., *Military and Civilian in Roman Britain: Cultural Relationships in a Frontier Province* = *BAR BS* 136: 187–218

KIRK, G. S. (1970) *Myth: its Meaning and Functions in Ancient and Other Cultures.* Cambridge

KIRK, G. S., RAVEN, J. E. AND SCHOFIELD, M. (1983) *The Presocratic Philosophers: a Critical History with a Selection of Texts.* 2nd edn. Cambridge

KNIGHTS, B. A., DICKSON, C. A., DICKSON, J. H. and BREEZE, D. J. (1983) 'Evidence concerning the Roman military diet at Bearsden, Scotland, in the 2nd century AD', *Jl Arch. Sci.* 10: 139–52

KOMLOS, J. (1989) *Nutrition and Economic Development in the Eighteenth Century*

Habsburg Monarchy: an Anthropometric History. Princeton

LAKS, A. and MOST, G. W., eds. (1997) *Studies on the Derveni Papyrus.* Oxford

LAFITAU, J. F. (1724) *Mœurs des sauvages amériquains, comparées aux mœurs des premiers temps.* 2 vols. Paris (Engl. tr. by W. N. Fenton and E. L. Moore, *Customs of the American Indians Compared with the Customs of Primitive Times* (Toronto, 1974, 1977))

LAUFFER, S. (1971) *Diokletians Preisedikt.* Berlin

LAURIOUX, B. (1988) 'Le lièvre lubrique et la bête sanglante. Réflexions sur quelques interdits alimentaires du haut moyen age', in Bodson (1988a), 127–32

LAZER, E. (1995) 'Human skeletal remains in Pompeii', unpubl. PhD thesis, University of Sydney

LEACH, E. (1974) *Lévi-Strauss.* London (Fontana Modern Masters)

LEHRER, A. (1972) 'Cooking vocabularies and the culinary triangle of Lévi-Strauss', *Anthr. Ling.* 14: 155–71

LE ROY LADURIE, E. (1979) 'Amenorrhoea in time of famine (seventh to twentieth century)', in his *The Territory of the Historian* (Fr. publ. *Le territoire de l'historien* (Paris, 1973)). Hassocks: 255–72

LÉVI-STRAUSS, C. (1966) 'The culinary triangle', *Partisan Review* 33: 586–95 (tr. of 'Le triangle culinaire', *L'Arc* 26 (1965), 19–29)

    (1970) *The Raw and the Cooked: Introduction to a Science of Mythology* I. London (Fr. publ. *Le cru et le cuit: Mythologiques* I (Paris, 1964))

    (1978) *The Origin of Table Manners.* (tr. of *L'origine des manières de table: Mythologiques I.* (Paris, 1968)). London

LÉVY-BRUHL, L. (1922) *Primitive Mentality.* London

LIEBER, E. (1970) 'Galen on contaminated cereals as a cause of epidemics', *Bull. Hist. Med.* 44: 332–45

LIEBESCHUETZ, J. W. H. G. (1972) *Antioch: City and Imperial Administration in the Later Roman Empire.* London

LLOYD, G. E. R. (1983) *Science, Folklore and Ideology: Studies in the Life Sciences of Ancient Greece.* Cambridge

LONG, T. (1986) *Barbarians in Greek Comedy.* Carbondale and Edwardsville

LONGO, O. and SCARPI, P., eds. (1989) *Homo Edens: Regimi, miti e pratiche dell'alimentazione nella civiltà del Mediterraneo.* Milan

LORAUX, N. (1981) 'La cité comme cuisine et comme partage', *Annales ESC* 36: 614–22

    (1990) 'Herakles: the super-male and the female', in Halperin et al. (1990), 21–52

LOUSSERT, R. and BROUSSE, G. (1978) *L'olivier: techniques agricoles et productions méditerranéennes.* I Paris

LOWE, J. C. B. (1985) 'Cooks in Plautus', *Cl. Ant.* 4: 72–102

MACMULLEN, R. (1974) *Roman Social Relations: 50 BC to AD 284.* New Haven and London

MAKLER, P. T. (1980) 'New information on nutrition in ancient Greece', *Klio* 62: 317–19

MALTHUS, T. R. (1798) *An Essay on the Principle of Population.* (Harmondsworth (Penguin), 1970)

MANCHESTER, K. and ROBERTS, C. (1995) *The Archaeology of Disease.* 2nd edn. Stroud

MARKLE, M. M. (1985) 'Jury pay and assembly pay at Athens', in P. Cartledge and D. Harvey, eds., *Crux: Essays in Greek History presented to G.E.M. de Ste Croix on his 75th birthday.* London: 265–97

MARTIN, D. L., ARMELAGOS, G. J. and HENDERSON, K. A. (1988) 'The persistence of nutritional stress in Northeastern African (Sudanese Nubian) populations', in R. A. Huss-Ashmore and S. Katz, eds., *Famine in Africa,* 1. New York: 163–87

MARTIN, D. L., GOODMAN, A. H. and ARMELAGOS, G. J. (1985) 'Skeletal pathologies as indicators of quality and quantity of diet', in Gilbert and Miekle (1985), 227–79

MASCIADRI, M. and MONTEVECCHI, O. (1982) 'Contratti di baliatico e vendite fiduciarie', *Aegyptus* 62: 148–61

MASON, P. (1987) 'Third person/second sex: patterns of sexual asymmetry in the *Theogony* of Hesiod', in J. Blok and P. Mason, eds., *Sexual Asymmetry: Studies in Ancient Society.* Amsterdam: 147–89

MATTHEWS, J. (1989) *The Roman Empire of Ammianus.* London

MATTINGLY, D. J. (1988a) 'Oil for export? A comparison of Libyan, Spanish and Tunisian olive oil production in the Roman empire', *JRA* 1: 33–56

(1988b) 'Olea mediterranea?', *JRA* 1: 153–61

(1988c) 'The olive boom. Oil surpluses, wealth and power in Roman Tripolitania', *Libyan Studies* 19: 21–41

MAURIZIO, A. (1932) *Histoire de l'alimentation végétale depuis la préhistoire jusqu'à nos jours.* Tr. F. Gidon. Paris

MAUSS, M. (1925) 'Sur un texte de Posidonius. Le suicide contre-prestation suprême', *Rev. Celt.* 42: 324–9 (= *Œuvres* 3: 52–9. Paris)

(1990) *The Gift: the Form and Reason for Exchange in Archaic Societies.* London (Fr. publ. *Essai sur le Don* (1925))

MCCARTNEY, E. S. (1925) 'How the apple became the token of love', *TAPA* 56: 70–81

MENNELL, S. (1985) *All Manners of Food: Eating and Taste in England and France from the Middle Ages to the Present.* Oxford

MENNELL, S., MURCOTT, A., and VAN OTTERLOO, A. H. (1992) 'The sociology of food and eating: a trend report and bibliography', *Current Sociology* 40: 1–152

MIGEOTTE, L. (1990) 'Distributions de grain à Samos à la période hellénistique: le "pain gratuit" pour tous?' in *Sacris Erudiri: Jaarboek voor Godsdienstwetenschappen* 31: *Opes Atticae: Mélanges offerts aux professeurs R. Bogaert et H.van Looy.* The Hague: 297–308

MILLETT, P. (1983) 'Maritime loans and the structure of credit in fourth-century Athens', in P. Garnsey et al. (1983), 36–52

(1989) 'Patronage and its avoidance in classical Athens', in A. Wallace-

Hadrill, ed., *Patronage in Ancient Society.* London: 15–48

(1991) *Lending and Borrowing in Ancient Athens.* Cambridge

MINTZ, S. W. (1985) *Sweetness and Power: the Place of Sugar in Modern History.* New York and Harmondsworth

MOLLESON, T. I. (1993) 'Pt. 2: The human remains', in D. E. Farwell and T. I. Molleson, eds., *Excavations at Poundbury 1966–80* vol. 2: *The Cemeteries.* Dorchester: 141–214

MOORE, G. F. (1927) *Judaism in the First Centuries of the Christian Era: the Age of the Tannaim.* 3 vols. London

MORCOS, S. and W. (1977) 'Diets in ancient Egypt', *Prog. Fd. Nutr. Sci.* 2.10: 457–71

MORFORD, M. (1977) 'Juvenal's fifth satire', *AJPh* 98: 219–45

MORRIS, I. (1992) *Death-Ritual and Social Structure in Classical Antiquity.* Cambridge

MORROW, G. R. (1960) *Plato's Cretan City: a Historical Interpretation of the Laws.* Princeton

MROZEK, S. (1987) *Les distributions d'argent et de nourritures dans les villes italiennes du Haut-Empire romain.* Brussels

MURRAY, O. (1983a) 'Symposion and Männerbund', in P. Oliva and A. Frolikova, eds., *Concilium Eirene XVI, Proc. 16th Internat. Eirene Conf., Prague 31.8–4.9.1982,* I 47–52

(1983b) 'The symposion as social organisation', in R. Hagg, ed., *The Greek Renaissance of the Eighth Century BC: Tradition and Innovation: Proceedings of the 2nd Internat. Symp. at the Swedish Instit. in Athens, 1–5 June, 1981.* Stockholm: 195–9

(1983c) 'The Greek symposion in history', in E. Gabba, ed., *Tria Corda: scritti in onore di A. Momigliano.* Como: 257–72

(1985a) 'Symposium and genre in the poetry of Horace', *JRS* 75: 39–50

(1985b) 'At the Etruscan banquet', *TLS* 30 Aug., pp. 948, 960

(1990a) 'The affair of the Mysteries: democracy and the drinking group', in Murray (1990b), 149–61

ed., (1990b) *Sympotica: a Symposium on the Symposium.* Oxford

(1990c) 'Sweet feasts of the grape', *THES* 6 July, pp. 13, 17

(1996) 'Hellenistic royal symposia', in P. Bilde et al., eds., *Aspects of Hellenistic Kingship.* Aarhus: 15–27

MURRAY, O. and TEÇUSAN, M., ed., (1995) *In Vino Veritas.* London

MUSURILLO, H. (1956) 'The problem of ascetical fasting in the Greek patristic writers', *Traditio* 12: 1–64

NELSON, M. C. (1988) *Bitter Bread: the Famine in Norrbotten, 1867–1868.* Uppsala

NELSON, M. C. and SVANBERG, I. (1987) 'Lichens as food: historical perspectives on food propaganda', *Svenska Linnésällskapets Årsskrift* 1987: 7–51

NEUSNER, J. (1973) *The Idea of Purity in Ancient Judaism.* Leiden

NEWMAN, L. F. et al., (1990) 'Agricultural intensification, urbanization and hierarchy', in L. F. Newman, ed., *Hunger in History: Food Shortage, Poverty, and Deprivation.* Oxford: 101–24

NIPPEL, W. (1990) *Griechen, Barbaren und 'Wilde'. Alte Geschichte und Sozialanthropologie.* Frankfurt

(1995) *Public Order in Ancient Rome.* Cambridge

(1996a) 'Facts and fiction: Greek ethnography and its legacy', *Hist. and Anthr.* 9: 125–38

(1996b) 'La costruzione dell'"altro"', in S. Settis, ed., *I Greci: Storia cultura arte società*. 1. *Noi e i Greci*. Turin: 165–96

NUTTON, V. (1995) 'Galen and the traveller's fare', in Wilkins et al. (1995), 359–70

OLENDER, M. (1990) 'Aspects of Baubo', in D. M. Halperin, J. J. Winkler and F. I. Zeitlin, eds., *Before Sexuality: the Construction of Erotic Experience in the Ancient Greek World*. Princeton: 83–114

OLIVER, G. J. (1995) 'The Athenian state under threat: politics and food supply, 307 to 229 BC', unpubl. D. Phil. thesis, Oxford

ORTNER, D. J. and PUTSCHAR, W. G. J. (1981) *Identification of Pathological Conditions in Human Skeletal Remains*. Washington, DC

OSBORNE, C. (1995) 'Ancient vegetarianism', in Wilkins et al. (1995): 214–24

PARKER, R. (1983) *Miasma: Pollution and Purification in Early Greek Religion*. Oxford

PASSARIELLO, P. (1990) 'Review essay: Anomalies, analogies, and sacred profanities: Mary Douglas on food and culture, 1957–1989', *Food and Foodways* 4: 53–71

PASSERINI, A. (1934) 'La *truphe* nella storiografia ellenistica', *St. It. Fil. Cl.* 11: 35–56

PAUL, G. (1991) 'Symposia and deipna in Plutarch's *Lives* and in other historical writings', in Slater (1991), 157–70

PAVIS D'ESCURAC, H. (1976) *La préfecture de l'Annone: service administratif impérial d'Auguste à Constantin*. Rome

(1987) 'A propos de l'approvisionnement en blé des cités de l'orient romain', in E. Frézouls, ed., *Sociétés urbaines, sociétés rurales dans l'Asie Mineure et la Syrie hellénistiques et romaines: actes du coll. Strasbourg (nov. 1985)*. Strasbourg: 117–30

PELLETIER, A. (1962) *Lettre d'Aristée à Philocrate* (SC 89). Paris

PETERSEN, W. (1979) *Malthus*. London

PETIT, P. (1955) *Libanius et la vie municipale à Antioche au IVe siècle après J.-C.* Paris

POMEROY, S. B. (1984) 'The Persian king and the queen bee', *AJAH* 9: 98–108

PRICE, T. D., ed., (1989) *The Chemistry of Prehistoric Human Bone*. Cambridge

PUCCI, G. (1989) 'Consumi alimentari', in *Storia di Roma* IV: *caratteri e morfologie*. Turin: 369–88

PURCELL, N. (1985) 'Wine and wealth in ancient Italy', *JRS* 75: 1–19

(1995) 'Eating fish: the paradoxes of seafood', in Wilkins et al. (1995), 132–49

RATHBONE, D. (1983) 'Italian wines in Roman Egypt', *Opus* 2: 81–98

REA, J. R. (1972) 'Public documents: the corn dole in Oxyrhynchus and kindred documents', in *The Oxyrhynchus Papyri* vol. 40 (London), 1–30

RENFREW, J. M. (1973) *Palaeoethnobotany: the Prehistoric Food Plants of the Near East and Europe*. New York

RICHLIN, A. (1984) 'Invective against women in Roman satire', *Arethusa* 17: 167–80

ed. (1992) *Pornography and Representation in Greece and Rome*. New York and Oxford

RICKMAN, G. E. (1980) *The Corn Supply of Ancient Rome.* Oxford

RILEY, J. C. (1994) 'Height, nutrition and mortality risk reconsidered', *Jl. Interdisc. Hist.* 24: 466–88

ROSE, J. C., CONDON, K. W. and GOODMAN, A. H. (1985) 'Diet and dentition: developmental disturbances', in Gilbert and Mielke (1985), 281–305

ROSELLINI, M. and SAÏD, S. (1978) 'Usage de femmes et autres 'nomoi' chez les "sauvages" d'Hérodote: essai de lecture structurale', *ASNP* 8: 949–1005

ROSSI, P. F. et al. (1996) 'Stress e adattamento in età romana imperiale', in *L'adattamento umano all'ambiente passato e presente. Atti XI Congresso degli Antropologi Italiani, Isernia, 13–16 sett. 1995*: 343–54

ROTBERG, R. I. and RABB, T. K., eds. (1985) *Hunger and History: the Impact of Changing Food Production and Consumption Patterns on Society.* Cambridge

ROUSSELLE, A. (1974) 'Abstinence et continence dans les monastères de Gaule méridionale à la fin de l'antiquité et au début du moyen age: étude d'un régime alimentaire et de sa fonction', *Hommage à André Dupont: études médiévales languedociennes*: 239–54

(1988) *Porneia: on Desire and the Body in Antiquity.* London (Fr. publ. *Porneia: de la maîtrise du corps à la privation sensorielle* (Paris, 1983))

ROWLAND, M. G. M. (1986) 'The weanling's dilemma: are we making progress?', in B. Wharton, ed., *Food for the Weanling.* London: 33–42

ROYSTON, E. (1982) 'The prevalence of nutritional anaemia in women in developing countries: a critical review of available information', *World Health Quarterly* 35.2: 52–91

ROYSTON, E. and LOPEZ, A. D. (1987) 'On the assessment of maternal mortality', *World Health Quarterly* 40.3: 214–24

RUBIN, M. (1991) *Corpus Christi: the Eucharist in Late Medieval Culture.* Cambridge

SALLARES, R. (1991) *The Ecology of the Ancient Greek World.* London

SAMTER, E. (1901) *Familienfeste der Griechen und Römer.* Berlin

SCHAPS, D. M. (1985–88) 'Comic inflation in the marketplace', *Scr. Cl. Isr.* 8–9: 66–73

SCHEID, J. (1988) 'La spartizione sacrificale a Roma', in C. Grottanelli and N. F. Parise, eds., *Sacrificio e società nel mondo antico.* Rome: 267–92

(1990) *Romulus et ses frères: le collège des Frères Arvales, modèle du culte public dans la Rome des empereurs.* Rome

SCHEIDEL, W. (1995) 'The most silent women of Greece and Rome: rural labour and women's life in the ancient world, I', *G&R* 42: 202–17

(1996) 'The most silent women of Greece and Rome: rural labour and women's life in the ancient world, II,' *G&R* 43: 1–10

SCHMELING, G. (1970) 'Trimalchio's menu and wine list', *CPh* 55: 248–51

SCHMIDT, M. (1976) *Die Erklärungen zum Weltbild Homers und zur Kultur der Heroenzeit in den bT-Scholien zur Ilias.* Munich

SCHMITT-PANTEL, P. (1990) 'Sacrificed meal and *symposium*: two modes of civic institutions in the archaic city?', in Murray (1990b), 14–33

(1992) *La cité au banquet. Histoire des repas publics dans les cités grecques.* Rome

(1997) 'Public feasts in the Hellenistic Greek city: forms and meanings', in

P. Bilde et al., eds., *Conventional Values of the Hellenistic Greeks.* Aarhus: 29–47
SCHNAPP, A. (1989) 'Eros the hunter', in C. Bérard et al., *A City of Images: Iconography and Society in Ancient Greece.* Princeton: 71–88 (Fr. publ. *La cité des images. Religion et société en Grèce antique* (Lausanne and Paris, 1984))
(1997) *Le chasseur et la cité: chasse et érotique dans la Grèce ancienne.* Paris
SCOBIE, A. (1986) 'Slums, sanitation and mortality in the Roman world', *Klio* 68: 399–433
SCRIMSHAW, N. (1975) 'Nutrition and infection', *Progr. Fd. Nutr. Sci.* 1.6: 393–420
SCRIMSHAW, N., TAYLOR, C. E. and GORDON, J. E. (1968) *Interactions of Nutrition and Infection.* Geneva
SEGAL, A. F. (1990) *Paul the Convert: the Apostolate and Apostasy of Saul the Pharisee.* New Haven
SEN, A. (1981) *Poverty and Famines: an Essay on Entitlement and Deprivation.* Oxford
SHACK, W. (1978) 'Anthropology and the diet of man', in Yudkin (1978), 261–80
SHAW, B. D. (1982–83) ' "Eaters of flesh, drinkers of milk": the ancient Mediterranean ideology of the pastoral nomad', *Ancient Society* 13/14: 5–31
SHERO, L. (1923) 'The *Cena* in Roman satire', *CP* 18: 126–43
SHIPLEY, G. (1987) *A History of Samos, 800–188 BC.* Oxford
SIMOONS, F. J. (1961) *Eat Not this Flesh: Food Avoidances in the Old World.* Madison
(1991) *Food in China: a Cultural and Historical Inquiry.* Boca Raton
SIPPEL, D. V. (1987) 'Dietary deficiency among the lower class of late Republican and early Imperial Rome', *Anc. World* 16: 47–54
SIRKS, A. J. B. (1991) *Food for Rome.* Amsterdam
SLATER, W. J., ed. (1991) *Dining in a Classical Context.* Ann Arbor
SMITH, P., BAR-YOSEF, O., and SILLEN, A (1984) 'Archaeological and skeletal evidence for dietary change during the late Pleistocene/early Holocene in the Levant', in Cohen and Armelagos (1984), 101–36
SMITH, P. and PERETZ, B. (1978) 'Dental pathology in the period of the Roman empire: a comparison of two populations', *Ossa* 5: 35–41
(1986) 'Hypoplasia and health status: a comparison of two life-styles', *Human Evolution* 1:1–10
SOLER, J. (1979) 'The semiotics of food in the Bible,' in R. Forster and O. Ranum, eds., *Food and Drink in History.* Baltimore and London: 126–38. (Fr. publ. 'Sémiotique de la nourriture dans la Bible', *Annales ESC* 28.4 (1973): 943–55
(1996) 'Les raisons de la Bible: règles alimentaires hébraïques', in Flandrin and Montanari (1996), 73–84
SORABJI, R. (1993) *Animal Minds and Human Morals: the Origins of the Western Debate.* London
SPARKES, B. A. (1981) 'Not cooking but baking', *G&R* 28: 172–8
SPENCER, C. (1993) *The Heretic's Feast: a History of Vegetarianism.* London
SPERBER, D. (1975) *Rethinking Symbolism.* Cambridge. (Fr. publ. *Le symbolisme en général* (Paris, 1974))
SPURR, S. (1986) *Arable Cultivation in Roman Italy 200 BC to AD 100.* London
STEINHAUER, G. (1994) 'Inscription agoranomique du Pirée', *BCH* 118: 51–68

STROUD, R. S. (forthcoming) *An Athenian Law on the Grain-Tax in the Islands*
STRUBBE, J. H. M. (1987) 'The *sitonia* in the cities of Asia Minor under the
Principate, I', *Epigr. Anat.* 10: 45–82
(1989) 'The *sitonia* in the cities of Asia Minor under the Principate, II', *Epigr.
Anat.* 13: 99–122
STRUBBE, J. H. M., TYBOUT, R. A. and VERSNEL, H. S., ed. (1996) *Energeia: Studies
on Ancient History and Epigraphy Presented to H. W. Pleket.* Amsterdam
STUART-MACADAM, P. L. (1985) 'Porotic hyperostosis: representative of a childhood condition', *Am. Jl. Ph. Anth.* 66: 391–8
(1989) 'Nutritional deficiency diseases: a survey of scurvy, rickets, and iron-
deficiency anemia', in Işcan and Kennedy (1989), 201–22
SUSSMAN, L. (1978) 'Workers and drones: labor, idleness and gender definition
in Hesiod's beehive', *Arethusa* 11: 27–41
TCHERNIA, A. (1986) *Le vin de l'Italie romaine: essai d'histoire économique d'après les
amphores.* Rome
TEÇUSAN, M. (1990) '*Logos Sympotikos*: patterns of the irrational in philosophical
drinking: Plato outside the *Symposium*', in Murray (1990b), 238–62
TEMKIN, O. and TEMKIN, C. L. (1967) *Ancient Medicine. Selected papers of Ludwig
Edelstein.* Baltimore
TENGSTRÖM, E. (1974) *Bread for the People. Studies of the Corn-Supply of Rome during
the Late Empire.* Stockholm
THACKERAY, H. ST. J. (1917) *The Letter of Aristaeus.* London and New York
THÉLAMON, F. (1992) 'Ascèse et sociabilité. Les conduites alimentaires des
moines d'Egypte au IVe siècle', *Rev. Et. Aug.* 38: 295–321
THYLEFORS, B. (1987) 'A simplified methodology for the assessment of blind-
ness and its main causes', *World Health Statistics Quarterly* 40.2: 129–41
TOMLINSON, R. A. (1970) 'Ancient Macedonian symposia', in B. Laourdas and
C. Makaronas, eds., *Ancient Macedonia: First Internat. Sympos. Thessaloniki,
26–29 August, 1968.* Thessaloniki: 308–15
TONER, J. P. (1995) *Leisure and Ancient Rome.* Oxford
VAN REEN, R., ed. (1977) *Idiopathic Urinary Bladder Stone Disease.* Washington,
DC
VERNANT, J.-P. (1981a) 'The myth of Prometheus in Hesiod', in Gordon (1981),
43–56 (Fr. publ. *Mythe et société en Grèce ancienne* (Paris, 1974), 177–94))
(1981b) 'Sacrificial and alimentary codes in Hesiod's myth of Prometheus', in
Gordon (1981), 57–79 (Fr. publ. 'Sacrifice et alimentation humaine à propos
du *Promethée d'Hésiode*', *ASNP* 7.3 (1977), 905–40)
VEYNE, P. (1976) *Le pain et le cirque: sociologie historique d'un pluralisme politique.* Paris
(Engl. tr. (abridged) *Bread and Circuses: Historical Sociology and Political
Pluralism* (London, 1990))
(1985) 'L'empire romain', in P. Ariès and G. Duby, eds., *Histoire de la vie privée*,
1 pt 1. Paris (Tr. as *A History of Private Life* (London, 1987))
VIDAL-NAQUET, P. (1981) 'Land and sacrifice in the Odyssey: a study of religious and mythical meaning', in Gordon (1981), 80–94 (Fr. publ. 'Valeurs
religieuses et mythiques de la terre et du sacrifice dans l'Odyssée', *Annales*

ESC 25 (1970), 1278–97)

VIRLOUVET, C. (1985) *Famines et émeutes à Rome des origines de la République à la mort de Néron.* Rome

(1995) *Tessera frumentaria: les procédures de la distribution de blé public à Rome à la fin de la République et au début de l'Empire.* Rome

VON REDEN, S. (1989) 'On meat and grain: food as symbol', in Garnsey (1989), 177–92

VOTH, H.-J. (1996) *Going Short and Working Little? Labour Intensity and Energy Availability in Eighteenth-Century England.* Camb. Gp. Hist. Pop. Soc. Str. Working Paper Series: no. 4

WALKER, S. (1983) 'Women and housing in classical Greece', in A. Cameron and A. Kuhrt, eds., *Images of Women in Antiquity.* London: 81–91

WALKER BYNUM, C. (1987) *Holy Feast and Holy Fast: the Religious Significance of Food to Medieval Women.* Berkeley

WALLACE-HADRILL, A., ed. (1989) *Patronage in Ancient Society.* London and New York

WARD, B. (1987) *Harlots of the Desert: a Study of Repentance in Early Monastic Sources.* Oxford

WATERLOW, J. C. (1989) 'Diet of the classical period of Greece and Rome', *Eur. Jl. Clin. Nutr.* 43 suppl. 2:3–12

WELLS, C. (1975) 'Ancient obstetric hazards and female mortality', *Bull. of NY Acad. Med.* 51: 1235–49

WEST, M. L. (1983) *The Orphic Poems.* Oxford

WHEELER, E. F. (1991) 'Intra-household food and nutrient allocation', *Nutr. Res. Review* 4: 69–81

WHITE, K. D. (1976) 'Food requirements and food supplies in classical times in relation to the diet of the various classes', *Progr. Fd. Nutr. Sci.* 2: 143–91

(1984) *Greek and Roman Technology.* London

WHITEHEAD, R. G. (1989) 'Famine', in L. Friday and R. Laskey, eds., *The Fragile Environment.* Cambridge: 82–106

WHITEHEAD, R. G., PAUL, A. A. and COLE, T. J. (1989) 'Diet and the growth of healthy infants', *Jl Hum. Nutr. & Dietetics* 2: 73–84

WHITTAKER, C. R. (1985) 'Trade and the aristocracy in the Roman empire', *Opus* 4: 49–75

WHITTAKER, C. R. and GARNSEY, P. (1998) 'Rural life in the later Roman empire', in *CAH* XIII: 277–311

WIESEHÖFER, J. (n.d.) 'Zur Ernährung von Säuglingen in der Antike' (typescript)

WIET, G. (1962) *Le traité des famines de Maqrizi.* Leiden.

WILKINS, J. and HILL, S., eds. (1994) *The Life of Luxury: Europe's Oldest Cookery Book: Archestratus.* Totnes

WILKINS, J., HARVEY, D. and DOBSON, M., eds. (1995) *Food in Antiquity.* Exeter

WILLETTS, R. F. (1955) *Aristocratic Society in Ancient Crete.* London

WILSON, R. MCL. (1985) 'Alimentary and sexual encratism in the Nag Hammadi texts', in U. Bianchi, ed., *La Tradizione dell'Enkrateia: Motivazioni*

Ontologiche e Protologiche, Atti del Colloquio Internaz. Milano, 20–23 aprile 1982.
   Milan: 317–39
WING, E. S. and BROWN, A. B. (1979) *Paleonutrition: Method and Theory in Prehistoric
   Foodways.* New York and London
WINKLER, J. J. (1990) *The Constraints of Desire: the Anthropology of Sex and Gender in
   Ancient Greece.* New York and London
YUDKIN, J. (1978) 'Physiological determinants of food choice', in J. Yudkin, ed.,
   Diet of Man: Needs and Wants. London: 243–60

Index

Italic page numbers indicate the main treatment of a topic.

abstinence 9 n. 21, 85–6
acorns 40–1
Adam 1, 95–6
Aetius Amidenus 46–7
Africa, North 20, 31, 46, 60, 122
age, age group 49, 130
agriculture 1–2, 5, 67, 79, 110–11, 120, 127,
 145; *see also* peasants
agronomists 15–17; *see also* Cato, Columella,
 Varro
aigilops 39
Ainos 38
Alexandria 30, 46, 93, 126 n. 29
alterity 62–81
ambrosia 65 n. 6
amenorrhea 97
America, North, Americans, native North
 xiii, 49–51, 59 n. 35, 100, 129 n. 2, 146
amicitia 137; *see also* friends
amino acids 16 n. 6, 20; *see also* protein
Amphidromia 128
anaemia 20, 48, 56, 104, 108
animal products 16–17, 20; *see also* meat
animals 83 n. 6, 86–9, 91–3, 119, 139–40, 148
Anthimus 4, 145
anthropology xii–xiii, 1, 4, 93–5, 141–2, 144,
 146–7
Antigonids 131
Antioch 30
aphrodisiacs 9 n. 20
Apicius 37, 115, 121–2
Apollonius of Tyana 98
apples 8, 44 n. 5
archaeology xi, 28, 115, 121–2
Archestratus 74 n. 20, 115, 121–3, 145
Argos, the Argolid 27–8, 37 n. 9
Aristaeus 92–3
Aristarchus 77 n. 25
aristocracy 31, 80, 124, 126, 128, 130–1, 133,
 135–7, 144
Aristotle xii, 22, 29, 52, 65, 76 n. 24, 87–9, 106

army 16–18, 44, 59, 66–7, 89, 115, 120,
 125–6, 128, 145
Arval Brothers 132, 135
asceticism 9, 95–9, 124, 143, 147–8; *see also*
 monks
Asia Minor 115, 140
Asia, East, South 46
Athenaeus of Attaleia 102, 105
Athenaeus of Naupactus xiii, 9, 15–16, 63,
 73–7, 81, 88, 110, 115–16, 118, 121, 130–1,
 145
Athenians, Athens 10, 16, 18–19, 29, 31, 33,
 38, 64, 76, 110, 116–17, 121, 123, 127–8,
 130, 133 n. 13, 132–4, 140–1, 146
athletes 75, 89
Augustales 135
Augustine, St 6 n. 10, 97
Augustus 28, 66, 125
Aurelian 125

babies *see* infants
bacon 44 n. 5, 122, 125–6
bakers 41, 102, 120
banqueting *see* feasting
barbarians 6, 62–71, 80, 110–11, 124, 136,
 140, 146
bark 40
barley 15, 18–21, 66, 68–71, 75, 91, *118–21*
Barthes, R. 7–10, 144, 147
Basil of Caesarea 96, 129
Baucis and Philemon 128
beans, broad 15, 40, *87–91*, 113, 121
beef 17 n. 8, 44 n. 5, 90; *see also* meat
beer 44 n. 5, 67, 118
beri-beri 19
berries 36
birds 68, 77, 83 n. 5, 90 n. 21, 92, 125
Bithynia 15, 71
bladder-stone *see* calculi
blood 56–7, 65–6, 84 n. 7, 97, 126, 139, 143;
 see also sacrifice